Only When I Laugh

PAUL MERTON

Only When I Laugh

A MEMOIR

EBURY
PRESS

3 5 7 9 10 8 6 4

Ebury Press, an imprint of Ebury Publishing
20 Vauxhall Bridge Road
London SW1V 2SA

Ebury Press is part of the Penguin Random House group of companies whose
addresses can be found at global.penguinrandomhouse.com

Copyright © Paul Merton 2014

Photographs first plates section: p1–5 author's own; p6 © Rex Features, © Getty
Images; p7 courtesy of The Comedy Store; p8 courtesy of Pozzitive Television.

Photographs second plates section: p1 © Rex Features; p2–3 courtesy of Hat Trick;
p4 © Rex Features; p5 courtesy of Hat Trick; p6 © BBC, © PA Images;
p7 author's own, © BBC; p8 © Andy Hollingworth, author's own

Paul Merton has asserted his right to be identified as the author of this Work
in accordance with the Copyright, Designs and Patents Act 1988

First published by Ebury Press in 2014

www.eburypublishing.co.uk

A CIP catalogue record for this book is available from the British Library

ISBN 9780091949341

Printed and bound in Great Britain by Clays Ltd, St Ives plc

Penguin Random House is committed to a sustainable future for
our business, our readers and our planet. This book is made
from Forest Stewardship Council® certified paper.

Laughter is the shortest distance between two people

Victor Borge

Contents

1

And the Fishes Ran Away

I used to enjoy sitting inside my parents' wardrobe. At the age of five, I was small enough to squeeze into it but sufficiently strong to hold the door closed behind me. I often sat in the darkness amidst the aroma of mothballs, imagining the great adventures that could be had if only I could find a secret door that would lead to a strange and wonderful world where small shy boys were prized for their ability to sit inside large items of furniture. I enjoyed being slightly scared in the darkness. I was in another world. Invisible. An outsider inside. That fascination for hidden worlds has never left me.

In the centre of London I'm always intrigued by those bits and pieces that only a few of us ever see. The other side of the houses and offices that you pass in the street. Rooftops and iron fire escapes leading from obscure doors down to unsuspected alleyways leading to who knows where. A landscape of air-conditioning units and air vents. I always look out the back windows whenever I find myself in Soho, or around Fulham where I spent my early childhood, and I'm seldom disappointed. Occasionally you glimpse the prize that is a rooftop garden, with dozens of green plants and a couple of deckchairs. Up high where no one at street level can see you. A patio in the sky. An ordinary part of our world, but secretly set apart from it, somewhere you can drift off to.

Just like the inside of my head.

My father always enjoyed telling people that he had first met my mother in bed. It is perfectly true. He was a patient in the Fulham Hospital and she was one of the nurses.

The year is 1955. He is Albert Martin, a plasterer in his late twenties, born and bred in Fulham, and she, Mary Power, of a similar age from County Waterford in the Republic of Ireland. They are both of medium height. Dad lives with his father, also called Albert, in a council flat off the Fulham Palace Road.

Too shy to ask Mum out directly, Dad wrote a letter to that effect and gave it to another nurse to pass on to Mary. Luckily for him – and me – she agreed to a date, and the two of them embarked on a courtship that involved many a Saturday night twirling around the dance floor of the nearby Hammersmith Palais. Dad had a lively sense of humour and in Mum he had found an always appreciative audience. Mum was funny as well but she was a much quieter character than Dad.

Within a year of their first date they were married, and after a July weekend honeymoon in Ramsgate Mum also moved into the council flat with Albert Martin Senior, whose wife – my grandmother – had died a few years before. And so there they were, the three of them. Happily rubbing along together until one day, about a year later, a mysterious stranger suddenly appeared.

I was born on 9 July 1957 at five past five in the afternoon in the Parsons Green nursing home right next door to the White Horse pub. I had no name and no past so mysterious stranger summed me up nicely.

Naturally, Mum adored the miracle that was me, but Dad was less convinced. Perhaps he saw this newly formed bundle of joy as a rival for his affection, and he wasn't too happy about it. As for my grandfather, Albert Senior, he was a rather grumpy man with a club foot who I never saw laugh in all the time I knew him. The man not the club foot. Perhaps because of this I always got the feeling that my birth had a somewhat mixed reception, as Grandad contemplated sharing his living space with a crying, weeing blob of humanity.

Our council flat in Robert Owen House was a cosy affair and beautifully situated in grounds set back from the Fulham Palace Road. The flats were built in the mid-1930s to accommodate those made homeless by the slum clearance programme around the environs of Wandsworth Bridge.

Grandad's club foot guaranteed us a ground floor flat because, although the flats ran to four floors, there were no lifts. We had a living room, a small kitchen, a short hallway with a couple of bedrooms off it, and a toilet. I remember my parents' bedroom and my room, but not my grandad's. I suspect I was never allowed in there. However, one thing I do remember all too clearly is the wallpaper in my room. It's one of my earliest memories and still gives me the shudders to this day. My room was decorated on all four walls with a grotesque tableau featuring gnomes and goblins with distorted evil faces, long prominent noses and dark black eyes. Some of them were mending shoes. Others were sitting upon giant toadstools. As light seeped through cracks in the curtains, I would glimpse malignant faces grinning at me. The stuff of nightmares stuck on your wall, staring at you forever!

I've also always been afraid of balloons bursting. I see a brightly coloured balloon and I recoil at the prospect of it suddenly popping. To explode from a buoyant globe of fun, floating in slow motion, to sudden, ragged scraps of torn rubber is a traumatic event which-ever way you look at it. Especially if you're a balloon.

The keen amateur psychologists amongst you will be pleased to know that this phobia can be directly traced back to an incident that I have no memory of, but which my mother told me about many years later. It's a simple story involving a twelve-month-old baby, his father, a big red shiny balloon and a pin. According to Mum, I was holding the balloon with gurgling delight and bubbling laughter when Dad stuck the pin in sharply and literally burst my world, causing me to cry uncontrollably for the best part of half an hour.

Did Dad really hate me so much to upset me so unnecessarily? Or was he in a rather unthinking way simply playing a rather stupid joke which he thought might get a laugh? I'm sure it's the latter, because he could be a fun and caring parent. He once taught me the following nonsense poem that he had learnt as a child:

> One Dark Night in the Middle of the Day
> The Thames caught light
> And the fishes ran away
> The blind man saw it
> The deaf man heard it
> The man with no legs ran to get the fire engine
> Which was drawn by two dead horses
> Who ran over a dead cat
> And half-killed it.

Dad was always looking to make funny remarks. How much of my subsequent ambition was inspired by his example is hard to say.

*

Although we had the relative luxury of living in a ground floor flat, we didn't have a garden. Instead, our back windows looked out on to a meadow that was about 500-foot long and 100-foot wide. An incredible sight and the stuff of the perfect childhood, you would think! Frustratingly, though, the key feature of this meadow was it had a six-foot-high iron fence all around it with one gate, presumably for access, which was always locked. When I was little I remember wanting to run amongst the wild flowers, but my mother said it was forbidden. Instead we had to content ourselves by looking out of the living room window at the charming field with its gently waving grasses, never knowing what it would be like to walk amongst them. Clearly parts of the world were off limits, even if they appeared to be within easy reach.

Outside our front door, though, there was plenty of opportunity to play within the confines of Robert Owen House. Built back from the main road there was lots of space, with no worries about traffic. In my time living there I don't ever remember seeing a parked car. Nobody owned one, although the man next door did have a motorbike with a sidecar attached. His young son Kevin was my first real friend as opposed to the many imaginary creatures that bubbled up from my brain. (I used to play on my own with my fingers and thumbs, investing each one of them with a character. They had conversations between themselves. An only child finds games to play.) Kevin looked like an angel with his white mop of curly hair.

He was a couple of years younger than me so I was generally in the position of coming up with games and ideas. Once I tore up a sheet of white paper into tiny pieces and, with Kevin by my side, I threw these scraps up into the air from the height of a third-floor balcony. We watched them flutter up and away in the wind.

'Do you see these bits of paper flying away?' I asked.

'Yes,' said Kevin, watching them with wide-eyed wonder.

'Later, those bits of paper will turn into white butterflies,' I said.

'Will they?' said Kevin, his voice full of excitement.

'Yes, I bet we see one tomorrow.'

And he believed me. I didn't feel I was playing a trick on Kevin because I half-believed it myself. Imagine the beauty of such a feat! We saw quite a few white butterflies over the next couple of days, and we were both very excited to see the paper transformed.

The freedom to run around the flats was much cherished. Just a few yards from our front door was a long building with a pitched corrugated roof. This was the drying shed where tenants' wet washing was taken to be placed over warm air heaters. I'm hazy about the interior detail because my chief fascination was with the aforementioned roof. I would throw small pebbles onto its irregular surface and then attempt to catch them as they hurtled towards me, often with a late change in direction. Around the back of the flats was a large space devoted to a children's playground with its usual swings and roundabout. Ball games were allowed on an adjacent half-size football pitch with its tarmacadam surface.

The sensation of living in a small world was exacerbated by attending a Catholic school and going to church every Sunday. If there was anything guaranteed to bring me back down to earth with a bump, it was church. I was bored right from my first experience, which was a Mass conducted entirely in Latin. At the age of five I just really didn't get the holiness and it all seemed so dull. We used to attend St Augustine's Church in Fulham Palace Road at the Hammersmith flyover end. It's still there. At such an early age I couldn't really grasp what it was supposed to be about.

At times you would sit or kneel or stand according to what

everybody else was doing around you. On one occasion, the boredom so overwhelmed me I produced a toy car out of my pocket and pushed it along the wooden pew making low 'vroom vroom' noises as I did so.

Mum was pretty angry and she told me in no uncertain terms to behave myself or the priest would put me on a swing and push me really hard so I would swing really high. This was something I hated. Obviously Mum said it to frighten me into behaving appropriately. But, like the bursting balloon, it's always stuck with me. Ever since, I have been wary of priests.

For me the greatest joy was leaving at the end of the service and getting back out into the daylight of the real world. A roast chicken Sunday lunch, with crispy roast potatoes and greens slowly cooking in the oven at home, helped quicken the pace away from the incense-burning atmosphere of the church.

Then one day, DISASTER! There I was, a perfectly happy (if occasionally frustrated) only child, when all of a sudden everything changed. My sister Angela arrived when I was four-and-a-half. I can still recall the absolute shock that hit me upon seeing my newborn sister for the first time. Mum had gone to hospital but nobody had told me why. As a family we always made a point of not talking about anything important. I was taken to stay with one of my mother's nursing colleagues in Brentford for a few days, and upon my return to the family council flat I was asked to go into my parents' bedroom.

There, lying in a pink little carrycot, was a pink little baby.

'How dare they do this to me?' I thought. *'Behind my back as well!'*

'Paul, say hello to your new sister,' said my seemingly proud mum.

I looked down at the helpless thing lying there.

'Oh,' I said. 'I'm going into the other room now to play.' And I walked out of the room.

I was four-and-a-half years old and my world had just turned upside down. I had always been the centre of attention as far as my mother was concerned, so what on earth was she doing bringing something more adorable into the house without consulting me first?! I was perfectly adept at playing games on my own, so a baby was no good to me at all. Really I might have been consulted. As Mum had increasingly gained weight, I had been kept in the dark. I just thought she liked her food. In fairness, after Angela was born Mum did lose the extra pounds quite quickly. In fact, she was one of the first women in Robert Owen House to fully embrace low fat yoghurt.

I can picture the young Paul Martin playing his solo games. There I am watching Joe Loss & His Orchestra playing on our black-and-white television and standing in front of the set, imitating the actions of the band leader conducting with a knitting needle in my hand. I didn't want to be a member of the orchestra. I wanted to be the man standing out front, soaking up the applause.

I fantasised about running a theatre that ran continuous shows twenty-four hours a day, seven days a week, for an audience of children who could watch the show sitting in comfortable seats which would, at the touch of a button, convert into a bed so they could sleep when they wanted. I'd thought it all through! I, of course, was the person onstage, apparently forever entertaining the audience by constantly making up amusing stuff.

These frankly egotistical solitary games were inspired by a life-changing visit to the Bertram Mills Circus in Olympia the previous Christmas. I was four. The circus was huge. It could seat an audience of thousands. I'd never been anywhere before that contained so many people indoors. We sat in a row of benches some distance from the sawdust ring. I soaked it all up. The buzz from the audience before the show, the musicians tuning up, the ringmaster's announcement, 'Ladies and Gentlemen, boys and girls, welcome to Bertram Mills Circus', as a string of smartly groomed white horses entered the arena and trotted round and round accompanied by rousing music. This, I really enjoyed. I also liked the trapeze artists swinging above my head. The colour, the swooping spotlight, the spectacle all created a buzzy excitement in my growing brain. But the best was yet to come.

My jaw dropped open, my eyes widened, I stopped breathing when I saw clowns for the first time.

Clowns, in their white-painted faces, their big long boots, their huge baggy multicoloured trousers and their buckets of whitewash, coupled with perilous ladders balancing on small tables. Clowns, with their custard pies, unicycles and backfiring cars that make the doors fall off, and strings of sausages lassoing a man in the front row. Floating on the waves of laughter inside that big top was the single most important experience in my young life. I'd never seen adults behave like that before and, quite frankly, I didn't know they had it in them. Normally grown-ups were much more serious. They were people who suggested that a priest would be happy to push me very high on a swing. My dad liked to make jokes, but clowns were something else! That night in the big top I heard the sound of massed laughter, and that buzz, once tasted, is forever with you. From that night on I wanted desperately to be part of it all. To be in the ring, to be in the middle, to be part of the creative spirit that sparks people into laughter. This is where I wanted to live.

At one point in the show, a clown asked for volunteers to go into the ring. My heart leapt at the very thought, but I was also frightened. I hesitated and other children put their hands up first. They were picked. And I sat next to my mum and dad and wished I'd had the courage to put my hand up first.

After the show I begged Mum to buy me a plastic moulded clown mask. It had two tiny holes in the eyes and a couple in the nostrils. It was hot, sweaty, hard on the face, and held on to my head with a piece of tight white elastic. It was extremely uncomfortable to wear and I loved it. I couldn't see much via the eye holes, it wasn't that easy to breathe through the nostrils, and the whole thing smelt of cheap nasty plastic. I was in heaven. I tumbled round the back of the sofa, occasionally hitting myself over the head with a rolled-up newspaper. The tight elastic created a couple of rips either side of the mask, which greatly irritated my skin but I still didn't want to take it off. When I looked in the mirror I looked like a clown. When I rolled over on the floor or fell backwards onto the sofa, I wasn't doing it for the rest of the family; I was doing it for myself.

I also loved the anonymity of the mask. Perfect for a shy kid. Hiding behind a cheap plastic layer of clown meant I could be seen without being seen.

Around this time I also discovered the power of the comedy costume. Dressing up funny. I put on Dad's clothes; his jacket and trousers which were way too big for me lent my figure a comedic aspect. It had the desired affect and my mother dissolved into peals of laughter when I entered the room – a tiny boy swamped in material. A little head sticking out of a mountain of casual wear. Miniscule arms hidden inside gigantic sleeves while voluminous trousers cascaded into a pile of cloth at my feet. All I had to do was just stand there and drink in the laughter. Mum's laughter.

*

I struggled through a period when I got all the usual childhood illnesses in a single year – chicken pox, measles, German measles twice and mumps. One of these illnesses gave me a raging fever that led me to standing upright in bed in my little pyjamas saturated in sweat, at half past two in the morning, humming alternately the theme tunes to *Dixon of Dock Green* and *Z Cars*. I can vividly remember doing it. Standing atop the blankets on my bed, my wet hair plastered across my sweaty forehead, the cotton pyjamas damply stuck to me. It must have been a richly comic tableau because when my mother came to see what all the humming was about she opened my bedroom door and laughed out loud.

Then, concern.

My temperature was high, my brow was fevered and I was humming. What on earth was I up to? I suppose that the fever nullified my shyness as a wannabe performer and gave me the courage to hum TV theme tunes loudly into the night. In another world I could have been a star. 'The humming Tot. Watch him sweat! He's a mini marvel.'

2

There's Only One Paul Martin

Bishops Park, adjacent to Fulham football ground, was a favourite place for us to visit as it was only a short walk down one of many numerous side streets, and was the nearest green space to us that wasn't locked. For me, Bishops Park held many points of interest. Firstly, unlike our meadow, you could walk straight in. There was a giant sand pit and an equally enormous paddling pool with a man-made island in the middle. And there was a creamy coloured ice cream van that sold vaguely vanillared ice creams with chocolate flakes. There was an open-air theatre, which staged musical events throughout the summer. The usual offerings were brass bands playing patriotic songs and occasional variety acts. Once there was a juggling clown, who my dad later spotted walking through the crowd without his make-up or costume on, but with a telltale smudge of white greasepaint behind his right ear. I excitedly ran after the off-duty clown to get a good look at him. He walked through the crowd, but nobody recognised him other than me and my dad.

The open-air theatre was in the middle of Bishops Park and I once saw onstage a bonniest baby contest. Fifteen proud mothers each holding, in their eyes, the most beautiful, bonniest baby since babies began is a guaranteed recipe for angry exchanges amongst the nappies. And yet these contests were staged year after year, before common sense finally kicked in.

The park also had a beautiful riverside walk that ran from Fulham Football Club to Putney Bridge. I remember standing with my father looking over the water to the other bank. There was so much I wanted to know about the world.

'Dad,' I said, 'what's on the other side of the river?'

'Nothing,' he said. 'There's nothing over there.' He wasn't in the mood for conversation.

'Can you walk on that side?' I asked.

'No,' he replied.

And I believed him. The river was the border. The opposite bank was nowhere land. Dad didn't realise how impactful his words were upon me. I took his casual remarks to be the truth.

He wasn't always so taciturn. On other occasions he would talk animatedly about great comedians, prompted by my seeing vintage films on our black-and-white television.

'Who's he?' I said one day, pointing at Charlie Chaplin silently falling about.

'He used to be the most famous man in the world,' my dad replied, and I looked for reasons in the speeded-up action to justify such an exalted status.

Before he was married, Dad had visited a couple of music halls on the dying variety circuit and had witnessed Peter Sellers, amongst others, struggling for laughs in bare, grim theatres. He saw himself as an aficionado of comedy, although he never would have used the word himself. As a household, we liked watching comedy shows more than any other television programme. Arthur Haynes, Morecambe and Wise, Bruce Forsyth compèring *Sunday Night at the London Palladium*, were unmissable events in the weekly calendar.

I took what Dad said or did to heart much more than he realised.

One incident sticks in the mind. After I'd been born, Dad had left his job as a plasterer and joined London Transport as a Tube driver, and I saw him drive a District line train across a railway bridge in Fulham. I had pestered for a few days to be taken to a spot where I could see this event, but Dad was reluctant. Eventually, for a quiet life, my parents gave in and Mum took me to the Putney End of the New Kings Road at the agreed time of just after eleven. Holding my mother's hand, I looked up at the iron bridge, my little heart beating with anticipation.

And there he was. A big red District line train being driven by my father. He looked down to where we were and waved in a half-hearted manner, almost as if he was a little embarrassed to be doing what he was doing, whereas I was beside myself with excitement. Dad could never see this intensely proud moment of my early life from my point of view.

'There's my dad driving a train,' I shouted, which made Mum laugh. But the truth was that Dad looked upon it as a rather lowly job and so didn't see it the way I did when I was five years old. I wanted my dad to be a hero, but he wasn't having any of it. I think he would have liked to be in show business or playing professional football. He was a keen amateur player and won medals for Robert Owen House's team, Owen Villa, in the West Fulham Football League.

Perhaps the root of some of this lay with his relationship with his own father. Albert Senior himself was no barrel of laughs. He wasn't particularly strong on empathy, so I don't think the two of them had much of a close relationship. Grandad liked geraniums and smoking Weights cigarettes. These unfiltered thick, white tubes of very strong tobacco left heavy yellow stains on his fingers. His hobbies were eating pigs' trotters and mending his own shoes, resoling and reheeling them in the living room. Fags and feet. Grandad once worked as a theatre electrician at the Royal Court Theatre in London, and our one proud family heirloom was a copy of a souvenir programme commemorating 1,000 performances of a play called *The Farmer's Wife*. This was our family's one connection to show business.

Dad, on his part, enjoyed watching the horse racing on the telly. For a few races I became convinced I could predict the winners. Dad was never much of a gambler; he only ever bet very small stakes – a shilling here, a shilling there. I remember watching some racing and telling Dad that horse number 22 would win. And it did! Despite this feat of incredible clairvoyance, Dad didn't seem to be as impressed as I was. I'm sure I got the next race right as well, but instead of realising that I was a budding genius when it came to matters of the turf, I was told 'that's enough now'. And so it was.

In the early 1960s household items often pretended to be something they weren't. This was a source of fascination for all of us. For starters, we had an electric fire with a pretend coal fire effect, which was achieved by a little fan rotating underneath the plastic moulded top and a red light bulb that threw up flickering shadows, optimistically intended to resemble dancing flames.

It was decided one day that we would put new wallpaper up in the living room. Despite my tender years, this was to be the scene of a major creative triumph on my part. While we were looking at wallpaper patterns I saw a design that greatly excited me. It took a while to convince my parents – after all, how many people let a five-year-old make decorating decisions? But somehow I managed to persuade them. Perhaps it was the passion or the breathtaking scope of my vision. The wallpaper I had selected had a brick wall pattern printed on to it. We papered only one wall, just above the fireplace. People admired it and I wasn't slow in telling visitors that it was my idea. I was excited by the fun of it. The humorous wallpaper that made you smile, rather than grimacing at terrifying gnomish cobblers, which I had learnt to tolerate in my bedroom.

Fablon was another sensation. How do you transform a rather ordinary table into a stunningly beautiful coffee table with swirls of woody-looking pattern, resembling top-quality craftsmanship and materials? Easy. You stick a piece of plastic with such a pattern printed on it directly on to your cheap-looking table, and, hey presto, you now have a cheap-looking table with a layer of plastic stuck on top of it! The world of plastics was upon us. We were living in the future!

I remember the sudden arrival of plastic flowers. Individual yellow tulips with long green stems, all moulded from plastic. We were told that plastic flowers were so much better than the real thing because they didn't need watering and they would never die or fade. They had no scent or softness, no attraction to passing insects, but from a distance they looked like the real thing. Petrol stations were giving away free plastic flowers with every gallon of petrol sold, but nobody was convinced.

Other novelties were more entertaining and some of them were seasonal. Once a year, at Christmas, we transformed our black-and-white television into a colour TV simply by utilising the transparent yellow wrapping around the soft toffees in the Quality Street tin. Looking at the monochrome screen through the sweet wrapper magically converted boring greys into vibrant living yellow. You could do the same with the golden wrapping around a bottle of Lucozade, but that was a slightly darker hue. There was a product advertised in the back of the *Daily Mirror* which claimed to turn your humble telly into a glorious Technicolor experience.

It was nothing more than a large sweet wrapper with a twist. You fitted a transparent plastic screen over the TV screen, but, unlike the Quality Street wrapper, this special device displayed more than one colour. The top third was blue, the middle section was a sort of pink flesh colour, while the bottom bit was green. It would appear realistic if you were looking at a white person standing on a lawn with a cloudless sky above them. For everything else it would have been a mess.

In fact, in some ways, watching TV like that wasn't as good as a brilliant little toy I had, my Give-A-Show Projector that projected animated slides of cartoon characters onto flat white surfaces. Ideal for ceilings. Before going to sleep at night, I would shine the projector onto the white ceiling above me and push the slides through one at a time. I would supply the voices of the characters portrayed. A real challenge for scenes involving Snow White and the seven dwarfs. Once I'd exhausted the fun of that I would then do my best to get to sleep – carefully avoiding the eyes of the evil pixies on my wallpaper.

Real Technicolor was available on a huge screen at the local ABC cinema, over the river in Putney. Now this was the real deal. Saturday morning pictures was an immensely popular institution with children as well as their parents, who could leave their kids somewhere safe for three hours. Mum or Dad would walk me to the cinema through Bishops Park, over Putney Bridge, at about nine thirty, and pick me up again just after twelve. In between, I sat in a cinema full of screaming kids watching a selection of Bugs Bunny cartoons brighter and richer in colour than any live film could hope to be. The deepest blues, the strongest reds. These cartoons made your eyeballs pop and I loved them. The surreal humour also made a vivid impact. Characters walked off cliffs without falling and survived huge explosions on an hourly basis.

Also showing were cheaply made serials from 1940s America. The one I vividly remember is the *Adventures of Captain Marvel* who was clearly inspired by Superman. When not being a super-hero the Captain was a mild-mannered, weak-looking, young man in his early twenties who, nevertheless, upon uttering the magic word 'shazam', transformed himself into a much burlier, older actor. The Captain wore the obligatory tights and cape. Captain Marvel could fly and this special effect was achieved by our hero running and then leaping out of frame. The film then cut to a very poor Captain Marvel lookalike dummy, crudely suspended by a couple of dodgy-looking wires. The dummy's arms were posed outstretched to convince you that, yes, a man could fly.

I wasn't bothered by the non-special effects but I was annoyed by the cliffhanger endings. One episode finished with Captain Marvel's alter ego, the mild-mannered youth, locked inside a speeding car as it raced along a mountain pass. We see him trapped in the car, and in the next shot we see the car plummet off the cliff and into a deep ravine where it explodes on impact. 'Don't miss the next episode of Captain Marvel,' intoned the deep American voice dramatically. I spent the next week eagerly awaiting that next episode. How could the good Captain survive? I tell you how – the whole thing was dishonest.

The following Saturday I was sitting in the ABC cinema in Putney High Street impatiently waiting. The other films flashed by, but they held no fascination for me – I needed to find out what had happened. The *Captain Marvel* episode began as they always did, with a quick recap of the previous cliffhanger. Here again was the speeding car, racing along the mountain pass. And here was our callow youth, trapped inside the speeding car. And here is the callow youth jumping out of the fast-moving vehicle safely onto a grass bank, where he can watch from a distance the car hurtle into the ravine. What? He didn't do that last week! He didn't jump out of the car then!! I would have seen it!

I was extremely disillusioned. How dare entertainment lie to me? I knew it was cheating the audience and insulting our level of intelligence. It wasn't right. The whole affair left me feeling thoroughly disgusted.

I resolved that the entertainment that I provided would be better!

At school, I used to do my best to make the kids in the dinner queue laugh. My first junior school was a Catholic school in Fulham called St Thomas's. I was in a class with thirty other kids. I had a couple of other friends by this time, one of them was called Ken and, although he was six, in my memory he had the demeanour of a much older man. The same could be said of another boy, whose name I cannot recall but he was a perfect double for Tony Hancock. The same weary demeanour and world-weary eyes, except on the face of a child. The comedian was the subject of a ribald playground riddle with his name easily spelt out by touching four different parts of the body. Toe, knee, hand – you get the picture …

Every dinner time, I queued up with my classmates to make the short walk to another nearby school that, unlike ours, had canteen facilities. One day, as we lined up in this distinctively cobbled yard with its heavy wooden fences and air of dark foreboding, I was reminded of the exterior set of *Steptoe and Son*, then the most popular comedy on British television. To entertain my classmates, I imitated as best I could the two leading characters. Harry H. Corbett's 'Oh my good gawd' and 'You dirty old man' were firm favourites. I distinctly remember making an effort to entertain the queue on the occasion of my seventh birthday, and precociously thinking, *I'm making my classmates laugh now but I have to improve the quality of my jokes all the time because next year I will be eight and so will they. They will be a bit more clever than they are now and so I must keep improving.'* At this time I harvested my jokes from old *Beano* and *Dandy* annuals.

'What's yellow and white and travels at a hundred miles an hour? A train driver's egg sandwich.'

By the time I was eight and Angie was four (I won't guess at how old Grandad was), the little flat in Fulham was becoming a tight fit for the five of us. I enjoyed living in Robert Owen House, with its own world set back from the main road. But we needed more room.

Just before we left the area a minor incident in school left me rather shaken. One day I was introduced to a new pupil who was joining our class. The teacher called me over to meet him. Something seemed to be amusing her.

'Could you come here for a moment, Paul Martin?'

'Yes miss.'

'I want you to meet Paul Martin.'

I stood there dumbstruck. My face burned with anger. He just smiled. *'How dare this boy have exactly the same name as me?'* I remember thinking. *'That's the same as being me and I'm me. There's only one Paul Martin. That's my name and it always will be!'*

3

We Cross the River But Fail to Reach the Moon

All of a sudden our world got a lot bigger. We moved to Morden, the last stop on the Northern line, which was a long way over the river. You could get there by bus. The 93 ran from Putney Bridge to North Cheam via Morden, which I thought was the country-side when I first saw it. There was green space everywhere. Dad had partially taught me to cycle a couple of years earlier and here was the environment to really enjoy a bike. Three minutes' up the road from the new house was St Helier Avenue, a mile-and-a-half stretch of dual carriageway with a safe separate cycle lane alongside. Morden Park had acres of greenery and a large public swimming pool.

Opposite our new home where we lived in Morden Hall Road was a huge area of parkland with beautiful streams running through it. Our council house was a great novelty with its two floors and a small garden out the back. Laid to lawn with a concrete path down the middle, there was room to cut a couple of holes into the grass to practise putting. My parents didn't need much persuasion and Dad was always keen to play competitive sport, be it make-shift putting across rough grass or table tennis across the dining room table. When we played each other he showed little mercy and would gleefully smash the table tennis ball past me to score another point. This would infuriate me to the point of tears.

'You've got to give me a chance,' I would say.

'Give Paul a chance,' Mum would say.

'Alright,' Dad would say, and then proceeded to lob me a couple of easy ones before eventually smashing another one past me. This resulted in big tears on my part.

Solitary games were easier. I converted our dining table into a rudimentary snooker table by laying some green baize cloth across it with books acting as cushions. I left gaps between the books to act as pockets and bought twenty-one ping-pong balls and coloured them appropriately. The little putter I used for our garden golf doubled up as a cue when used handle first.

The house and garden were exciting enough, but Morden itself to an eight-year-old boy also had great attractions. Firstly, it had a magnificent Odeon cinema that had been built, and opened to great fanfare in 1932. It had an organ that went up and down, and an organist that went up and down with it. This picture house opened at a time when luxurious, comfortable surroundings were seen as a priority to help make the moviegoing experience feel extra special. The Morden cinema had a huge screen and a stage big enough to host variety acts. Its position directly opposite the Tube station was dominant but not overpowering. Mum would take me to see the latest Morecambe and Wise or Norman Wisdom film, which always looked extra-impressive in such surroundings.

There was another competing house of fun in this small town. The big supermarket, just over the road from the picture house, was not just impressive because of its vastness, it also had a magical aspect that in turn amused, baffled and sometimes frightened the inhabitants of Morden. The entrance and exit was via a pair of sliding glass doors that opened and closed automatically, according to the customer's movements. We are familiar with these doors today and don't think of them as advanced science fiction, but it was different back in the mid-1960s, in Morden. For the shopper laden with bags, the doors suddenly opening was enough to make them reel back in astonishment at this paranormal activity. Fear of invisible mechanisms that couldn't be trusted compelled old ladies to hurry through with a desperate urgency, less they be trapped between two sliding panes of glass. Morden was a small town, but I found fun everywhere.

One sunny Sunday afternoon, I witnessed a sight that I will never forget. I was walking around Morden town centre just for something to do. I walked round the back of Crown House when a sudden strong wind whipped up behind me, almost lifting me off my feet.

On the corner of the street in front of me a man's grey hat then appeared, moving at great speed from left to right. It tumbled along the pavement in a straight line, over a distance of twenty-five yards or more, before disappearing from view.

Of course, a runaway hat promises the owner in quick pursuit, but what emerged was so much better. First, I heard an offstage cry of 'No! No!' and then, superbly, a cheap ginger wig appeared, which half-flew and half-bounced along exactly the same path as the hat. Again, this thing moved at speed and disappeared quickly from view.

And then the owner appeared. Magnificently, he was a great fat bloke with a big red face, puffing away as he pursued the other two competitors in this Hat-Wig-Man race. He blustered across my line of vision in pursuit of his dignity, and then disappeared. I looked around quickly to see if anybody else had seen it, but there was no one else about. I had been in the right place at the right time to witness a brief few seconds of magic that I've never, ever forgotten.

*

Moving to Morden meant attending a new church, St Teresa's, which was next to the school of the same name. I was to spend hundreds of bored hours in that church. In fairness, there was one time I was transfixed for well over twenty minutes, as I saw a bus ticket floating in the hot air rising through the grill on the floor. It bobbed up to a comfortable height of thirty feet and hovered around and about at that altitude for the rest of Mass. The ticket's graceful moves were hypnotic, and something about its aerodynamic shape and weight kept it up in the air. Unless of course I was watching a white butterfly. Unfortunately, further attempts in later Masses to replicate this magnificent flight were never successful. Several of us tried.

It was in that church that I ran through the process of giving my first confession, when I was nine. The Catholics amongst you will recognise the procedure. You enter a box stood up on one end and divided in the middle. You sit down and directly to your right there is a small grill behind which sits the priest to whom you confess your sins.

Your first confession is a pretty big deal. A priest promised us that we would leave the confessional box after that first time feeling that our feet were floating on air! The lightness we would experience would be the direct result of our soul being cleansed for the very first time. Catholics believe that we are all born with the 'stain' of original sin on our souls. The first confession would wipe the slate clean.

We had a couple of rehearsals where I had to make sure I had learnt my words. The first thing I had to say was, 'Bless me father, this is my first confession and I accuse myself of …' Now this next bit was difficult. Obviously I didn't want to list every perceived sin, and I sought generalisations that could cover any eventuality. I came up with 'I have been disobedient to my mother and father', which, if pressed, I could concede meant not keeping my bedroom tidy. The priest would then tell you how many times you had to say the 'Our Father' prayer or the 'Hail Mary' in order to serve your penance. Then, that would be it, job done. Soul cleansed, walking on air.

We rehearsed this twice so that we wouldn't muck it up when we did it properly. After the second practise I came out of the confessional box to rejoin one of my fellow pupils who was kneeling in one of the pews.

'What was it like?' he whispered.

'It was alright, it was just like last time,' I said.

'But that was IT, just now,' the other boy whispered back. 'That was your first confession!'

'I thought it was another rehearsal!'

'No,' he said. 'That was IT!'

I'd managed to give my first confession without even knowing it. I hadn't realised it was the real thing. My feet, I'm sorry to report, did not feel as if they were walking on air.

My relationship with the church was being put under an even greater degree of strain.

In the school next door, you will be pleased to know that I was enjoying much greater success. Miss Gately was our teacher and I thrived under her. Particularly in the English lessons. Miss Gately was in her mid-sixties with a lovely wrinkly face and she was very encouraging towards me, asking me to read to the class sometimes, and on a couple of occasions I took other children for reading lessons. I owe a huge debt to my mother, who taught me to read from an early age. I loved reading books and before I went to sleep at night I generally read ten to fifteen pages of whatever fiction was entertaining me at the time. At the end of the school year, I was voted the most popular pupil in the class.

Sad to say, I would never ever be as good at school again.

I wasn't the only winner in the summer of 1966; the England football team surpassed all pessimism by actually winning the World Cup in a tense final against the Germans at Wembley Stadium. At the time, prior to kick off, the whole country was paralysed with fear at the prospect of losing. Just over twenty years since the end of the Second World War, many viewers watching the match at home had memories of loved ones lost in battle or their own houses bombed by the Luftwaffe. We couldn't lose to the Germans. Not on our home soil. To be defeated at Wembley would be humiliation.

That's why the England team played so nervously throughout. It seemed that their desire not to lose was outweighing their desire to win. When the Germans equalised just before the end of normal time it was a cruel extension of the misery to be endured.

My father, sat in front of the telly, groaned with despair. We clutched at straws. The ball bounced off the crossbar and onto the goal line. We claimed a goal and the Russian linesman agreed with us. We were all guilty of wishful thinking. The fourth goal, scored by Geoff Hurst, was probably celebrated in every English household in a similar way. As Geoff collected the ball just around the halfway line it was obvious he had a clear run on goal. 'Go on,' shouted my dad from the sofa. 'Run!' Geoff heard him and started running.

'Go on, go on,' shouted Dad, urging greater effort. 'Hit it!' And Geoff hit it so hard the ball flew past a startled keeper, who seemed to be distracted by a number of fans running on to the pitch.

'YES!' shouted my dad at the same time as 12 million other people. We had won. The release of joy was intense. The match itself had been extremely anxious, but now the final whistle had blown and the country could breathe a huge sigh of relief. Now we had won it once, it would be that much easier never to win it again.

Naturally, if the Germans had won, the blow to national morale would have been immense – but at least we would have had them surrounded.

That summer we went to a holiday camp in Great Yarmouth, which I absolutely loved. We spent a week there staying in a tiny chalet, but as we only ever really used it for sleeping, it didn't matter how small it was. We were used to little rooms but outside was a different world altogether. A world of Glamorous Granny competitions where women were rewarded for having children at a very young age. Knobbly knee contests where men of a certain vintage were encouraged to roll their trousers up to show off their lower legs. The volume of audience applause for each pair of knees decided the winner. There was always something to do during the day, which began with a communal breakfast in a huge room capable of seating 500 people. Being amongst so many was a buzz in itself, but there were also a couple of rituals that helped the mood along. One was the occasional sound of metal dinner trays smashing to the floor somewhere in the kitchen, which always got a big cheer from the amused diners. I noticed that it only happened when it was raining and people needed cheering up.

At the end of breakfast, the holiday camp's chief entertainer ran through that day's events. A treasure hunt starting at ten o'clock down by the swimming pool. Bingo at eleven and then indoor horse racing in the ballroom at two. This unlikely sounding event was actually films of American horse races projected onto a screen. Having informed us about our organised fun, the chief entertainer finished off by shouting out 'See you later alligator' to which it seemed everybody else shouted back 'In a while crocodile'. This happened every morning the week we were there, and it puzzled me just as much at the end as it did at the beginning. I asked my mother about it.

'Mum, why are people shouting out "in a while crocodile"?' I queried. 'And why is the man saying "see you later alligator"?'

I have previously remarked on the quality of some of our family conversations. This was to be no exception. My mother had no answer and neither did Dad. They weren't rock 'n' roll fans and had no idea that these words featured as a call and response in Bill Haley's big mid-1950s hit 'See You Later, Alligator'. I didn't know it either so it remained a mystery to us all.

As much as I enjoyed the sheer space of the outside areas of the holiday camp – the swimming pool, the football pitch – it was the spectacular indoors that set my heart pounding. There was firstly the snooker room with its half-a-dozen full-sized tables, their smoothly immaculate green baize surfaces brightly lit from above. The brightest lights I had ever seen in a room, making the coloured balls ping their hues into my visual cortex. That was exciting, but this room was a mere support act to the main event. The ballroom. The magnificent ballroom, with its polished wooden floor, red seating and gantry of coloured lights hanging above ... THE STAGE! The very place I dreamt of.

At one end of the room, there it was, around four-and-a-half foot off the floor, and by standing on my tiptoes I could see across its surface, right to the back.

My first visit was in daylight shortly after arriving at the camp, and I was fascinated by the specks of dust illuminated by the sunlight pouring in through the double doors. The room was big and smelt of last night's beer. Small, round, brown, stained tables were scattered throughout the seated area. Each surrounded by four red leather stools. It was so grown-up and intoxicating, and this was when it was empty. At night, with the dancers, the singers, the musicians, the spotlights picking out soloists and hundreds of happy campers all swaying along, it was overpowering. I wanted to be on that stage more than anything. A few days later an opportunity arose, and it was to be extremely disappointing.

A children's magician was putting on a show for us kids. He asked for a volunteer to join him. I put my hand up straight away and he picked ... me! I walked up the few steps to the stage. My heartbeat increasing as I approached my idea of heaven. Just three steps and I was there standing next to the magician, who towered over me. He held a red sparkly cylindrical tube up to my face and asked me to put my hand through to make sure there was nothing inside. I put my hand in as he looked through the other end.

'Oh, you tweaked my nose!' he shouted in outrage as he clutched the tip of it with the fingers on his left hand. He staggered back holding his nose and going, 'Ooohh.'

I was confused because I was certain I hadn't gone near his nose, let alone tweaked it. I looked at the audience and said my first line ever onstage. 'I didn't touch his nose!' I was outraged by the suggestion. The conjurer was lying and reeked of Captain Marvel and his cheating ways. What a serious little boy I could be.

The conjurer quickly ushered me off. It was all over, far too soon.

I was perplexed by his behaviour and later spoke to my mother about it. 'The magician said I tweaked his nose, but I didn't.'

'Perhaps it was meant to be a joke?' suggested Mum, but I didn't think so. There was nothing remotely funny about the way the magician acted! So it seemed to me that he was just lying to the audience and also blaming me for something I hadn't done. The whole thing was very fishy.

My second stage appearance happened a couple of days later courtesy of four older boys who were putting together some sketches for a show. This time it went slightly better. I got cast as a person sitting on a park bench reading a broadsheet newspaper. All I had to do was hold the newspaper up in front of me, but my hands were shaking with excitement and I had to be told to keep steady. How can you keep steady when you're erupting with joy? The show went well and, even though my role was tiny, when I walked down the steps afterwards I felt like I was walking on air.

And I hadn't even been to confession.

The next day I landed back on earth with a bump when I fell off a donkey. I was sitting on this ass next to five other kids sitting on theirs. The starting pistol was fired, and my donkey reared up and threw me to the ground, where I lay until the thunder of hooves had passed. I stood up to the sound of laughter, but entirely the wrong kind.

My dad approached me, about to make things worse.

'I bet five shillings on you to win,' he said.

'Don't blame me,' I said. 'Blame the ruddy donkey.'

This, it has to be said, provoked more laughter from the onlookers. I stormed away fuming, not really having any idea what had gone on.*

---

* Later, my mother told me exactly what had happened. Upon the pistol being fired, my dad had smacked my donkey so hard on the arse it lost all interest in having a race and instead adopted another pursuit, i.e. throwing me to the ground. It was the balloon thing all over again.

If that was the lowest point of the holiday, the highlight was undoubtedly the variety show staged in the grand ballroom the night before we left. One act was unforgettable, although it only lasted four minutes.

He made his entrance wearing a beautifully tailored dinner jacket and trousers, white shirt and tie. His large head was made to appear bigger by a bushy grey-black beard that also leant him the air of a ship's captain. His stature commanded attention as he approached the microphone. He began to sing, 'Have you ever been across the sea to Ireland?' His baritone voice immediately captivated his audience further. He sang a verse, a chorus, and then something strange happened.

At first it looked like it was an optical illusion, but then, as the act progressed, you realised that his arms actually were getting longer. Slowly but surely, as he sang, his upper limbs were visibly extending: two minutes in and they're six foot long. The audience are now in hysterics as he continues the song accompanied by extravagant long arm semaphore. His jacket is built in such a way that the sleeves endlessly extend. He hits the line 'where the hand of friendship is extended' just as his arms reach their maximum limit which he indicates by waving them both above his head. He finishes the song to rapturous applause, he bows and he's gone. Dragging his long limbs behind him.

The summer holidays of 1966 came to their inevitable close and it was time to return to school. The beginning of a new school year and a new teacher. This, I'm afraid, is where it all went wrong. This teacher was a nun. Her name was Sister Galista and she was a woman with far too many teeth.

She was tall and walked with a long purposeful stride up and down the corridors of our junior school. She wore the standard nun's black habit and black headwear, with a band of white at the top. She looked like an angry pint of Guinness. She always seemed to be annoyed about something or other. Perhaps she didn't like children because she certainly made it very clear that she didn't like me.

The two of us got off to a bad start. I had been the golden boy with my previous teacher Miss Gately, so it was with some degree of surprise that I first encountered Sister Galista's attitude towards me. She asked the class to write an essay entitled 'What I did during my summer holidays'. I loved writing essays. 'For my summer holidays I went to Great Yarmouth to a holiday camp for a week,' was how I started. It was the next line that proved controversial. The class handed our essays in and the following day saw Sister Galista enter the classroom at an above-average speed with our exercise books tucked under her arm.

She stood in front of us. 'Paul Martin, will you stand up?' Her tone of voice suggested I was in trouble and her next words confirmed it.

'You have written a terrible essay. I shall read it to the class.'

She opened my exercise book with disdain, as if lifting up a rock to see creepy-crawlies underneath. She began.

'"For my summer holidays I went to Great Yarmouth to a holiday camp for a week."' Here she paused for a sneer before continuing. '"One day a space ship landed on the beach and took me to the moon. It was lovely on the moon. I walked around and met a moon lady,"' Sister Galista snapped the book shut and glared straight at me. 'You can't write about things that aren't true,' she said. 'A spaceship did not land on the beach and you did not go to the moon. Did you?'

'No, Sister,' I mumbled through my shock, as I stood there red-faced and humiliated. The Golden Boy fallen and now looking distinctly tarnished. I honestly didn't know what had hit me as I sat down dazed, trying to deal with intensely wrong criticism. In Miss Gately's class the prize I was given for being voted the most popular pupil was a paperback book written by Spike Milligan called *Silly Verse for Kids*. Spike was making stuff up all the time, so to comment that 'You can't write about things that aren't true' was clearly nonsense in its own right. But there was more to come. Sister Galista set the topic for our next essay: 'What I see on my way to school.'

I set about writing a straight non-fictional account of my fifteen-minute walk to school. It was very dull. Nothing unusual happened along the way, and that's how I wrote it. Dull but true. Sister Galista collected our essays and delivered her verdict the following day. She quickly moved into the classroom her face showing that she was absolutely livid. Somebody was in trouble and I was glad it wasn't me. The rest of the class would now know how it felt to be berated by her.

One kid had written about finding a submarine in the sewers after lifting up a loose manhole cover. Another wrote vividly about the difficulties of keeping a tiger in her back garden. Sister Galista tore into them all, each and every one, but her condemnation had an unexpected twist.

'You have all written terrible essays. Full of all this fantasy nonsense,' she paused for effect. 'This is all YOUR fault Paul Martin. Stand up!' I stood up so dazed I was on the brink of a coma.

Except this was more of a living nightmare. 'How can this be my fault?' were the unspoken words which she answered anyway.

'You have poisoned the minds of your classmates with your ridiculous stories. I shall have no more.' So there I was, deeply humiliated again.

I'm honestly not exaggerating when I say that I felt the pain of that moment for many years. It shaped me for a long time afterwards. Sister Galista definitely made me a shyer child and less able to express my ambition to become a comedy performer.

I don't know why this nun bullied me, but if she expected me to kowtow to her point of view she was very mistaken. I knew imagination wasn't wrong. Her attitude gave me something to kick against. She honestly helped to define me. Her very opposition was enough to earn my loyalty to whatever it was that she didn't like. She certainly had no sense of humour and despised it in others, which naturally further fuelled my belief that laughing was the best thing around.

At home, I listened to comedy shows on the radio, memorising the best jokes so I could retell them in the playground. Professional beyond my years, I would always credit the original source.

'I heard this joke on *The Ken Dodd Show*. Ken Dodd says, "And the follow-up record to 'I Left My Heart in San Francisco' is called 'I Found My Kidneys on Clapham Common'".'

I knew a lot of other peoples' jokes.

The year with Sister Galista passed slowly. I kept my head down and there were no further incidents.

The next couple of years at school were uneventful and I continued to absorb as much good comedy as I could find, no matter what the source or the vintage. In some ways I was ahead of my contemporaries, in others I was fifty years out of date. I was one of the first kids at school to discover *Monty Python's Flying Circus*, which had just started broadcasting on BBC2, late on Sunday night. It was 1969 and I was twelve. Anarchic, strange, revolutionary, I got it straight away. Even the not-so-successful episodes had extraordinary moments that stayed with you.

But I also enjoyed 'The Golden Silents', a series devoted to the films of Charlie Chaplin and Buster Keaton, amongst others. This fascination for these comedies led me into a new hobby. I began collecting silent films on Super 8 mm, which I projected onto a white bedsheet hung on my bedroom wall. My parents bought me a cheap projector for seventeen quid as a birthday present, and my mum made me a set of heavy curtains to block out the daylight. I was extremely fortunate that one of the very few shops in Britain that sold films of this vintage was only one stop away on the Northern line, in South Wimbledon.

Perry's Movies was the name of the business in Kingston Road, and I blush now to think just how shy I was in those days. I was always tongue-tied, red faced and easily put off my stride whenever I was in that shop. On some occasions I might have a question but I couldn't summon up the nerve to ask it.

I really wasn't very good at talking to people, especially on the telephone. There used to be a cinema in Oxford Street that ran a Buster Keaton film festival every summer and I found it really difficult to phone the venue to find out times of showings. This was information I really wanted to know but, standing in our hallway looking at the wall-mounted phone, I was unable to summon up the nerve to use it. It's silly but that's how I was when I was twelve, thirteen, fourteen. I was such a shy dreamer. I couldn't pick up the phone and yet I would practise walking down the stairs pretending I was making an entrance on the Michael Parkinson talk show!

In this period I got my first job, which was a newspaper delivery round every weekday morning. At Christmas time it was the tradition that the newspaper boy would knock on the front door of his customers to elicit a seasonal donation. This would prove to be a real test of my shyness, but there was money involved and it had to be done. Nevertheless, it was with faltering steps that I approached the first couple of houses. I rang the bell and … there was nobody in. It was seven o'clock in the evening and perhaps people hadn't got back from work. My nerves were in shreds!

Unfortunately, in the third house I tried, somebody was in. I'd practised my words over and over again in the privacy of my bedroom, but now I was facing a woman who had just opened her front door and I found myself hesitating.

'Err. Ah. Hello,' I said. 'Hello, I'm your um, er … daily paperboy.' This was the line I'd rehearsed and the customer was meant to infer from this that I was now expecting them to give me money. I know it's not very clear, but this is what I'd come up with. What else could I say? 'Hello can you give me some money?' is just plain begging so I was seeking nuance, you see. Anyway, this woman looked at me and she clearly had no idea what I was talking about. That's the trouble with nuance.

I repeated the line. 'Hello, I'm your, er, weekly paperboy.' I got the words out better this time but it didn't really help because it was the words that were the very things that were puzzling her.

After an age she realised what I must be implying, and she disappeared back inside before re-emerging with a threepenny bit.

'Thank you,' I said, glad the ordeal was over. I took a couple of deep breaths and steeled myself for the house next door.

You will be relieved to know that I improved as I repeated the line from door to door. Everybody else understood what I was vaguely going on about, and I finished the evening with about sixteen quid in coins, which was very healthy and heavy in my pockets.

I carried on being a paperboy for the next twelve months, so I had the chance to relive the experience of knocking on people's doors soliciting money at Christmas time. The following year, I approached the third house with a certain apprehension. I knocked on the door. The same woman opened it.

'Good evening,' I said in a confident manner, 'I'm your weekly paperboy.'

'Oh yes,' she said, 'I won't be a moment.' She came back with her purse and generously donated to the cause. I was pleased with the way it had gone.

'Actually, I'm glad it's you,' she continued as she handed me the money. 'We had a right idiot come round last year.'

4

Going Rapidly Downhill

With its bold Gothic architecture, its grand hall with vastly high ceilings, thick wooden beams and oil paintings of former pupils hanging on the wall, Wimbledon College was a daunting prospect. Highly intimidating to me, in a *Tom Brown's School Days* way, it was a warren of thin brown corridors. The school was run by Jesuit priests and had been a grammar school since the 1940s, but had been forced to become a comprehensive in 1969. And in the summer of 1970, attending secondary school for the first time, I was to be part of the first ever comprehensive intake.

My initial view of the place was in the company of my mother. It was a Saturday morning and we had been asked to attend to be measured for the official school uniform from the official school outfitters, Kinch & Lack.

Up to that point in my school career my blazers had come from the Co-op. Off the peg. At ten o'clock the two outfitters arrived wearing smart suits with tape measures around their necks. They were very well spoken as they started to professionally measure the first boy in the queue. His mother asked a pertinent question: 'How much is this going to cost?' she said. Our parents had all been sent letters by Wimbledon College instructing us to turn up this Saturday morning, but with no indication of prices. 'Eighteen guineas for the blazer,' said the softly spoken besuited gentleman. The cost was treble what my mother normally paid for a Co-op blazer. Word quickly spread through the queue. Nobody had the money to pay three times the price.

The two outfitters were puzzled. I dare say this was a unique experience for them. We were not the usual clientele and we were irate. As the queue broke up, other mums arriving with kids were told about the huge expense of the uniform. The outfitters tried insisting that the purchase of their clothes was obligatory, but quietly backed down when the parents' anger became apparent. No school uniforms were purchased that day. I never did find out the cost of the trousers.

A few days later, we received another letter from the school informing us that they understood the expense involved but we must also realise that the school did have an official uniform. As a special generous offer Kinch & Lack were prepared to knock 10 per cent off the cost, but that was no good to us either. In the end, because you can't insist people spend money they haven't got, we were allowed to wear our ordinary black blazers with simple black trousers.

My first impressions of Wimbledon College garnered on that first visit were backed up when I started the school proper a few weeks later. The headmaster Father Carty addressed the pupils in the grand hall with its oil paintings of old boys. He told us what a fine school Wimbledon College was. It had a rich tradition. Did we know that the last Governor of Burma was educated at Wimbledon College? Also Major Pat Reid, the first man to escape from Colditz, was an old Wimbledonian. It all felt so alienating. What were we doing there, us working-class kids standing in the same hall with the grammar school boys? A cursory glance would tell you that although we were all wearing the school uniform, our blazers did not come from Kinch & Lack. I expect the rest of the school was appalled by our arrival. Snotty-nosed urchins with their shirts hanging out. We were the enemy within. I didn't see it like that at the time, I was too busy trying to fit in to this strange world I'd been plunged into – Gothic towers, priests patrolling corridors that led to parts of the school you weren't allowed into, and strange physical punishments administered with enthusiasm, often on the slightest pretext.

Proud to be a grammar school, it saw no reason why the comprehensive kids should be allowed to pollute their world. The grammar school boys occupied sets 1 to 4, while us lot, who had failed our eleven-plus test, were in sets 5 to 7. Set 7 consisting of three boys who were semi-literate. I was in set 5, confusingly called Lower Grammar 5. But sets 1–4 were taught a whole array of different subjects to us.

The first day was bewildering. As well as being in Lower Grammar 5, apparently I also belonged to Fisher House, which entitled me to wear a red strip of cloth above the school badge on my blazer. One of the older boys gave us a cursory tour of the buildings. 'This is rogues' gallery,' he said as we walked swiftly down one of the many dimly lit corridors. It was a couple of years before I realised that I had misheard and its actual name was Ruds' gallery, an abbreviation of Rudiments, which was the name of the year below us. Wimbledon College was a place that used unnecessarily strange words.

One of our first tasks was to choose which one of three subjects we wanted to study. French, geography or metalwork. In preparation for the comprehensive intake, the Jesuits had built a modern complex away from the main building. Pride of place was a metalwork classroom equipped with a forge and two dozen work benches fitted with vices. Perfect for the incoming working-class kids of south London.

The problem was that, given the choice, the majority of us picked either French or geography. It turned out that very few of us wanted to become blacksmiths when we left school. Personally, I chose French. It made sense to me. I'd rather speak the language of our nearest European neighbour than make a trowel. Unfortunately, too many people had opted for French, so it was decided that everyone who had chosen it would sit an exam and the top 30 per cent would be able to take the subject.

The grammar school boys had been studying French three times longer than us and none of set 5 passed. All was not lost, however, as I noticed that German O level was also taught. I went along to the class to sign up.

'What do you want?' demanded the teacher curtly.

'I've come to do German,' I said. She looked at me with unconcealed contempt. On the blackboard, she wrote a word that was thirteen letters long and asked me to pronounce it. I couldn't and she asked me to leave. That was the end of my linguistics career.

Over the course of the next two years I think it's very fair to say that my expertise in my subsequently designated subject – metalwork, of course – never truly emerged. The first item we were taught to produce was called a centre punch. Basically, you file a piece of metal down to a point. One boy in the class completed the entire task inside the first lesson. After three months of working on my bit of metal, it had become so misshapen and unfit for purpose I pushed it into the forge and left it there in the hope it would have a better life being melted. In the two years I attended metalwork I didn't learn a thing. I'm not suited to carrying out practical tasks. I'm not one for making things. We all wore aprons and mine had Buster Keaton's name written on it in biro. Others opted for David Bowie.

Corporal punishment was alive and kicking at Wimbledon College. The weapon of choice was called a ferule. It was made of hard leather and depending on the severity of the crime you might receive four, six or eight ferule strokes across the palms of your hands, administered by one of the teachers. Everyday somebody or other was getting the ferule. Either at lunchtime or directly after school. It happened to me once. I'd always struggled with mathematics, from the early days of trying to unravel the mysteries of 'if it takes three men four days to dig a hole eleven-foot deep, how much faster will the Flying Scotsman arrive at Kings Cross station given that steam pressure is 20 per cent lower than the price of eggs in Istanbul?'

That was hard enough. So by the time we moved on to algebra, $x-y=b/9$, well, I'm screaming for the exit. It makes my brain go funny, as if part of it has been clamped and rendered useless.

Father Spring was my first maths teacher at Wimbledon College. If his name conjures up images of freshness and purity, and light-hearted frolicking amidst fragrant meadows, forget it. Father Spring was a bastard. A young Jesuit priest with pinched-thin lips and a cold heart of stone, he had no discernable sense of humour, which is always a major failing in a human being.

Father Spring set the maths homework, algebra, and I didn't understand a single letter of it. But I did try, spending three hours working at the dining table at home in the evening. I went to sleep late. I woke up late, dashing out of the house and onto the bus before realising I'd left my homework on the dining table. Frustratingly, it was too late to do anything other than contemplate explaining it all to Father Spring first thing, as maths was the first lesson of the day.

'Hand in your homework, boys,' Father Spring instructs.

'Sir,' I say, with my hand up, 'I've left my homework at home.'

'Four ferules!'

I was stunned by the ice-cold ruthlessness of this holy man. I started to protest.

'But Sir …'

'EIGHT ferules.'

Tears formed in my eyes at the sheer injustice of it all. I stopped any protest right there. I was later whacked across both palms of the hand four times. I was unlucky to get one of the vicious teachers. The first couple of blows to each palm stung like crazy but after that, so did all the others. *

Wimbledon College and its environs was all another world to me. A posh world where people lived in big houses, seriously big houses, with two acres of lawn out the back. The school was surrounded by such properties. It was a pleasant world to stroll past on a sunny afternoon.

After a few months the idea occurred to a few of us comprehensive boys to kick a tennis ball around the playground after school. An impromptu game of football which gave us a sense of territory. One early evening, one of the grammar school boys was crossing the playground on his way to somewhere else when our tennis ball rolled towards him. Instead of ignoring it as was the custom amongst his tribe, he started dribbling with it before taking a shot at goal. We encouraged him to join us and we played together for about twenty minutes. After he'd gone I remember we said what

---

* Of course, as much as I detest institutionalised violence, I must say that corporal punishment improved my algebra no end, and now I happily while away a winter's evenings working out the true value of pi, to the nearest kilometre. I've always equated pain with learning and I'm a fervent believer in punching myself in the face whenever I learn a new fact. This is why I've never appeared on *Celebrity Mastermind*. I fear the general knowledge round would render me unconscious.

a nice bloke he seemed. This was my first interaction with one of 'them' and it would be a long time before it happened again.

We were kept apart from the rest of the school in our own little set 5 bit. Our English teacher, Mr Winter, was enthusiastic with a good sense of humour. I always looked forward to Friday's lesson in particular. The class would be split into four groups of five and we would ad-lib a sketch each. It wasn't called improvisation, but it was still all about making it up as you went along.

The other teacher that made a very good impression was Richard Milward, who was my history teacher. He was a noted historian specialising in the Tudors and Stuarts, with an expert knowledge of Wimbledon and Merton in that period. He was an excellent communicator of his enthusiasms but initially he found some of my fellow classmates bafflingly ignorant. One boy was semi-literate and his spelling of 'countryside' sadly lacked that all-important letter 'o', which greatly angered Mr Milward who believed insubordination, rather than ignorance, was afoot.

Richard Milward looked how a teacher should look. He wore a black gown that swirled around him as he bustled about the school. It's quite easy for me to picture him striding through Oxford cloisters, a selection of textbooks under his arm. He would cycle to and from the school, even giving you a cheery wave as he went past. I can remember the first time he did it and how proud I felt. He wasn't judging me or treating me any differently to the grammar school boys he was teaching. He once completely staggered me during a discussion about the English Civil War. I said that Thomas Fairfax deserved a biography of his own and Mr Milward agreed and suggested I should write it!

'Me?' I said.

'Yes,' he said. 'You're quite capable of it.'

*

My self-imposed barriers were quite rigid and I could not see what he evidently did. My shyness deepened as puberty advanced. There was now much more stuff to be shy about.

I think it was around this time, and in this environment, that I started to adapt to being a different kind of boy. Essentially, I was shy and anxious about fitting in. My school mates were into rock music: Bowie, Genesis, Pink Floyd. I had a poster of Charlie Chaplin on my wall and an LP called *The Jolson Story*, which I played regularly. I was truly out of step with those around me. And I was always telling jokes. Actually, I wasn't just telling jokes, I was, to be honest, wisecracking every few minutes. Taking the piss out of my classmates was a popular sport with me. Not so much with them.

There was one incident in that first year which I didn't tell my parents about at the time as it would have terrified them. It was at the end of the school day, the autumn leaves were falling and one of my classmates, Mick, had a lovely new racing bike. As he was walking it through the main gate I asked if he minded me borrowing it to ride down Edge Hill and I would meet him at the bottom. He readily agreed. I climbed on the bike and started cycling downhill. But I had made a potentially fatal error. I hadn't familiarised myself with the bike and, as I picked up speed, I realised with a sudden cold sweat that I didn't know how the brakes worked. Edge Hill is steep in the middle and I was now approaching twenty miles per hour. I was going too fast to steer myself into the next side road. Straight ahead at the bottom was a busy road, and it was rush hour and I was heading straight for it. I was going too fast to deviate. The traffic ahead was constant, with gaps of a second or so between vehicles.

I pull on what I think are the brakes, but nothing happens. As I approach the main road I look to my right to see a lorry coming towards me. From now on everything slows right down in my head, but in reality my speed doesn't alter.

It was clear that this could be it. I was experiencing every microsecond to its full capacity. I crossed the road at speed, narrowly missing the lorry coming towards me by a margin of just ten yards. One second later and I would have been under its wheels. Once that bit was out of the way, I then crossed over the second line of traffic, this time running from left to right. I went directly between two cars, both of them doing around thirty miles per hour, but with a generous twenty-foot gap between them. The bike hit the kerb on the side of the road, I toppled off and landed on my arse. I was completely unhurt.

And so was the bike. No buckled wheel, no scratched paint work. No bruising, broken bones or death.

The lorry driver stopped his vehicle fifty yards up the road and came running back to where I was sitting on the pavement. 'What did you do that for?' he shouted at me. I didn't have a ready answer. I was too stunned with shock to say anything beyond 'the brake's not working'. I had just survived a near certain death situation and this lorry driver seeks an explanation for my actions. But he's in shock too. He's nearly killed a schoolboy on a bike.

Upon getting to my feet, I picked up the remarkably unaffected bike and squeezed what I took to be the brakes. Now, they worked fine. I leant the bike against a wall and stood next to it, taking deep breaths into me. My legs were wobbly as I realised just how lucky I'd been. Mick, who was still ambling down the hill, arrived a few minutes later. I tried to briefly describe what had just happened, but my account lacked dramatic 'oomph' because quite clearly both myself and the bike had never been in better physical shape. My internal mechanisms were all of a jitter, but that wasn't immediately apparent.

'You can ride it a bit more if you like,' he said, but I quickly refused his offer.*

The schoolboy whose bike I had borrowed, Mick, gained a fleeting taste of celebrity a couple of years later in our school when he appeared on *Top of the Pops* and was briefly interviewed by whichever DJ was hosting that week.

'What's your name?' enquired the DJ.

'Mick,' said Mick.

That was the end of the exchange. But in our part of the school it might as well have been *Frost/Nixon*.

Small as it may seem, this was an important moment for me. Knowing someone who had been on telly seemed to make it somehow possible that it might happen for me one day. Obviously, I would aim for a career rather than a one-word appearance. But you get the gist. How that was going to happen, though, I had no idea. There was no map of how to get there.

Other than my general wisecracking, opportunity to practise any kind of performance was in short supply. But I did read voraciously, particularly the lives and careers of the pre-eminent silent comedy stars. I absorbed Charlie Chaplin and Buster Keaton's attitude to their work. Always strive to do your best, and improve and refine your work as you go on. A total dedication to your craft was necessary for success and even then there were no guarantees.

I remember one phrase that leapt out at me when I was reading a book on the history of the music hall, which detailed the suicide of a performer long past his peak who threw himself off a bridge into the Thames. According to the book his 'particular brand of

---

* It was some time before I climbed back on to a bike and I avoided all hills and any potential of runaway danger. An exercise bike suits me fine these days.

red-nosed humour had gone out of fashion'. It struck a chord with me.

And so I progressed, if 'progressed' is the right word, through the years at Wimbledon College, up to O levels and heading towards the outside world.

The summer holiday that followed was an anxious time. If my O level results weren't good enough I would have to leave school and either find some kind of job or try and get into a technical college to study God knows what.

I knew that I wanted to be a comedian but I had no way of achieving this ambition. I was sixteen, it was 1973, and there simply were no comedy clubs in London. Staying on at Wimbledon College was the least scary option of all, which, looking back, indicates my supreme reluctance to start living in the outside world.

My first tentative steps into full-time paid employment took me to the giant Sainsbury's supermarket in Cheam. That summer I worked in the meat-packing department, behind the scenes away from the customers. My job was to shovel pink mince into a tray using a white plastic scoop, and then to place that tray on a conveyor belt, which transported the meaty delight through a machine that wrapped clear plastic film over the contents and automatically stamped the appropriate price and weight.

I never got promoted beyond scooping the mince. No further responsibilities were given to me. My lack of promotion was undoubtedly due to my complete inability to achieve a consistent weight of scooped mince. Doing something mechanically over and over again is not one of my strong points.

Unlike Bill. Bill did the same simple task repeatedly day after day, year after year. He worked at a table on his own with his back to the rest of the workforce. Everybody wore white coats and white hats. Some of us were qualified butchers who could skilfully cut pieces of meat into chops while, yes, others simply shovelled mince. But Bill packed chickens. Dead chickens. Into boxes. He created the boxes from flat-packed cardboard. He'd push the sides together and a box would pop up and a chicken would pop in. All beautifully manipulated by Bill. The boxed bird was then placed on top of a growing pile of the same.

Bill, the master of his trade, completed four boxes a minute while all the time maintaining a conversation over his shoulder, and not once looking at what he was doing. Apart from chickens, Bill's other specialist subject, and the general topic of his conversation, was racism.

'Do you know how they stop a bus in Brixton?' Bill quipped one day. 'They use a blowpipe to fire a poison dart into the driver's neck.' Charming man. Some people said this stuff all the time back then.

Sitting in the staff canteen and listening to the workers' banter during tea breaks was a twice daily occurrence. The working-class voices around me were deeper and older in tone than the ones I had gone to school with, but the humour and values were the same. One radical difference was that amongst the men were women. Real women. Yes! Young sexy women, dressed in tight-fitting Sainsbury's work clothes.

The sixteen-year-old version of me found a couple of the young women working there particularly attractive. They may have only been two or three years older but they were properly adult. They had clearly done it. The combination of a glimpse of bare thigh and the sensuous curve of a breast was enough to send me back to the meat department in a complete tizzy – where I could handle leg and breast to my heart's content. Providing it was chicken.

I hope I'm not being too ungallant when I suggest that one of the subjects of my desire had a definite air of tartiness about her. Let's call her Rita. I had the feeling that she enjoyed herself and wouldn't be too put out helping a young, nervous, shy boy into the world of manhood, round the back of the bins. That was my fantasy anyhow. I never once summoned up the nerve to talk to her, but planning how I might, and imagining what might happen later, occupied a great deal of my 'leisure time'. I would somehow contrive to bump into her on the stairs. That was the plan in my head. I would say, 'Hello do you like mince?' and that would be it!

But it was impossible. I was tongue-tied, nervous, easily embarrassed, and at the age of sixteen I was producing so much testosterone there were times I could barely function as a human being.

I did get talking to one of my co-workers one tea break in the canteen. He was a young boy the same age as me and he was also awaiting exam results. He was better spoken than I was and seemed rather out of place working in the meat-packing department of a supermarket.

'How many O level results are you expecting?' he asked me.

'Four,' I said. 'English, English Literature, History and Sociology.'

'Oh,' he said. 'Isn't ten the usual number?'

I blushed red and said, 'I don't know. Is it?'

Not for the kids in my class at school it wasn't. I didn't even know there were ten subjects you could take for O levels.

This posh boy was keen to put me down perhaps to deflect questions away from his own situation. I mean, what was a well-educated lad doing in that environment, unless he's been sent there as some kind of life lesson to help him fully appreciate how lucky he really is? Setting fire to the school tuck shop might warrant a six-week sentence shovelling tripe into plastic trays, but none of this occurred to me at the time. I didn't know whether school tuck shops even existed outside the realms of schoolboy fiction. I knew as little about his world as he knew about mine. I glimpsed the poshness at Wimbledon College, but I was never part of it.

Geoff was my boss in the meat-packing department. Geoff was a butcher. He was in his late forties, balding, and proud of his work. His knives were always well looked after. I sometimes cleaned them but Geoff always sharpened them. He read the *Daily Mirror*, he didn't like bad language in the workplace, he was an honest, decent sort. He wasn't racist. He didn't make suggestive remarks to the young women working there. He had a sunny disposition and he was respected by his co-workers. Geoff, in the meat-packing department, was the man you looked up to.

At the end of one lunch break I found myself standing next to him. We were both washing our hands in adjacent sinks. The slim tablet of almost transparently thin soap passed between us. Suddenly, apropos of nothing in particular, Geoff said, 'Do you know I've always had one ambition in life. But I don't know. It's possibly too late now.'

Naturally my ears pricked up at this. At sixteen years old I was very conscious that the large majority of people in work don't really like their jobs. So when Geoff mentioned he'd always held an ambition close to his heart, I was eager to know what it was. Perhaps he could tell I had a secret passion because he had one himself. Maybe he had yearned to be a jazz pianist, a mountaineer or maybe a wildlife photographer, crouching in camouflaged huts poking a long lens towards unsuspecting zebras. It was none of these.

'What was your ambition, Geoff?' I asked.

Geoff paused, turned to me, and looked me straight in the eye. 'I've always wanted to work for Safeway,' he said. 'They really know how to look after their staff.'

5

Mozart's Crème Brûlée

There's no other way to put this. General horniness was becoming a problem. Particularly in warm weather, with summer dresses and all the rest of it. Floaty, beautiful women flowing down a busy street, while I followed them at a discrete distance, drinking in their shape, utterly hypnotised by their gentle swaying. I was always twenty or so yards behind them.

It was desperately important that they never knew I was there. If any woman had approached me and smiled, I'm pretty sure I would have gone extremely red-faced and then caught fire. Consumed in flames of lust shooting ten feet high, which is quite easy to achieve when you're sixteen.

I used to walk up and down Wimbledon Broadway a fair amount when I was in the mood.

Quite often there would be the most delicious dilemma. While discreetly following one beautiful girl, I would see another beautiful girl walking towards me. Oh, what do I do? Shall I change direction or keep going as far as the Odeon cinema? On more than one occasion I became rooted to the spot with my head swivelling from left to right as a seemingly endless parade of bare shoulders, long hair, short hair, bare midriffs, covered midriffs, tight-fitting jeans, floral-patterned dresses floated by.

My fixation on physical appearance is easily explained by my total ignorance of what women were like, and how you approached them or even spoke to them in a flirty context. It was way beyond my capabilities to ever attempt to 'chat up' a girl. They were a completely alien species to me. My parents' attempt to make sure that I knew all about the birds and the bees consisted of my mother hurling a sex education booklet, produced by the Catholic Church, across the living room at me one morning, before quickly shutting the door in a state of high embarrassment. The booklet was entitled *Becoming a Man*, and featured several black and white photographs of a priest shaking hands and generally relaxing with a group of adolescent boys. We would look at such a publication with different eyes today. Back then I felt as embarrassed as my mother did on the other side of the door. Dad's only offering on the subject of growing up was that I 'should always dry underneath yourself after having a bath'. This vague advice could equally apply to the floor I suppose. An admirable health and safety tip to pass on from father to son. None of us wanted to talk about sex, so we didn't. I knew the basic facts anyway so the booklet was no good to me.

Wimbledon College was an all-boys establishment with very few female teachers. My sister Angela was four-and-a-half years younger than me, and so of course were all her friends. I simply didn't meet any girls my age. There was one girl who regularly walked past our house in Morden on her way to the shops. She wore short dresses and had long shapely legs that were further extended by her high-heeled shoes. She had a long stride that mesmerised me whenever I happened to be glued to the front window, gasping my appreciation on the glass as she walked by. Then, not having seen her for a few months, I spotted her again. She had the same stride, the same brevity of clothing and the same high-heeled shoes. But now she was pushing a pram with a tiny baby in it. She didn't look like she was ready for the big bad world. I knew I wasn't. Staring out the window was enough excitement for me.

When I got into the sixth form I was profoundly relieved that I had another two years of school ahead of me. Postponing the inevitable, if only for a while, was a blessed relief. I wasn't yet ready to break out of my cocoon or do anything to change the status quo. Fortunately, or unfortunately, for me, depending on how you look at it, my friends had other ideas. The kids I hung around with at school were people I had met the year before going to Wimbledon College. Our mutual astonishment at arriving at such a place had bound us together. I didn't feel as if I was part of a gang but, nevertheless, Jim, Tony, Edward and Sam were also in set 5, and it was they who I played football with in the playground after school. The rest of them socialised together at the weekends, going to football matches and drinking beer in pubs where the landlord turned a blind eye to how old you really were. I spent my weekends sitting at home, often alone, up in my bedroom reading show-business biographies and running silent films on my projector. At school the four friends I had suddenly stopped talking to me in November 1973.

They ignored me during registration and that was that from then on. It's easy to tell when people have stopped talking to you, but woefully hard to find out why. Looking back now, I can see that on occasions my ready wit was used to embarrass or attack a contemporary; picking on somebody's large nose or levelling fun at a chap's flat head. At sixteen I was as anxious as anyone as to what kind of physical specimen I was turning into, and by verbally attacking others that made it less likely that they would have go at me. If I had a pop at a classmate's pimples I was establishing a higher status than him. Or so I thought, but of course people can be alienated very easily by somebody scoring cheap laughs at their physical appearance. And so they stopped talking to me. All of a sudden.

'Hello.'

Nothing back.

Demonstrating once again a streak of stubborn individualism, instead of trying to ingratiate myself back into the group I looked round for other people to talk to. The idea of being in the sixth form on my own – desolate in a forest of tweed jackets – was daunting, but I had no choice. I had been lonely enough in my summer holiday's solitude, but to be friendless in a roomful of spotty adolescents seemed a fate worse than death.

I soon found two other boys to talk to. And although Tom was fat and Luke had a pudding bowl haircut, I didn't make fun of either one of them. They were nice guys who found the things I said hysterical. I took the sting out of my humour and felt all the better for it. And then I met John Irwin properly for the first time.

We had first been introduced five years earlier by a well-meaning pupil who used the rather unfortunate phrase, 'This is Paul Martin, he's the class comedian.' I winced at the description with its heavy tone of being a right pain in the neck, always heartily joking or dishing out lame puns. And that's exactly what John thought too. So after that poor start we never engaged with each other much over the next few years. Although we both attended Wimbledon College at the same time, John resided in set 4 while I was in set 5, so our paths didn't cross again until I found myself sitting a few seats away from him in the sixth form common room. I don't know why I said what I said, but I said it …

'I was hearing the other day that Beethoven invented the rice pudding,' I said with a perfectly straight face.

'Yes, I heard that too,' said John with an equally straight face.

'He only wrote his music to finance his researches into desserts,' I said. 'That was the stuff that really interested him.'

'Yes,' said John, 'and Mozart invented the crème brûlée.'

At that moment I recognised a fellow spirit. Somebody with the same sense of humour, who could return a strange thought back to you with added comic spin.

Mozart's creation of the crème brûlée seems a happier fit to me than Beethoven's rice pudding. Something about the caramelised topping conjures up an atmosphere of harpsichords played in golden palaces by periwigged flunkeys. Now I think about it, there's also something strangely authentic about the image of Beethoven in a dimly-lit cellar, moodily stirring the contents of a vast cauldron while muttering Germanically about the inconsistency of locally grown rice.

John was one of the more obviously individual students in the sixth form. At six foot two, he was the same height as me but he had shoulder-length straw-coloured hair and more eccentric clothes. He wore workman's boots, dark trousers and a rather tightly cut light-grey jacket, which fitted snugly across his broad shoulders. Our quick exchange made us both laugh and we began to seek out each other's company during the lunch breaks.

After one particularly mirthful chat in which I roared with laughter, I was brought crashing back to earth by a fellow sixth former who took me aside and said, 'It's scum like you that gives this place a bad name.'

I was poleaxed by this verbal assault. This other guy was a grammar school boy who had clearly had enough of me and my kind polluting his world of tweed jackets and very large gardens with our unsophisticated working-class vowel sounds and roughness. But getting to know John was the antidote to all that, and soon after I first began talking to him we experienced an afternoon of such sustained hilarity that I got to the point where my nervous system was twanging with joy. I hadn't laughed so long and so hard in my life, before or since. Over the course of three hours, the two of us sat in the corner of the sixth form common room at first just saying silly things – odd juxtapositions to each other that soon became a verbal jazz that built on emerging themes.

Other sixth formers gathered around us, ostensibly looking at their text books but also laughing at the stuff that John and I were coming up with. This went on at least for a couple of hours. I remember one boy suddenly getting to his feet and exclaiming, 'Shit, I should have been in geography ten minutes ago.'

Everybody laughed at that as well. It was an extreme, heady buzz that left me literally holding my sides with laughter, the ache made pleasurable by the morphine-like natural endorphins that were flooding through my brain. After a particularly intense burst of laughter we would take a rest, which was generally well observed until one of us would then pick at a comic thread and start ravelling it away in another direction, taking us on to further peaks of hilarity.

Eventually, two or three elements came together in such a way that, to our astonishment, a bona fide joke emerged with a proper punchline. Being there at the heart of its creation, as disparate efforts flew together, was thrilling for us and the dozen or so other sixth formers sitting around. It doesn't matter what the joke was because that's not really the point of the story. The point is that seven years later the exact same joke was told to me by a profes-sional illustrator in his house in Wrexham, North Wales. I was astounded. Had John and I created a joke that had been spread by the boys listening to us in that sixth form common room, or had we accidentally arrived at an already existing joke? I felt the latter explanation was unlikely, but unless the joke is found in an old joke book which predates 1974 I don't suppose we'll ever know.

*

One afternoon, the maths teacher decided to ask each pupil in his class what careers they were going to pursue when they left school. I always avoided this kind of questioning if I could. If cornered, I might just mutter something about being a journalist, but my real ambition would remain undisclosed. I didn't want people putting me off by dismissively laughing at the very notion that I could somehow become a comedian. The teacher asked a boy in the front row the dreaded question, 'What are you going to do when you leave school?'

The boy replied in a dull voice, 'I'm going to work for Sunlight Laundry.'

The teacher's cheeks flushed purple with anger and the veins in his face throbbed furiously. 'What a pathetic answer,' he roared. 'You are young, you have the world in front of you. Don't limit your horizons, you must aim higher in life.' He paused for breath. 'And why on earth do you want to work for Sunlight Laundry?'

'It's only at the end of my road. I can walk there,' came the feeble reply.

'What a dismal lack of ambition,' said the teacher, who then turned to the next pupil. 'And what are you going to do?' he said.

'I'm going to work with him,' the boy replied.

The sixth form master was a Jesuit priest called Father Cooper. He was a heavy smoker and his white hair had a brown nicotine streak at the front. Father Cooper offered careers advice and I spent a lot of time dodging his eye, because although I knew what I wanted to do, I couldn't see how he could help.

'Hello Father Cooper, I'd like to work in comedy.'

'Fine, how does a twelve-week summer season in Blackpool with Ken Dodd and The Tremeloes suit you?'

I didn't have much faith in the careers advice process, but an appointment had to be made. I can remember it clearly. In a small office two floors up, with windows overlooking the playground and the old gym, Father Cooper sat behind a large wooden desk, shelves filled with box files behind his head. I knocked on the door.

'Come in, Paul.'

I walked in and closed the door tentatively behind me. I was nervous in the face of authority, even though it reeked of Benson & Hedges.

'Sit down, Paul.' I sat down. 'Have you thought about what you're going to do when you leave school?'

Here was my big opportunity. The chance to proclaim my ambition, to lay it on the table and, alright, it might invite ridicule, but my belief and commitment would withstand robust examination. I spoke without hesitation.

'I don't know really.'

He looked at me in a very 'well clearly you have no idea about anything' sort of way and offered up the usual options.

'Are you interested in being in the services? The Army perhaps?'

'Not really.'

Father Cooper sighed and looked at the shy, uncommunicative boy unable to make proper eye contact, and perhaps came to the conclusion that he was dealing with a no-hoper. Naturally, I'm guessing at his thoughts but this interpretation certainly explains what happened next. He stood and reached for the very top shelf behind him, and lifted up a box folder coated in dust. He blew the dust into the main body of the room. As I watched the particles of grey matter briefly catch the weak sunlight, before settling into the carpet, I was momentarily distracted from the purpose of our interview. I was brought quickly back to banal reality by the leaflet that Father Cooper had removed from the dusty box file and was now pushing towards me. The words in big bold black type will haunt me forever and, in truth, I shudder at the prospect of writing them now. The leaflet was part of a series collected under the generic title of 'If I were a …' and then a job like car mechanic, perhaps with a description of the skills that would be needed.

The 'If I were' leaflet in the series that was propelled across the brown-stained desk by brown-stained fingers was 'If I were a … Shelf-Filler'. Shelf-filler! In a supermarket filling shelves!

I muttered something that hopefully reflected my jaw-dropping astonishment at this dismally low view of my employment prospects.

'Thank you,' I seem to remember was my response.

The impending world of work led me to hear about a rather strange job from one of the boys at school. In the Jewish faith, boys are circumcised at a very early age and this boy's uncle got talking to the man who carried out this task. They were at a party and for the want of something to say the uncle asked, 'Tell me, what do you do with all those foreskins. Do you just throw them away?'

And the other man said, 'Oh no, they're not wasted. In fact I skilfully turn each one of them into a tiny purse.'

'But what's the point of that?' said the uncle.

'Well, if you rub them they turn into a set of luggage.'

Forgive me for smuggling that in, but that's the joke that John and I came up with between us, over the course of a couple of hours one rainy Thursday afternoon in the corner of the sixth form common room. I wanted to surprise you with it.

Talking to John was a daily joy and we had fun inventing new lyrics to popular songs. I remember one verse from our rewriting of 'Bachelor Boy', which we renamed 'Bachelor's Boy' with its implication of being born out of wedlock. We enjoyed singing our spoof verses:

When I was young
I said to my Pa
'Can I go on the hunt?'
And he looked at me
And he said with a smile
'Of course you can, you can.'
He said, 'Son, you are a bachelor's boy
And that's the way you'll stay
Son, you are a bachelor's boy until your dying day.'

Around about this time I wrote a frankly rude poem devoted to the art and practise of masturbation, or self-love as we might more delicately call it. Although the subject matter is clearly distasteful, in my defence I was a teenage boy. I never agreed with the religious orthodoxy that this act was wrong in itself. When a priest told me it was sinful, I thought, *'It must be the way you're doing it because it feels fine to me.'*

Which leads me to speculate upon the personal habits of one of the founding fathers of the United States. This poem was a writing exercise on my part, undertaken after the undeniably catchy couplet 'Benjamin Franklin couldn't stop wanking' popped into my head all of a sudden one sunny afternoon.

Benjamin Franklin
Couldn't stop wanking
So he consulted his priest
He said in confession
He's just had a session
And the priest said
'This practice must cease.'

So, young Ben,
Went back to his den
And made a big effort to stop.
He welded his zip
Tied his hand to his hip
But the cum shot out of his sock.

I blame the hormones coursing through my veins. There were other verses but mercifully I can't remember them. Looking back at it now, I'm rather impressed. It rhymes nicely enough and the words jostle together harmoniously – although of course the subject matter leaves a lot to be desired. It was a writing exercise in the end, but at least I was writing about what I knew.

I'd realised early on that developing my comedy writing skills was something that I could do on my own and didn't cost anything. I could write without having to interact with other people. Although it's a bawdy ditty and goes against my general hostility towards getting cheap laughs from poo, wee and bum jokes, I do recognise that the lines have a certain comic bounce. And anyway, it was never for public consumption! I think I've apologised enough.

Around this time John and I went to see Mel Brooks's new movie *Young Frankenstein*, which was a parody of the Universal horror films made in the early 1930s. The two of us had played around with the idea of a film that combined the distinctly different genres of a Cliff Richard musical, blended with a gothic horror landscape of corpses swinging from gibbets as feral children sang 'Darling, we're the young ones'. The savage incongruity of these two styles provoked much laughter between us. We imagined a scene set at a railway platform where a passenger leans out of a train window and enquires of a porter, 'Pardon me boy, is this the Transylvania station?' – a parody of Glenn Miller's tune 'Chattanooga Choo Choo', with its reference to Pennsylvania station.

Well, we were stupefied as we watched *Young Frankenstein* because there, suddenly on the screen, was the scene as we had imagined it, including the above line of dialogue. It was completely astonishing to us. But as we later talked – once we had discounted the suspicion that Mel Brooks had hired spies to listen in on our corner of the sixth form common room – I reasoned that it showed we could create material that was good enough for the screen. This, we agreed, was good news.

My English teacher in the sixth form was Mr McClave. Mr McClave was tall and thin and from Belfast. He somewhat resembled the former Spurs and Northern Ireland goalkeeper Pat Jennings. He had prominent cheekbones with a ridge of dark hair growing along each one. He had a wry sense of humour. Our A level syllabus consisted of *King Lear*, *Coriolanus*, *The Canterbury Tales* and one English novel.

There had been some speculation as to the identity of the last book and there were groans all round the classroom when Mr McClave walked in with several copies of *Northanger Abbey* by Jane Austen. Not the stuff for a bunch of straight sixteen-year-old boys. Mr McClave quelled the objections with the following words: 'Now I got this book for two reasons. Firstly, I think it is one of the best books ever written. And, secondly, it's the only one I could get.'

Mr McClave had been my English teacher the year before and was greatly encouraging even though we didn't always agree. I had the feeling he enjoyed reading my essays. At the end of one adventure story I wrote: 'I then ran out of the house, hailed a passing taxi and was never seen again.' Mr McClave wrote at the bottom in red ink: 'You can't say you were never seen again. Only other people can say you were never seen again.' I tried to argue the point but he was adamant.

In my previous year he had encouraged me to read out a couple of my essays to the class. The only detail I can remember is that one of them briefly featured a budgie called Amos the Turk.

I also wrote a poem about a football match. A first-person account of playing the game. At one point I got the ball and started running with it.

> *I swerved to the right*
> *I swerved to the left*
> *And then I remembered*
> *I was the Ref.*

Now in the sixth form, he gave me permission to perform a short sketch in front of the class. I wrote, learnt and rehearsed it. This was me pushing myself into getting some performance experience. I performed the sketch and it actually went very well. There were laughs in all the right places.

At the end, Mr McClave clapped enthusiastically and so did the majority of the kids. I felt a huge wave of achievement rushing over me. I had found the nerve to ask the teacher, if I could perform this sketch the week before and I had the temperament to perform it in front of classmates who I didn't know particularly well. I felt a real triumph.

This was an English A level class and I was in with a group of boys who had risen through the grammar school part of Wimbledon College, so they weren't necessarily an easy crowd.

He looked at me and spoke the words I'd been waiting to hear from a responsible adult all my life. 'You ought to go on the stage,' he said.

After our discussion about whether I could say 'I was never seen again', I finished another essay with something like the following paragraph: 'So there I was in the middle of the Amazon jungle, surrounded by three tigers and a circus acrobat, when I suddenly ran out of the clearing, hailed a passing taxi and was never seen again.'

Mr McClave didn't make any comment in red ink this time, which rather disappointed me. My next essay finished with: 'Gentlemen, as the Commander of this nuclear submarine may I make it quite clear that I have no alternative but to fire myself out of the torpedo tube, hail a passing taxi and never be seen again.'

'Alright,' he scrawled, 'that's enough.'

6

Tomato Soup

On my sixteenth birthday my parents had cashed in an insurance policy to which they had been contributing 25p a week since the day I'd been born, and that they had been hoping would help me to get a start in life. The policy had matured and I was given £100. After discussing it with the family it was clear that £100, although a nice sum, was not worth anything like as much as it had been in 1957, and sadly wouldn't quite be up to the job of giving me a start in life. So instead I bought a really nice record player with two fairly huge speakers and a built-in amplifier for ninety-five quid.

This gave me great pleasure, particularly as the system had a headphone socket, which was a far from common feature back then. I spent a lot of time up in my bedroom, door closed, listening to records through big headphones that were heavy but had a marvellous sound. Hearing the Goons performing together in this way allowed me to feel I was onstage with them, waiting for my cue. I had also finally caught up with popular music and had borrowed all of the Beatles' albums one by one from Sutton library. This is how I spent a huge amount of my sixth form years at home, discovering popular music from ten years before. The Kinks, Simon and Garfunkel, and the Beach Boys all became favourites.

The next year my family went on holiday without me. I was three weeks past my seventeenth birthday and no longer comfortable with the family environment. Being told what to do was something that I didn't really enjoy, and the prospects of living on my own in the family home for seven days seemed pretty appealing. I remember thinking I could use this opportunity to start writing a book. A work of fiction. A detective novel! I had a title which I liked – *How do you Spell Marguerite?* One brilliant plot point being that a suicide note left by somebody called Marguerite had misspelt her name. I gave it a good stab and I wrote sixteen pages, but came to an inevitable stop as invention dried up. It dawned on me that I had very few life experiences to draw on at this stage. The characters were paper thin, the 'comedy' was inspired by stuff I'd seen elsewhere. I wasn't deliberately setting out to copy other people's material, but it couldn't help but seep through. That's the danger of having such a retentive memory for jokes.

Although I used the seven days away from other people to practise writing, the truth is that I also took the opportunity to go slightly off my bonce due to the almost complete lack of human contact over that time. I fell into the habit of listening to the late-night phone-ins on the then extremely new LBC station. I found myself talking back to the radio. During the day I didn't speak to anybody other than bus conductors or shop assistants. I ate a lot of soup bulked out with torn slices of bread. I had fish and chips at night, and sometimes Kentucky Fried Chicken. I took the 93 bus back to Fulham, alighting at Putney Bridge and then walking through Bishops Park and on to the flats at Robert Owen House. I was looking for something. The secure past. My life in the flats before moving away at the age of eight was a time before I worried about what would happen after I left school.

But now my head was full of crippling post-puberty shyness and the terror of trying to find a job. Not having any human connection was beginning to affect me more and more. At one point, I walked through the fields opposite our house holding aloft a small tin of Heinz tomato soup, while declaiming loudly, 'Do not overheat as this will impair flavour,' in a mock-Shakespearean actor's voice.

The daftest thing I did in the whole week was to sit on a park bench in Hyde Park, from 5.45 a.m. to sometime after half past eight in the morning, hoping that Michael Crawford, the star of *Some Mothers Do 'Ave 'Em*, might run past. I was a huge fan of his television show and he was starring in a musical called *Billy* at the Theatre Royal Drury Lane, which was based on the *Billy Liar* novel written by Keith Waterhouse. Billy wanted to become a scriptwriter for a television comic called Danny Boon, whose beautifully bad catchphrase was 'It's all happening'. The lavish musical might have been staged especially for me.

That week I spent home alone I saw the show three times. The cheapest seats at the very top were only 75p. I read a newspaper interview with Michael Crawford where he spoke about running through Hyde Park every morning to help him keep in shape for the demanding role of Billy.

So, I went to Hyde Park very early the following morning and sat on a bench in the hope that he would run past. Hyde Park is extremely large. The chances of Michael Crawford running past the park bench I had selected were beyond remote. There were a few joggers around, but none of them was Michael Crawford.

I conjured up moments of excitement as I persuaded myself that the far distant figure gradually approaching might be him. But it wasn't. Even if it had been, what would I have done? I have an awful feeling I would have just sat there on the bench, astonished to be so close to him and everything he represented.

Shy, slightly bonkers, obsessed with the world of comedy, but with absolutely no idea of how to get there, I simply sat on a bench in a park, waiting for show business to turn up.

That summer I floundered around. Looking back now, I was trying to figure it all out. I went to Morden library every week where I'd found they stocked a copy of the theatrical newspaper *The Stage*. I was particularly fascinated by the small ads placed by acts struggling near the bottom rungs of the showbiz ladder. The fabulous 'Winola and her Syncopated Snakes', the hilarious 'Victor Buffoon – Rib Tickler to Royalty'. Old-time variety acts that hadn't retired. There were photos of juggling Cossacks in huge furry hats, a big fat man playing a tiny xylophone, another large man folding balloons into the shape of a poodle.

I imagined that all these acts knew each other and that there was a camaraderie between them. I had an LP of some of Morecambe and Wise's early BBC material, and I was particularly struck by the photo on the front cover. Eric stood with his arm proudly around Ernie as a gesture of solid fraternity. From the outside, I imagined show business was stuffed full of friends who enjoyed each other's work. I saw glimpses of this happiness on episodes of *This is Your Life* whenever comedians were featured. They all seemed to have a good time together.

As a clear comparison to how far away I was from taking my first step into show business, there was a young man the same age as me who I saw make a big impact on a talent show called *New Faces*.

Lenny Henry had buckets of charm and supreme coolness under pressure. At sixteen he was doing live television and relishing it. He was being what I wanted to be, but with such accomplishment. His act consisted of impressions and the audience loved him.

He had a cheeky grin, but also fantastic timing and stage presence. I was envious of him being that good that early in life, while I was in Morden library reading the small ads in *The Stage* or sitting in my bedroom.

Although sure about what I wanted to do, I was still very unsure about myself. I could be easily crushed. Occasionally my mother would drive us to Epsom to enjoy the greenery and space. Amidst all the nature was a golf course that had a road running through one of the fairways. I'd recently bought a simple golf club second hand for 75p, and a couple of badly scuffed greyish golf balls. It seemed a good idea to take club and balls with me the next time we drove to Epsom. We could park near the road that traverses the course and I could have a little practise just knocking a couple of balls around.

And so we did. I was standing to one side of the fairway with my club in hand, with its wooden shaft and metal head. I was wearing a short-sleeved shirt, a pair of shorts and sandals. I hit the ball and it didn't go anywhere near where I had intended it to. I saw a man walking towards me. He was pulling a golf bag crammed with drivers, wedges, putters and irons. He called out to me in a posh voice, 'You there.' Immediately embarrassed, I turned towards him.

I say nothing.

'Are you a member of the club?' he barks.

Club? What club? I thought I was on a common that happened to have a golf course on it. There were no signs saying 'Private – Keep Out'. I'd assumed it was a public course and I'd also assumed that nobody would really mind if I tried to hit a couple of golf balls along a bit of fairway. I was wrong.

'No, I'm not,' I said, acutely aware of my sartorial shortcomings.

I mumbled some short apology and walked back to the car red-faced and embarrassed. I was in the wrong place and I didn't belong there. This place wasn't for me. It was like the other side of the river. Or the locked meadow. One of those places that you're not allowed to go.

My two years in the sixth form came to an unexceptional end when I sat my three A level exams. I'd felt reasonably confident with English literature, but the other two subjects, oh dear! History was split into one paper on the English Civil War, while the other covered European history from the fourteenth to the seventeenth century. The English Civil War was taught by Richard Milward, while the European stuff was taught by a rotund balding Jesuit priest called Father Blundell.

He was popular with the pupils and I liked him well enough. He wasn't a very good teacher though. He talked away but none of it sunk in. I felt strong on the Civil War but I was woefully under-prepared for three centuries of European tussle. If my prospects in history were in doubt then my third subject, chemistry, was a cast-iron certainty. I knew nothing. For two years I'd attended the lessons and watched the young idealistic priest religiously chalk equations onto the blackboard while explaining complex formulas. Two years! And at the end of it, all I knew for certain was that lime water turned milky. I didn't know what you had to do to it to achieve this cloudy effect, but I remembered it clearly from an experiment carried out in the classroom. I wish there had been more educated people in my class.

I sat the English A level and that went well. But I couldn't be complacent because history was three days away. The English Civil War was a breeze but, as expected, the European section was far more challenging. The first question was: 'Charles the Fifth of Sweden was influenced by his evil ministers. Discuss.' I wrote: 'Charles the Fifth of Sweden suffered greatly at the hands of his evil ministers. One minister was so evil he used to make his wife wear a bucket on her head while he threw Brussels sprouts at her and complained loudly that she smelt of bacon.'

'*Well,*' I thought, '*If I am going to fail this exam I might as well enjoy myself.*'

A week later I sat my chemistry A level. I opened up the paper and read the first question. And with calm authority I wrote the words 'Lime water turns milky'. The exam was two-and-a-half hours long, so I wrote them again. 'Lime water turns milky.' I then, over the course of the afternoon, managed, with application, to fall asleep. It was a sunny day and when I left the examination hall it was with a lightness of step and a youthful heart. I knew that chemistry would never bother me again. And neither would school for that matter. I couldn't postpone the moment any longer.

It was time to leave.

7

An Experiment with a Powerful Psychedelic Drug Leads to a Career in the Civil Service

'So, what sort of work are you looking for, then?' asked the guy in the employment office.

'I'm not sure really,' came my emphatic reply.

I had looked at the jobs offered on the vacancy board and none of them resembled a career in show business. There was a plethora of office jobs on offer, but they didn't appear to be the sort of work I would want to devote the next forty-five years of my life to. I was new to the world of unemployment and had yet to develop the sad-eyed, doleful expression that can afflict the long-term unemployed.

'Well,' he said. 'You've got to make a decision. What about factory work? Do you like working with your hands?'

'No, that's not for me,' I said. 'I probably wouldn't fit in to that environment.'

'Yes,' said the guy behind the counter. 'Factories can be very strange places. I've heard stories about vats of processed peas that would make your hair curl.'

'Yes I'm sure,' I said.

'How about working somewhere like this?' he said, gesturing to the employment office around us.

I looked around at the room, with its grey metal filing cabinets, its cream painted walls, its 'you don't have to be mad to work here' signs, and said 'OK'. Then he gave me some forms, which I took home to fill out.

It was 1977 and punk music was raw, brutal and swearing on our tellies. Although the perfect age (twenty) to be going to music gigs, my innate shyness precluded anything so bold. Nevertheless, I did do a little rebelling. As if in one desperate attempt not to become the boring civil servant I seemed destined to become, I dropped half a tab of LSD with some friends on a piece of National Trust land, one warm but rainy Saturday afternoon that July. It was a couple of miles from Morden, quite near to Mitcham Junction. Someone knew someone with a key to the woodland.

I had gone to an old school friend's house where he and another friend had just taken some LSD, and they gave me the half a tab after I strongly suggested it was a good idea. It was reckless on my part but I got away with it. The experience was beautifully natural, with plenty of tree hugging and dipping feet into cold running streams, while making up poetic images and laughing about people watching weather reports indoors on television when they could be outside experiencing it for real. And the rocks in the river were the reddest rocks I'd ever seen. I'm not recommending that you ingest chemicals into your system. Far from it. I'm no expert on the subject, but take it from me: lime water turns milky.

I didn't tell my parents, of course, and I felt no need to unburden myself at confession. In fact, I hadn't gone to confession for many years. But still, the world of conformity beckoned and a letter through the post informed me that I'd got a civil service interview. At the interview, when they asked me what I thought I could bring to the job, I resisted the impulse to say 'a sense of the universal vibrations that all soul seekers search for within and without the cosmos'. Instead I said 'a keenness to work'. The man behind the desk said I would be notified by post in a few days' time.

I wasn't going to give up on my dreams though. In fact, I had persuaded John Irwin to co-write a television sketch show with me, which for a pair of twenty-year-olds was ambitious. Completely unsolicited, we had no other plan but to write something and send it off to the BBC. For three months we wrote for two hours every evening. John would arrive at my parents' house at around seven o'clock in the evening and we would go straight up to my room, where some tea and Jaffa Cakes would be waiting. We would write for a couple of hours, sitting in red matching armchairs, before setting off to the pub for a couple of pints at the end of the evening. It was a mishmash of different ideas and strangeness. I remember one character dressed in a black suit, huge black sunglasses, standing against a yellow sky with a blue sun shining down upon him. There weren't many great jokes but it had a strong visual content. It was a start.

One night on the way back from the pub, we took a detour and climbed on to the huge roundabout in Morden Hall Road. This roundabout was a hundred feet across and covered in bushes and small shrubs. And there in the middle of it, invisible to the traffic circling around us, John and I built a small fire from twigs and dried leaves and laughed at the absurdity of it all. Camping within feet of a busy main road.

All these ideas fed into this series we were writing on spec. I asked my sister Angela to type it up and, after making three photocopies, I posted one to the BBC.

*

Sadly, around this time Dennis, our neighbour, died. Dad was the first to break the news.

'I see Dennis has died,' he said.

'Really?' said Mum. 'How do you know?'

'I saw his coffin come out of the front door this morning,' he said.

'What, on its own?' I said.

Dad gave me a look. 'No, half-a-dozen funeral directors carried it out.'

'Well, we know he lived on his own,' said Mum.

'I wonder how long he was in the house dead before they discovered him,' I said in that rather morbid way that young people sometimes have.

'We don't know,' said Mum. 'Hopefully he was found quickly. I wonder if it was his heart. He must have only been in his forties.'

Poor Dennis. We never spoke to him, our family weren't expert at socialising, but we acknowledged each other with a nod in the street and now he was gone. To us he was simply a man in a flat hat, horn-rimmed glasses and nondescript grey raincoat.

The next day I saw Dennis walking past our house. He looked remarkably lively for someone who had been dead for three days. It turned out he had an invalid mother who was bedridden, who nobody else saw, who died in her sleep. It was her coffin that Dad had seen carried out the front door. It gave us a nasty turn I can tell you.

A few days later a letter arrived from the civil service offering me a job in the Department of Employment. I couldn't think of a good reason to turn them down, so I accepted and found myself working at Tooting employment office, just four stops along the Northern line from Morden.

As I go into work on my first day as a clerical officer, let's have a good look at me. I'm twenty years old, but shy and virginal for my age. My formal qualifications consist of one A level and a few O levels, but none of them maths. You can number me amongst the innumerate. As to my informal qualifications, I have studied all aspects of comedy, from live performances to radio, TV, cinema, the written word and cartoonists. Through my appreciation of the history of comedy, I have a good knowledge of acts who were stars long before I was born. I desperately want to be a comedian, but I see no obvious way into it.

I long ago identified the major pathways into becoming a comic. Firstly, the working men's clubs that were predominantly in the north. The people that played these venues were the unsuccessful versions of the guys who you saw on the television show *The Comedians*. As I wasn't from the north the idea of moving up there with no contacts, no act and no hope was obviously idiotic.

Another way towards becoming a well-known popular comedian was to join a holiday camp as a red coat and somehow gain the experience to take you up to the next level. The only other route that I could see was to go to Cambridge University and to successfully audition for the Footlights Revue. Given my lack of performing experience, my shyness and my Grade 5 CSE Maths, none of these options were remotely possible.

Nevertheless, to test my aptitude for stage performance I came up with a clever idea. The Royal Academy of Dramatic Art, the most famous stage school of them all, held auditions where, for a fee, you were watched by professionals as you performed two speeches. A Shakespeare and a modern piece. I turned up two hours early for the audition and practised walking up and down the steps into the building. I was so excited, my nervous system throbbing with anticipation. This was a real test for me. I was going to walk on to a stage and deliver two speeches which I had memorised. Would I be able to do it? Would nerves cause me to forget my words?

The time soon came. Ten o'clock in the morning. I walked up the steps and joined the five other applicants who were already there. They were a mixed bunch. The eldest was a man in his early thirties who had thick black eyebrows and a very heavy depressive air about him. He was nervous, as we all were, but my nervousness was entirely made of excitement. I had no anxiety about not being accepted as a student because that wasn't the purpose of the exercise. I waited in a room with the others and then my name was called, 'Paul Martin please.' I stood up. I felt alert but calm. Excited but in control.

A member of staff indicated the door I should walk through. Walking, I had practised earlier, so that was no problem. I moved through the door and on the other side was darkness. I was facing a high wall of black cloth right in front of me. Then, to my left, I saw a light, so I moved towards the source. I turned a corner and found myself on the stage. It was a small auditorium, maybe seventy seats or so, with two of them occupied by a man and a woman, both well dressed in their early thirties. They were looking straight at me. They were already appraising me before I'd even spoke. They were watching how I walked on to the stage. Did I look physically comfortable within myself? I knew I did because I felt it.

'And what are you going to begin with?' said the man down there in the darkness.

'Pardon?' I said suddenly feeling nervous. I had practised the two speeches but I hadn't given any thought to standing onstage as myself and attempting to answer questions.

'Will you start with your Shakespeare or will it be your modern piece first?' said the woman.

'Oh, Shakespeare,' I said.

'Which speech?' said the man.

'Oh, the opening speech of *Richard III*,' I said. I sensed my two examiners deflating.

'In your own time,' the man said.

I took a deep breath and adjusted my eyeline to a point above the two heads in the audience. Then I began.

'Now is the winter of our discontent. Made glorious summer by this sun of York,' I continued through the speech, growing in confidence as the words came easily, proving that I could deliver a memorised passage accurately under scrutiny. I got to the end of the Shakespeare and felt good about myself. I had enjoyed the sensation of acting. Even though I'm sure I wasn't very good, I nevertheless felt something was happening. I felt I was being somebody else. My modern piece was a Jimmy Porter rant from *Look Back in Anger*, which I also successfully negotiated.

When I left the building a few minutes later, after being told that sadly my audition had been unsuccessful, I wasn't remotely disappointed. In fact, I was quietly proud of myself. I'd stood onstage and had successfully repeated the speeches as learnt without stumbling over my words or, more importantly, feeling in any way self-conscious. Quite the opposite, in fact. Extraordinarily, I felt at home.

The conclusion I had drawn back in my early teens was that if I was to have any chance of succeeding as a professional comedian or actor, I would have to generate my own material. The acting profession is such a precarious one, I was absolutely convinced that writing and creating my own work at least gave me the chance of being noticed in something I might be good in.

The reasoning behind sending an unsolicited half-hour surreal television sketch show to the BBC was to at least make a start, and have our work looked at by a professional eye. Much in the same way that I'd paid for the RADA audition. John and I waited patiently for a couple of months and, aside from receiving an acknowledgement slip four days after posting our material, we heard nothing. We optimistically took this to be good news, thinking that if the BBC didn't like it they would simply send it straight back.

Meanwhile, back at Tooting employment office, all wasn't completely lost. In some ways it was a bold step forward. For starters, I had to quickly overcome my shyness about using the telephone. I was earning a salary with virtually no outgoings other than the money I gave my mother for my upkeep. Admittedly, I was still living at home at the age of twenty, but with cash in my pocket for the first time, pubs became a part of my life.

The night I first drank cider nearly killed me. Or would have done, if I hadn't remembered something my father had once told me.

I was sitting with a circle of friends in a pub called the The Railway Arms. Being unfamiliar with cider I was completely taken unawares by its potency. It tasted light and fizzy, but this was no harmless lemonade. I don't know how many pints I had that night, but when I left the pub at closing time I was incapable of walking in a straight line.

My immediate task was to try and cross the main road, and head into the entrance of South Wimbledon Tube station. This I managed without falling over, however, going down the escalators was another story. I tripped and ended up rolling around in a ball at the bottom. But that wasn't the dangerous part. I staggered on to the platform and then, much to the absolute horror of John Irwin who was with me, I jumped down onto the train track and walked into the tunnel.

I then very deliberately grabbed the middle rail in the sure knowledge that I would be safe because Dad had told me that only the furthest rail from the platform carried electric current. He was right, but I was drunk and stupid. I climbed back on to the platform a good minute or so before the next train arrived, my idiotic brain awash in alcohol. You won't be surprised to learn that I've never drunk cider since. Not a single drop.

Fully embracing the pub world, I also started smoking cigarettes. In pubs in the 1970s, the air was so thick with tobacco fumes that it felt like you smoked whether you did or not. Around the time I took up smoking, my mother stunned the rest of the family by suddenly announcing that she was giving up the habit. Now, my mother would never be considered an eccentric, but in one peculiar detail she was most odd. Of all the smokers I have ever known she was unique. She smoked the grand total of one cigarette a week. On a Thursday evening, around about eight thirty. So when she announced she was giving up, there was much laughter when I remarked, 'Give it up?! You haven't started yet.'

Three months into my civil service career we finally received a reply from the BBC. It had never occurred to us that we might phone them to check on our script's progress. I was content to adopt a wait-and-see approach. The letter was encouraging. A man called Ian Main liked what we had written sufficiently enough to pass it on to the then head of light entertainment, John Howard Davies. This was incredibly heady news. I knew that John Howard Davies was a former child film actor, memorably playing the title role in David Lean's production of *Oliver Twist* in the 1940s. He had since become a successful television director and producer, and the very fantastic notion that he was reading our work was incredibly exciting. I kept rereading the typed words written on BBC headed paper, my brain swimming with endorphins.

Yet, even though I wanted a career in comedy so much, I also knew that I had to try and temper my expectations. I knew that nobody ever began their TV career with an unsolicited script sent to the BBC. My idea to write the programme with John Irwin was to first of all test the waters, to see if we could write together as well as we ad-libbed. We could, and our collaborative efforts excited us both, but I had no expectations of this kind of early encouragement. It was exciting to dream of the possibility for a while. Ah, the innocence of youth. The script eventually came back some eight months later with a polite note saying sadly it wasn't what the BBC were looking for. It was great fun while the ride lasted.

I settled into life with the civil service while I wondered what my next move should be. I needed to find some way of gaining performance experience. I could write in my spare time, but how do you find a stage when there's no stage you can get on? Universities, working men's clubs, holiday camps, TV talent shows. I wasn't qualified for any of them. John and I wrote three more unsolicited scripts for the BBC, all of which were returned with thanks quite quickly. Looking back now, it might seem a silly strategy to pursue, but I couldn't see any other options.

The scripts we wrote were, I felt, steadily improving, but because of my full-time job at the Department of Employment it took roughly three months of working a couple of hours every weekday night to produce each one. The shows were surreal and fun to write, but I didn't know how funny they were. Each sketch flowed into the next, with parodies of Roger Moore in *The Saint* mixing in with visual images of a man screaming out of a train window as it passed through lovely countryside. One of my favourite ideas started with a tight close-up of an artist at work, showing his landscape canvas of a bucolic meadow with gently rolling hills. The camera then pulled back to reveal the artist and his easel sitting in a completely different landscape to the one he was painting. He was in a winter's scene where everything is covered in snow. A quirky idea, but perhaps not a rib tickler.

No matter how much you may want something, you do need enormous slices of luck to achieve it, and on 19 May 1979 I got very lucky indeed, although I didn't know it at the time. That was the night that The Comedy Store first opened in London, initially a joint venture between a Soho night club owner called Don Ward, and Peter Rosengard, a high powered insurance salesman. The two of them were familiar with the comedy clubs in LA and wondered why London didn't have an equivalent. So they opened one. But there was one huge difference between here and the States. In America there were dozens of comedians playing clubs in LA, Chicago, San Francisco, New York, whereas here there wasn't anyone. There were no comics because there were no clubs. The last comedy club to open in London had been Peter Cook's The Establishment club, which ran for a couple of years in the mid-1960s before closing for good.

Don Ward and Peter Rosengard held a series of auditions, prompted by an advert they had placed in *Private Eye* and London's then two newspapers, the *Evening Standard* and the *Evening News*, as well as the *Jewish Chronicle*. 'Comedians wanted for new comedy and improvisation club W1', and with those few words a new concept was introduced to the British comedy scene – democracy. From the 19th of May 1979, it didn't matter that you hadn't been to Oxbridge, or didn't live in the north, or were the wrong kind of person to jolly along holiday campers, you could still get onstage and give it a go, even though you might only last a few seconds …

I wasn't there on the opening night (in fact I wouldn't see the inside of the Store for another two-and-a-half years). In the early days each act could be 'gonged' off by the compère striking a gong when the audience demanded it. That wasn't for me. I was looking for stage experience not instant death.

My first full-on experience of what was to become known as 'alternative comedy', was in early 1980 when John and I went to see Alexei Sayle in a small Soho theatre around the corner from The Comedy Store. And when I say small, I'm talking about fifty seats.

I'd read about Alexei in one of the evening papers, and I made one of the best decisions of my life when I bought two tickets to see him live. He was compèring a show that featured three other acts. We sat in our seats, the lights dimmed, and Alexei Sayle walked on to the tiny stage. He was wearing an even tinier grey suit, with two short sleeves and a tight jacket buttoned across a rotund body, which was topped off with a large shaven head, upon which perched a pork pie hat pulled so far down over his eyes that the only way he could see the audience was by tilting his head as far back as it would go. He was loud, aggressive and Liverpudlian. Unlike every other comedian I had ever seen, he had no desire to be liked by his audience. He didn't care about that. His verbal delivery was intense, with punchlines spat out with a relentless vigour never before seen in British comedy.

'I work for a magazine called *What's On in Stoke Newington*. It's a piece of paper with "Fuck All" written on it.

'The other day I dressed as a circus clown with big boots, a white face and baggy pants, a red nose and then I thought, "hang on, this did fuck all for Mussolini".'

That joke exhilarated me. I'd never heard anything remotely like it. A deliberate non sequitur thrown in to provoke, puzzle, and who the hell makes jokes referencing Mussolini in 1980 for God's sake? Certainly nobody on the telly. Alexei introduced the

⬆ On my first birthday, sitting in Bishops Park.

➡ Happy and shy in the face of magic.

⬆ My first time at a holiday camp, with Mum and Dad – squinting in the sun.

⬅ Having another good squint.

⬇ Here's dad intercepting the ball for Owen Villa F.C.

A rare moment of accord between boy and donkey.

Baby Angela is clearly impressed by her brother's bow tie.

Angela and me on the family sofa in Morden. I always repapered the living room according to what colour shirt I was wearing.

→ Fellow Comedy Store Player Neil Mullarkey and I discover a passion for rolled-up trousers, London, 1986.

↓ With Julie in Brighton in spring, 1987. Time has not diminished my squint.

← Alexei Sayle, persuading me to leave the civil service.

← A superb double act. Julian Clary and Fanny the Wonder Dog.

➡ The Comedy Store reopened in Leicester Square in 1985, the same year The Comedy Store Players did their first Sunday night slot.

➡ When we were four. The Comedy Store Players: Mike Myers, me, Kit Hollerbach and Neil Mullarkey.

➡ The Players' first publicity shot, out in Leicester Square in 1985. Our first incarnation with Dave Cohen.

APPEARING TONITE
Dave Cohen
Kit Hollerbach
Paul Martin
Mike Myers
Neil Mullarkey

The cast of *The Big Fun Show* in 1987. Left to right, at the back: Tony Hawks, Neil Mullarkey, me, John Irwin. Josie Lawrence and Julian Clary are at the front.

other acts but it was him that held the attention. You were thinking about him even when you were watching someone else.

At one point he performed a routine that I later found out was called 'A Stream of Tastelessness'. In its rude simplicity it was without question the funniest thing I'd ever seen onstage. Alexei merely said every swear word you could think of in succession, without the distraction of any other words getting in the way. 'Fuck, bollocks, shit, wank,' was the beginning and he kept going in that vein, slowly building a head of steam as his body rocked rhythmically backwards and forwards in a frenzy of swearing. His speed and intensity increased as his arms pumped away, and the words tumbled out in whatever order he fancied, with no attempt at meaning. The cumulative effect was to convulse the audience into a trance-like altered state, where we became simultaneously weak with laughter but also empowered by it. I think it must have been at least a couple of minutes of solid side-aching laughter before Alexei finally relented and relieved us from our hysteria. Tears rolled down our faces and some of us gasped for breath. Seeing Alexei that night, so close up and volcanic, was the comedic equivalent of witnessing the Sex Pistols live, or America's first good look at the Beatles on *The Ed Sullivan Show* in 1964. The world had changed and would never be the same again.

Alexei Sayle changed my life. He showed that comedians who wore nice suits with frilly shirts and bow ties were dead in the water. This sea change wouldn't happen overnight, but the rumblings began with Alexei, who had been one of the first people to audition for The Comedy Store and had so wowed Don Ward and Peter Rosengard that he was immediately made the compère.

By sheer good fortune, a new kind of comedy venture had found a new kind of comedian. One who was contemptuous of celebrity or the standard crowd-pleasing tactics of saying 'Good evening Ladies and Gentlemen, and welcome to the show'. This comic looked like he'd rather headbutt you than tell you a joke. Alexei kick started The Comedy Store into life, and those who soon joined him there – amongst them Keith Allen, Nigel Planer, Rik Mayall, Ade Edmondson, Dawn French and Jennifer Saunders – were within a couple of years of becoming the new wave of television comedy. The first big successes were *The Young Ones* on the BBC, and the Comic Strip films on a brand new TV station called Channel 4.

As John and I sat in the pub after that Alexei Sayle performance, digesting what we had seen, one thing was very clear. It was time to leave my job.

I resigned from the civil service on 29 February 1980. I made it the special leap year day because I didn't want to forget it. My colleagues very thoughtfully bought me three boxes of good quality writing paper, which I promised to use once I'd been commissioned to write a television series.

8

An Incident at the Clement Attlee Massage Parlour

'Now, whatever you do,' said the landlord, indicating the meter, 'don't let the gas run out. Always keep it topped up with fifty pence coins.'

I nodded my agreement, I didn't want the gas to run out!

One of the few features of my new accommodation was a coin-operated gas meter high up on the wall near the door. The landlord, on first showing me the room I would be renting for eighteen pounds a week, was keen to emphasise the importance of this device.

The landlord collected the rent once a week, and while he was about it he emptied the coin box attached to the gas meter and put its contents, a dozen 50p coins, directly into his trouser pocket. I was so naive in the ways of the real world that I didn't question this and for the next few days I regularly fed the meter. A few more days passed and I fell out of the habit.

The next time I saw the landlord I said to him, 'I think there's something wrong with the meter.'

'What do you mean?' he said.

'I've forgotten to put my coins in but the gas hasn't run out. The fire is still going strong.'

'How puzzling,' he said, trying his best to look mystified. It was a little while before I twigged that this gas meter wasn't attached to any gas pipe and was simply a box for me to put money in. A simple scam. I had a lot to learn about the world outside and inside my bedsit.

Over the last year, now aged twenty-two, I had found that I was mainly living in my bedroom and keeping contact with my family at mealtimes. I had a portable black-and-white TV, so I often watched stuff on my own. It wasn't a particularly healthy or inspiring set up. It was time for me to move out of the family home.

Mum and Dad had probably thought it was time for me to go for a while, but they were very good at not mentioning it. Angela, my sister, still lived at home with them. They weren't so pleased about me leaving the civil service, but neither Mum nor Dad tried to talk me out of it. However, for the next eighteen months they did leave the local newspaper lying around their living room whenever I visited, with various jobs circled in the Positions Vacant column in black ink. So it was time to fly the nest to spread my glorious wings, to find somewhere big enough for me and my dreams! I found a bedsit in Streatham. One room the same size as my bedroom. Eighteen-feet long by thirteen-feet wide. I would still be popping home once a week to pick up my washing. This also allowed me the luxury of a proper bath.

Apart from the gas fire, there was a single bed pushed up against the wall and a small area with a sink, a fridge and a small electric oven. I didn't have a television set, but I did possess a small radio cassette player, which enabled me to record programmes directly off the radio at the touch of a button. I soon built up a library of comedy shows. One particular favourite was *Just a Minute*, which in those days featured the regular quartet of Clement Freud, Derek Nimmo, Peter Jones and Kenneth Williams. Chaired as always by Nicholas Parsons, the game could be played on your own while listening at home. Or in a bedsit.

The plan now was for John and me to write a sketch show that we could perform at the Edinburgh Fringe Festival. I knew this would be very hard work, but I believed by giving up my job I would be able to devote more time to the task of starting a career in comedy.

I hadn't taken into account the awful draining of morale and self-worth that happens when you sign on for more than a few weeks. Each day began with a bowl of porridge made with hot water. I bought big bags of jumbo oats from the local supermarket. At lunchtime I made sandwiches with white bread and fish paste, which came in small jars. How you extract paste from a fish is a question I shall leave hanging. None of this was nourishing, but it was cheap. It's easy to become depressed when you're eating such a diet.

It took a while to generate material for the show. I travelled up to Edinburgh and back by coach to look at a possible venue. I soon realised that there was absolutely no way we could afford to put on a show at the Fringe. The cost of putting details into the programme alone would have bankrupted me, never mind venue hire or accommodation. Money wasn't tight, it was non-existent. I could get by on eating fish paste sandwiches and living in a single room while claiming unemployment benefit chiefly because I was single and without dependants. I didn't know any girls or where you were supposed to meet them, so there was nothing at all to distract me from my goal – which was to write and perform a two-man sketch show with John.

John had found a job in another branch of the civil service after leaving school, and I would meet him two or three times a week to drink orange juice in one of the many nearby pubs. These evenings with John kept my spirits up as we spoke about possible sketch ideas and made ourselves laugh uproariously as we always did when we got together.

I remember telling him one evening that I had recently attended an introductory talk on Transcendental Meditation, or TM for short, at Streatham Library. The lecturer spoke of TM's ability to soothe the restless mind via a special technique, which would take you deep into a state of serenity. He spoke of a special induction course at his house in Balham, where he would give you your own personal mantra to guide you into an awareness of the eternal consciousness. He then asked if anyone had any questions and one man piped up, 'Yes, where's Balham?' The banality of the question amidst what we were hearing about universal consciousness tickled me greatly.

OK, Edinburgh was impossible. But a small note inserted into some Edinburgh details alerted me to the very first Swansea Fringe Festival. The entry fee was a very reasonable £5. This I could afford. And so, in October 1981, John and I travelled to South Wales to make our professional debuts. We could not have chosen a better place to start.

It was a two week festival and we were playing twelve nights with two Sundays off. I had suggested this schedule to give us plenty of practise onstage to hopefully develop some skills in a short space of time. We hired a church hall from St Jude's at a fiver a night.

We had now a show that was fifty minutes long, and that's all we knew about it. We didn't know if anybody other than us would find it amusing. I know I found John funny and treasured his support in this venture. He needed a little persuading but quickly saw that it might be fun. It also represented an extraordinary leap in the dark. John and I were very nervous. We had learnt and rehearsed our half-a-dozen sketches, but we hadn't shown them to anyone else. We had no director or any such luxury. It was just us.

On our opening night we sold eight tickets. Would any of it be amusing? We stood behind the curtain as our opening music, 'Amateur Hour' by Sparks, played on my cassette radio. We looked at each other in the semi-darkness. Neither of us had ever done this before but there was no stopping us now. As the music faded I took a deep breath, pulled back the curtain, and walked on to the stage. As I did, I felt like I had found the hidden door in the back of the wardrobe. I spoke my first words in front of a paying audience.

'Good evening Ladies and Gentlemen, my name is Mystero the Memory Man. Every day I learn 500 new facts. But I only started this morning. And I got up late. And then I went down the pub. Nevertheless I shall answer any question on any subject. Could I please have a question from a member of the audience?'

Here I paused. Nobody said anything. I hadn't reckoned on that so I repeated, 'Could I please have a question from a member of the audience?' and then somebody shouted out, 'What's the third highest mountain in the world?'

I replied quick as a whip, 'For the benefit of those at the back of the auditorium, I shall repeat the question. "Who won the cup final in 1957?"'

The audience laughed!

They laughed!

I was on a high throughout the rest of that first show. Our final sketch, which was nearly twelve minutes long, involved a rambling conversation between two old men describing the various toxic fumes around their neighbourhood. Halfway through the sketch I realised we had skipped six pages. We exchanged anxious glances, but I knew the words backwards and was able to steer us back to the missing pages, and then back on track to the end. Afterwards we congratulated ourselves for smoothly avoiding a calamity. It actually made us proud that on our very first professional experience, we had had the coolness of mind to adjust the script in our head, with no exterior sign that anything had gone awry. We finished to strong applause.

The adrenaline afterwards was intense. I was walking on air and feeling twice as sixpence. We had got through it, and it hadn't gone too badly either. Later we went to the Swansea Fringe Festival club bar, which was a room in the Dylan Thomas Theatre. A couple of acts, a classical guitarist and a sketch troupe provided impromptu entertainment, which all added to the exciting buzz of the evening. We drank beer to calm ourselves down.

Over the next two weeks, we performed the show another eleven times and it perceptibly improved in that short run. Socialising with other performers was also extremely exciting. To meet people who were living the life I wanted to live, and to drink beer with them, was thrilling. On some occasions I got rather overexcited. I spent fifteen minutes telling a complete stranger in the Swansea Fringe Club all about the secrets of fire-eating, which I learnt a few hours earlier, only for him to tell me that he was himself a professional fire-eater working at a nearby circus.

The festival over, and John and I made our way back to London on the coach. The two weeks had been a fantastically valuable experience. We had proved that the two of us could stand on a stage and make people laugh with words we had written ourselves. In the back of my mind, for so many years, had been the thought that despite my deep-rooted ambition I might not have the talent or the temperament to be a successful performer. Swansea dispelled a lot of that anxiety.

But what to do next? John and I agreed before we went to Swansea that we weren't a double act, and that was the right decision. Neither one of us wanted to be a straight man to the other. The only material from our Swansea show that could work as stand-up was the Memory Man act, but I knew there was a big leap from a dozen benign people in a church hall to The Comedy Store crowd in London.

Christmas came and went without any further ideas occurring to me. The holiday season gave me the chance to get away from the bedsit for a few days and stay with Mum and Dad in Morden. I must admit that I did miss the comforts of family life, and once I returned back to the basic bedsit room it felt like solitary confinement. Except, I suppose, I was the one with the key. I sat in the one armchair with an A4 notepad in front of me, holding a black ballpoint pen a couple of inches above the entirely blank page. My limited experience of life was poor preparation for launching myself as a stand-up. I couldn't think of jokes sitting in a depressing room on my own. It was hopeless. I had no initial sparks of inspiration that I could build on. Until I stopped looking.

It was a wet cold January night and I was standing in a shop doorway waiting for a 118 bus. I was wearing my olive green army greatcoat and desert boots, which always proved to be particularly absorbent. I needed cheering up. As there was nobody else about I began talking to myself in the manner of a stereotypical police constable. 'Now then, now then, what's going on here?' sort of stuff. Then, out of the blue, I immediately recalled a television documentary about a police investigation in the 1970s, code-named Operation Julie. Some people were making the hallucinogenic drug LSD on a vast scale and the police raided the premises. Unfortunately, some of them ingested LSD dust, which had somehow been floating around in the air in powder form. The bit that swam back into my mind was the interview with a bemused policeman recounting his accidental trip.

He was interviewed in a pub. In precise neutral tones in answer to the question, 'When did you first notice that something was wrong?' the policeman answered, 'I was sitting in this pub with Detective Sergeant Norris, when I noticed that my pint of beer was getting bigger!' That was the phrase that popped into my head.

The glorious comic contrast inherent in a formal, slightly stiff verbal delivery describing weird hallucinations was immediately appealing. As I waited for the bus I started writing the monologue in my head. I reasoned that I had to first set up the policeman as a rather slow-witted individual in as few lines as possible.

Then somehow, by mistake, he takes acid, and then goes on to describe his trip in the same sober tones as he started his evidence in. Although the set up was necessary, I had to make sure there were some laughs in it otherwise I'd quickly be in trouble with a rowdy crowd waiting for the first joke. The easiest solution to that was to have some mispronunciation of words. Completely absorbed, I forgot about the bus and went back home to write this down.

The first few sentences came fairly easily. 'On Wednesday 14th of October last at approximately ten forty-three hay em, I was pat-rolling along Streatham High Rd when I spotted a ver-hicle illegally parked outside the all night Clement Attlee Massage Parlour. I questioned the occupant, a Mr Jack E Stewart, who said, "Urinate off you effing love child." Mr Stewart then alopogised and offered me a candy-covered chocolate confectionary known to the uniformed branch as a Smartie. I accepted the Smartie and swallowed it. A Smartie that I now know contained an hallucino-genic drug. Thirty-five minutes later while …' and then I ran out of immediate inspiration.

The next line was crucial. I believed there was a huge laugh to be had in revealing the extent of the policeman's separation from reality, but what should he be doing? I wrestled with this for three days and eventually put the problem to John, who casually suggested 'Why don't you put him on a spaceship?' and I immediately knew this to be the answer.

I spent the next six weeks working on the rest of the monologue. Other than my Swansea experience, which was gentle, I didn't have much evidence that I might be an inherently comic person onstage, so I endeavoured to make the material as funny as possible. I wanted every line to be either a comic line or a set-up line. No waffle.

After much honing and re-writing I settled on a definitive version. I practised again and again in my bedsit, reading from a small black notebook in my hand.

The book was extra insurance. It actually contained the words of the monologue in case I forgot them through nerves. But now I had everything I needed. It was time to phone The Comedy Store.

Somewhere I'd read that you could, with prior notice, get up onstage and give it a go. I phoned a man who said, 'Come down next Saturday and you can do five minutes.' Blimey. I spent the next week living in an atmosphere of keenly rising anticipation. By Saturday, my heart was beating three times its normal rate.

The show started at midnight. The Comedy Store was situated in a dimly-lit alleyway in the dark centre of Soho. In 1982, Soho was a different place to today's gentrified tourist-friendly, convivial area. Then, women of the night leant out of upper floor windows, exhorting men to press their illuminated doorbells.

I arrived just after eleven fifteen. I spoke to the guy selling tickets on the door.

'Hello, I phoned last week about doing five minutes onstage,' I said.

'It's ten quid to come in,' he said. This wasn't going well.

'No, I spoke to somebody and they said I could do five minutes,' I insisted. I had to get on that night. I was fully prepared. The man looked me up and down. 'Alright. Go and speak to the compère upstairs.' I was in.

I hadn't been to The Comedy Store before, so I had a quick look around. I was completely taken aback to discover that instead of the usual stage facing a row of seats, the audience were seated around large tables upon which rested numerous glasses of alcohol. They were pissed, but I was completely sober so I wasn't going to worry too much about it. The compère, not knowing anything about me, put me on last. If I was really terrible no other act would have to follow me. I watched the show from the back of the room. Very few of the half-a-dozen acts were stand-up. Some of them were street acts from Covent Garden pleased to find a gig indoors. Poets, clowns, purveyors of comedy songs, were all part of the mix. Although some of the audience were drunk, they were an enthusiastic crowd who were there to see the comedy.

It came to my turn. I stood behind a glittery slash curtain waiting for the compère to announce my name. In my right hand I was holding my black notebook, and in my left one of those facsimile police constable helmets that the London souvenir shops sell. My plan was to walk onstage and straight up to the microphone to start the monologue immediately. No mucking about with 'Good evening Ladies and Gentlemen'.

'The next act has never appeared onstage at The Comedy Store before, so he might well be really awful. Put your hands together for Paul Martin.'

It was a little after 2 a.m. and the audience was already quite tired. None of the acts had wildly succeeded but equally none of them had died on their arse. That was about to change. I stepped up onto the stage, I felt I was jumping out of a plane while hoping I had packed my parachute properly.

I began.

'On Wednesday 14th of October last, at approximately ten forty-hay em, while pat-rolling along Streatham High Rd' (a few laughs on pat-rolling: good) 'I observed a motor ver-hicle' (chuckles) 'outside the all night Clement Attlee Massage Parlour' (a big laugh here: I was gaining confidence). Then I got to the big line 'Thirty-five minutes later, while sitting aboard an inter-galactic spaceship bound for the planet Zanussi' (massive laugh) 'I observed Constable Parrish approaching me disguised as a fort-night's holiday in Benidorm.' (This got the biggest laugh so far.)

'"Hello Constable Parrish," I said through the back of my neck' (more laughs here, particularly as I showed the policeman's embarrassment at having to repeat these ludicrous words in court) '"And how is my Lord Buckingham?"' (More laughter as the crowd totally tuned in to what I was doing. They were laughing at every single joke and even some of the set-up lines.)

'To which Constable Parrish replied, "You stupid git. Get off that bus shelter you stupid git." I then ate Constable Parrish. I was enticed down from the bus shelter by the very lovely Miss Marilyn Monroe, former screen starlet. We kissed, informally, until Marilyn, sweet tender Marilyn, revealed herself to me as Mr Brinsley Okomo, scrap metal dealer from Peckham. A panda patrol car flew past and three large uniformed pandas got out. I was charged by Chief Constable Warren with "Acting the goat", "Impersonating a Spaniard" and "Eating a Police Constable while in the course of his duty". I burst into hysterical laughter which lasted five months.

And that my Lord is the truth, the whole truth, and nothing but the truth.'

I stood back from the microphone and the audience went bananas. They were ecstatic. They applauded and cheered, and I stood there, stunned, soaking it up.

I stepped off the stage and the compère stepped on.

'More, more,' the audience shouted.

The compère comes over to where I'm standing. 'Can you do more?' he says.

'I haven't got any more,' I say. The compère tells the audience, 'He hasn't got any more.'

I shout out, 'I can do the sketch again,' and the audience shout out their approval, so I get up and run through the whole lot again. And the audience laughed again as I ad-libbed, 'Join in if you know the words.' It was an extraordinary moment in my life. To have such a good gig so early on was incredibly lucky.

I knew from all my reading and study of show business that beginners shouldn't get carried away. I had very little performance experience and there was a great deal to learn, but I had stood onstage and convulsed an audience with words I had written. I had performed it well, too.

I left The Comedy Store around two forty-five a.m. I was high. Everything I had ever dreamt about had just begun. I walked through Soho, past Trafalgar Square, past No. 10 and across West-minster Bridge. I looked down at the dark swirling waters. I told myself again I had done it. It was only one gig, and I might not get any laughs next time, but there was no doubt that there *would be a next time*. I didn't want to get the night bus, I didn't want the evening to end. I just kept walking. I thought about what lay ahead.

I resolved to serve a five-year apprenticeship; learn my craft. Everything I'd read about comedy showed me that those who had a great deal of experience before their success tended to have longer careers at the top. Priceless knowledge could be gained working in obscurity.

As I walked through Brixton, past the Tube and the Ritzy cinema, and up the hill towards Streatham, the first light of dawn appeared. I walked past a big church and I thought of Sister Galista. She had so hated my essay about a trip to the moon, and I don't suppose she would have liked a policeman flying to the planet Zanussi any better.

I got back to the bedsit just before seven. I sat on the edge of the bed feeling both drained and full. I'd walked all the way home.

I hugged myself, there being no one else to do it for me.

9

Learning French the Hard Way

Sometimes life changing experiences come in pairs. Within a few days of my stand-up debut, my friend Trevor invited me to a music gig in a pub just up the road from Clapham Junction station. Opposite the pub was the Odeon cinema where I had seen *A Clockwork Orange*, Stanley Kubrick's violent masterpiece that featured some female nudity, which at the time was about the only footage of a naked woman I had ever seen.

The music in the pub is loud, and normal conversation impossible. A girl sitting the other side of the table pushes a folded piece of paper towards me. I open it to read, 'Do you come here often?'

I laugh. I write something silly back. She laughs. She has long flowing hair. I write a note that says, 'Here is my address, 71 Lewin Road, Streatham. If you give me your address we can write to each other. My name is Paul.'

Writing notes was easy for me, it was talking to women that I was no good at. Over the next ten days we sent each other letters. We explored each other's sense of humour and communicated in a way that didn't make me blush all over. Her name was Leslie and I will be eternally grateful that she made that first move.

Inspired by the whole letter-writing thing, I sent her a slightly cryptic invitation to a first date. It took the form of a postcard. On one side was a full figure portrait of Cardinal Richelieu, and on the other was a simple message. 'Meet me in front of this painting at 2 o'clock Sunday?'

Although the Cardinal's portrait isn't easily classified as romantic, it was simple to find, as was the reproduction postcard sold in the National Gallery gift shop.

I approached the building at the appointed hour and made my way to the painting. She was there! My heart beat firmly in my chest as I walked up to her. She looked nervous.

'Hello,' I said as I sat down next to her on the bench opposite the painting.

'Cardinal Richelieu is a strange choice,' she said.

'I picked this painting because of the bench,' I said. 'If either one of us was late at least the other would be comfortable.' This explanation was accepted and we went for a walk in St James's Park. The sun was shining as we walked hand in hand beside the lake, with the grass at our feet. We talked all day and, after a quick snog in a doorway, I waved her goodbye as she boarded her train at Charing Cross station.

We met up again a few days later.

At her suggestion, she came to Streatham. I met her at the station and the two of us walked back to the bedsit. It was half-past twelve on a Saturday afternoon when I closed the door behind us and four thirty on the Sunday afternoon when I opened it again. And in those intervening hours the young gazelle became a man!

Not only was this a life changing, formative moment. It clearly did wonders for my creativity too, as, unbelievably, during one bout of high activity between us a fully-formed joke popped into my head! I knew what I had to do.

'Leslie,' I said, 'I'm sorry, do you mind if we stop for a moment?'

'Why?'

'I've just got to write something down.'

I stood up, found pen and paper, and jotted down, 'I learnt French the hard way – from a Spaniard'.

I was acutely aware that I needed lots of new material and I couldn't take the chance of forgetting a corking one-liner, even though to make a note immediately, I knew, lacked finesse. But then normal service was resumed.

I went to The Comedy Store the following Saturday. It was the first weekend of the Falklands War. The fleet had set sail for the islands and every comic on the bill that night wanted to go on first. Usually the acts wanted to avoid opening, as until you went on, you had no idea what the audience would be like. Watching somebody else opening told you if the crowd were rowdy or up for comedy. Generally, at the Store they were there for the latter, even if the late-night bar was also an attraction.

But that Saturday night every comic was begging the compère to let them open. Everyone had an Anglo-Argentinian joke, usually involving Osvaldo Ardiles in the punchline. Finding himself in a bit of a situation backstage, the compère asked each comic what their new jokes were so that he could avoid any potential clashes, if possible. Of course, I had no new topical jokes, as I was only a couple of weeks into my career and the Policeman on Acid was serving me well.

The compère opened the show … and immediately told all the

other comics' newly minted jokes. He even produced a can of Fray Bentos, which prompted an identical tin to be flung against the backstage wall in anger.*

There were some very strong performers in that period, whose ability to handle the audience was an education to see. John Hegley's poems and songs played on a mandolin with an intense comic focus always did really well at the Store, as indeed did Hubert and Hilary Haddock with their Fish and Fire Fantasy. I was there that night at the Store when a bored punter heckled the compère with the complaint that the previous two acts had been male stand-ups. He didn't know who was coming on next when he shouted out, 'Give us some variety,' so he was stunned to be whacked across the back of the head with a dead mackerel by Hubert Haddock as he made his way onstage to 'March of the Mods' by the Joe Loss Orchestra. He and Hilary danced with dead fish in various exotic ways, before finishing on 'What the world needs now is sprats, fresh sprats' as they hurled whitebait into the crowd.

Compared to these days, a surprising number of acts had a high visual content. None more so than Andrew Bailey, who regularly astonished audiences and the other performers with his fertile imagination and his willingness to take risks onstage. In a better world he would be a revered national treasure, if that didn't conjure up an air of cosiness entirely inappropriate to his oeuvre.

The first time Andrew played his character Podomovski, an East European with a pair of sinister dark glasses, a bright red

---

* It was a common ruse in those very early days for the compère to differentiate himself from the other acts. If they were bad it wasn't his fault. I was once introduced with the words, 'This next act has just signed a contract with Granada Television. Let's hope he can keep up the payments.' This derogatory comment placed doubt in the audience's mind, which an act would have to quickly dispel.

clown's nose, a black bowler hat and a long dark coat, he asked me to provide the offstage voice of the English translator. It was an honour. I had a script and a microphone.

Andrew said as Podomovski in a deep rich voice, 'Gudunk fang bow thin an Mitzi Perdanka,' and I read out the line, 'This woman reminds me of the town hall where I was born.'

He hummed the stripper music and peeled back his red nose to reveal a white one underneath. It got weirder after that. And the audience were with him every step of the way. Another character of his, Frederick Benson, who had a deathly white pallor, with huge dark rings around his eyes and massive shoulder pads under a glittery, sparkly, show-business jacket, looked like corpse entertaining on a cruise ship. He would often make his entrance with the hand mic fully in his mouth as he made deep guttural sounds, which eventually morphed into understandable language.

In his voice from the grave he would welcome us into his world. He had a large pane of magnifying glass, which he held in front of his head doubling its size as he told us about the fire exits. Working with such dedicated people as Andrew inspired a costume of my own. I chose a pair of red-and-white striped pyjamas.

It suited the policeman routine and immediately caught the audience's attention as something different. For the first few gigs with the new costume, I also stood on a ropey old duvet, which was my own private reference to the time as a young boy that I had stood on my bed humming TV themes feverishly.

Of course, I had been incredibly fortunate that my first time at the Store had gone so well. Others were not so lucky. I'm thinking particularly of Danny Knight. He would travel in from Hemel Hempstead every Saturday night for the opportunity to do five minutes at the end of the evening. His nerves always got the better of him and he never lasted more than a couple of minutes, but on one magical occasion he participated in the funniest performer/ heckler exchange that I've ever witnessed.

John Hegley, on the other hand, who was standing next to me at the back of the room, found it very sad. There speaks the soul of a poet.

Danny Knight was announced and he bounded onto the stage full of enthusiasm. He took the microphone from the stand and burbled a few pleasantries. The audience, who had been genial all evening, laughed lightly. This laugh, an extremely rare one for Danny, completely threw his concentration. He was so stunned that he physically froze. His face locked into shock as his eyes stared wildly into the near distance. Then he spoke. 'Where am I?' he said to the audience. 'I don't know what to do.'

Somebody from the middle of the room shouted out, 'Do an impression of the Queen.'

'OK,' says Danny, and then without changing his voice in any way he said, 'My husband and I … no that was shit. Give me something else.'

Then a new voice entered the conversation, easily distinguished from the others by the fact that its owner, a young man in a dark suit, was completely pissed. 'Tell us a joke,' he demanded loudly from a table near the back of the room. Danny turned to the direction of the heckle and then disastrously says the worst thing he could have done.

'If you think you can do any better, why don't you get up here and try it?' he said.

The number one rule is never invite a heckler up onstage ever, but Danny, out of sheer panic, has done just that.

The heckler gets to his feet unsteadily. He approaches the stage and climbs on. The drunk makes a grab for the microphone and after a brief toing and froing, Danny relinquishes it and the drunk is now in control. He sways a little as he begins his joke which makes no sense.

'There's this nun and a motorbike. The man driving the bike used to be a priest, but he isn't any more. He's got … traffic lights changing all the time, what's that all about? Green … and all the other colours, change, go, come, go.' The drunk is so drunk he's hilarious and the audience is lapping it up.

Danny stands at the back and looks mournfully on, as the man he invited on to the stage clearly is doing better than him. He has a thought and wanders over to the beat up piano at the back of the small stage, and starts picking out random notes. The sound of the piano spurs our drunk into his version of singing. He is hobbled by the fact that he has no fixed idea of either tune or words, but he does have enthusiasm. 'My town is here, London, London, it, it's a city,' he warbles off-key to much laughter.

Realising he somehow has to regain control of this gig that he's travelled in from Hemel Hempstead to do, Danny has a brief tussle over the microphone with the drunk before sending the pissed crooner back from whence he came.

Danny stands onstage and he takes a deep breath. This gig can still be rescued. Someone from the audience shouts out, 'Bring back the comic!'

Danny says. 'He's not coming back.'

A voice from the back says, 'Oh yes I am,' and the drunk again makes his way to the stage, weaving in and out of the tables. He and Danny tussle over the microphone before the drunk again takes control. The audience are hysterical as he once more embarks on a stream of unconsciousness.

'He told me he had a moped, I looked at it and said, "How many wheels has that got? And where's your side car?" He said, "Anyway this nun, forget her."'

Danny of course is watching all this totally aghast. He has now made the worst mistake a comic can make. Twice. Then a moment of pure inspiration on his part literally lifts the whole episode into the realms of comedy gold. Danny gets down on all fours and crawls between the legs of the intoxicated joke teller and then manages to stand up with the drunk essentially sitting across his shoulders almost six feet up in the air.

Not only is the move hilarious, with Danny's still mournful face framed by the trousered thighs of our drunk, what makes it even funnier is that the man with the microphone doesn't miss a beat as he is lifted into the air. He honestly didn't seem to notice that he was astride another man's shoulders as he just kept talking as before, 'Forget her … the priest lived near some Gypsies and he was shouting, "Lucky Heather, Lucky Heather, ten bob a pound."'

Gloriously he then stopped and looked down at the top of the head that was between his legs, noticing it for the first time. He ruffled the hair and laughed as Danny looked most uncomfortable down below. Then the drunk sat up straight, and looked slowly round to his left and then to his right. For the first time he was realising how high he was. His bemusement and growing awareness of his position was funny enough, but the whole episode was topped off with his sudden cry of, 'What the fuck am I doing up here?'

I laughed until I ached.

The underlying sadness on Danny Knight's face in the middle of all this accidental comedy lent the proceedings a tragic aspect from his perspective perhaps … but God it was funny.

The first Comedy Store on Meard Street closed on 23 December 1982. 1982 was a year of change for me. My first girlfriend, Leslie, although our relationship only lasted a couple of months, and a successful start at stand-up comedy were notable achievements in my book.

The Comedy Store effectively closed for two years while Don Ward searched for affordable new premises. But in that space of time the London cabaret circuit took root and flourished. New venues were springing up all over the place. Small function rooms above pubs became lively viable venues. The TV series *The Young Ones*, starring Alexei Sayle, Rik Mayall, Nigel Planer and Ade Edmondson, had alerted audiences to the new kind of comedy that was coming through, and hip London audiences were lapping it up. I was ideally placed to play each one of these venues as they became established. There weren't that many performers about and my Policeman on Acid routine always worked a treat. I was slowly adding to the act with bits and pieces as they occurred to me. I took my situation of living in a bedsit in Streatham, and embellished it for comic effect.

'Where I'm living in Streatham, I've got no facilities. Well, there is an outside toilet, but that's in Aberdeen. I've got a time-share with a bloke from Grimsby. I can't wait for the last two weeks in September.' As you can see, I was endeavouring to pack my material with funny lines. This piece had arguably three punchlines. Aberdeen, Grimsby and September. I further exaggerated my surroundings. 'I live opposite Brixton Prison and someone, I don't know who, has dug a tunnel from E-wing to the back of my fridge. I can't get to sleep at night; dozens of prisoners jumping out of my fridge at all hours of the morning. Half of them want minicabs.'

I invented a traumatic childhood. 'My Dad was a sadistic hairdresser who took it out on me. One evening he viciously re-styled my hair and I had to be rushed to hospital to be cut out from under a bouffant. I was once the mystery object at a barbers' convention in Didcot.' These lines have more than a whiff of patient construction about them, and that's often how I created stand-up material.

It very rarely ever came easy. One notable exception was a piece I wrote as a Raymond Chandler parody. A spoof American detective was an easy voice to conjure up, and I wrote a two-minute sketch in the space of half an hour.

'There was two of us in the room; one of us was dead. It didn't take long to figure out which one. It was Fatima. At first glance it looked like she'd been poisoned, but when I looked again I realised she had been harpooned and hung from the electric light.' And then later, 'He used to be something big in Hollywood. He'd been the bus station. He was the kind of guy who would burn down an orphanage just to keep his cocoa warm.'

When I wasn't writing in another character's voice I found that I struggled to come up with material. Even when I did write a good joke, it might take me ages to recognise it. One joke which I became identified with in my stand-up days lay in a notebook for eight months before I asked another comic's opinion about it. Much to my surprise, he thought it was hilarious. I tried it the next night and he was right. It stayed in my act for years and it always got its laugh.

'Good evening Ladies and Gentlemen. I'm a topical comedian. During the Blitz, in the Second World War, my dad used to say "Don't worry about the bombs. The only bomb you've got to worry about is the one that's got your name written on it." That scared the next door neighbours, Mr and Mrs Doodlebug.'

As 1983 turned into 1984, a flurry of jobs gave me my first experiences of working in television. I landed a bit part in *The Young Ones*, a three-minute spot featuring the Policeman on Acid in a Channel 4 show called *Stomping on the Cat*, and some background extra work in another Channel 4 programme called *Who Dares Wins*. I also appeared as a policeman who had lost his trousers in the back of somebody's garden, in a BBC2 documentary about a company that staged practical jokes. These were all important experiences, but I knew I still had a lot to learn. All of the above were filmed on location, apart from *Stomping on the Cat*, which was my first experience of working in a television studio. At a pre-production meeting the producer told us that twelve acts would be filmed, but only six would be used in the programme. I looked around the room at the other eleven acts and quietly fancied my chances. And I'm sure they all did the same. On the day, I turned up with my pyjamas in my holdall at one thirty and was handed a card with my dressing room number. With the other performers, I watched the other acts run through their five minutes for the purposes of a technical rehearsal. Some acts were nervous, others like me were relaxed but concentrated. At seven fifteen the studio audience filed in, and they didn't look like the people we were used to playing to on the cabaret circuit. They were much older and more working class. This was not an audience that was familiar with *The Young Ones*. As well as my pyjamas I wore a very small teddy bear pinned to the pyjama jacket, which was a present from Leslie. When my name was called I walked out and delivered the policeman monologue fearlessly in front of the cameras. The audience reaction was fine, but nothing compared to what I was used to. The idea of somebody on acid was still a fresh concept for people.

Stomping on the Cat was not a prime-time show. It went out one Tuesday night at five past midnight on Channel 4. This scheduling was typical of television's attitude towards acts on the cabaret circuit. It was great that Channel 4 were commissioning such shows, but they were still for the time being late-night fare.

Another programme, which I wasn't involved in, had the profoundly pessimistic title *Book 'em and Risk It*, which was filmed in the foyer of the Royal Festival Hall. Comedians were recorded performing their act walking in and out of lifts, looking out of giant windows, and generally making the best of it. They were outsiders.

Amongst the bits and pieces of television, I also landed a fantastic gig when I got a call out of the blue offering me a twenty-minute spot in a show with three other comics, Nick Revell, Arnold Brown and Norman Lovett. The show was called *Brave New Comedy*, and it would play dates throughout the year and also three weeks at the Edinburgh Festival. The three comedians needed a fourth according to the promoter, and my name came up and was instantly agreed upon.

This was a huge piece of luck for me. I had no problem in agreeing that I would open the show every night. I knew Nick from the very early days of the Store, and Arnold Brown was famous as one of the pioneers, while Norman Lovett was considered one of the best comics around. Both Arnold and Norman were much more experienced comedians and I was keen to watch them at work.

Our first gigs were at the Soho Poly theatre in London. They went very well and the four of us got on. The show was no more than four stand-ups one after the other, but each of us had a strong act and a distinctive individual voice. There was no danger of us beginning to sound the same through constant exposure to each other's vocal rhythms. I've seen it happen. Firstly, Nick was a Yorkshireman whose material reflected his political persuasions. He was a good old lefty as we all were. Some more active than others. Any Tories amongst the circuit performers certainly kept it to themselves.

Arnold Brown, a Glaswegian, has some of the best one-liners around. His jokes are beautifully constructed, honed and polished, with not a word out of place. His immaculate timing and presence on a microphone are always a joy to behold. In 1984, Arnold was three years away from winning the prestigious Perrier Award, which led unbelievably to him supporting Frank Sinatra at a huge arena gig in Glasgow.

'I asked Frank if he would address the Scottishness of the occasion by singing "Fly me to Dunoon".'

Norman Lovett's style is slower than most other comedians but for him it's a natural tempo. His fearless approach to pausing is an education in itself. Norman and I got on well. He had a TV idea he'd been kicking around for a while, and after a couple of months of occasional *Brave New Comedy* gigs he asked me to co-write the script with him. Norman had a nice flat near London Bridge and, as I was living in my single bedsit room, I volunteered to travel to Norman's every day for four weeks, including weekends.

I arrived every morning around ten, and after our first cup of tea of the day we got straight to work. Although our comedic styles are completely different, this made a good mix and the script was coming along rather nicely. We were both excited by the material we were creating. This excitement created momentum.

I arrived one Sunday morning bursting with ideas. With breaks we were working eight hours a day. I pointed out to Norman that Tommy Cooper was appearing on television that night and that we should arrange our work schedule accordingly.

As we progressed through the day, whenever we got stuck for a moment we conjured up the image of Tommy Cooper, laughed, and carried on. Looking forward to the programme made it more of an event in our minds. The added thrill of the show *Live at Her Majesty's* actually being broadcast live, keenly whetted our anticipation.

Norman turned the telly on in time to catch the opening credits. Jimmy Tarbuck was hosting. Tommy was introduced about twenty minutes in. He was magnificent. He wandered around the stage, fez on his head, a dazed look in his eye, picking up props apparently at random. He held up a large black cube and said, 'Look at that; Irish bowling ball.' He put the cube down and he looked into the wings. 'I thought it would go better than that, I did,' he said. He moves to the centre of the stage and clicks his fingers towards the other wing. A beautiful tall leggy showgirl walks onstage and drapes a voluminous golden robe over his shoulders. Tommy stands there like an emperor clothed in his finery. A man of immense stature he collapses suddenly to the floor. The audience laugh/gasp. The camera cuts wildly to another, which is pointing at one of the boxes. The theme music is quickly played and we're into a commercial break.

Norman and I talk about what we have just seen.

'That's a very strange ending,' I say.

Norman says, 'Maybe there's a joke when they come back. He'll be levitating or something?'

The commercials are over, the show is back on and Jimmy Tarbuck has gone up a gear. He's working hard and he's working well, but Tommy Cooper does not appear. At the end of the show Jimmy thanks all the performers but doesn't mention Tommy. Norman and I are baffled, but are fearing the worst.

The news immediately follows. It's read by Trevor McDonald. At the end of the bulletin he announces a late item of news. 'And we've just heard that Tommy Cooper has died following a suspected heart attack.'

We looked at each other stunned. I felt the emotional shock intensely and tears welled up in my eyes. I needed to take a walk. I wandered around for ten minutes before returning to Norman's flat and suggesting that we do no more work. Instead we went to the pub. We drank a couple of pints. Within a few minutes we were swapping reminiscences and quoting various parts of Tommy Cooper's act to each other.

Apart from all of his comedy magic I also really enjoyed his sketch work. One of my favourites was set in a train carriage. A group of actors, due to a mix up with the wardrobe department, have to travel in their costumes. They are dressed as high-ranking Nazis, with one of the cast made up as Hitler. He has the moustache, the hair and the same manic stare. When Tommy Cooper enters the carriage wearing a long brown coat and a bowler hat. 'Hitler' is reading a broadsheet newspaper and so is hidden.

Tommy sits opposite him. The newspaper comes down and Tommy is looking directly at Adolf Hitler. Tommy takes in the view for quite some time before eventually uttering the line, 'You ought to be ashamed of yourself.'

Already I was feeling better.

Nothing became of our uncommissioned script, but working with Norman was invaluable. There was a real satisfaction in creating decent material. As indeed was playing the Edinburgh Fringe Festival for the first time. We were lucky to get a good review in *The Scotsman* early on, and we had a very successful three week run.

There was also bitter disappointment, however. The other three, Nick, Arnold and Norman, had all appeared on a Radio 4 programme called *Aspects of the Fringe* the year before. The three of them assured me that I was bound to be picked for the show. This wasn't empty flattery. As hard as it may be to imagine today, there were only two other shows in Edinburgh that year that featured stand-up comedians. Six other comics in total. Three of whom were Mark Steel, Jenny Eclair and Rory Bremner. *Aspects of the Fringe* ran for two editions, so I assumed there would be room for a three-minute spot from me.

The producer came to see our show. Although we were sold out, a couple of seats were found. The show went well and I was happy with my twenty minutes. But I didn't get asked to appear on *Aspects of the Fringe*. When I talked to the producer about this a few days later he frankly told me, 'Yours isn't the sort of voice we are used to hearing on Radio 4.' I was gobsmacked. This was a barrier I hadn't been expecting. I believed up to that point that merit would count for a lot. If my act was good enough for *Aspects of the Fringe* then presumably I would be booked. But my voice, and by that I understood my accent, was deemed ... what? Too unfamiliar? Too working class, too London, too rough? All of the above I suppose. And when I thought about it he was right. My favourite shows on Radio 4, *I'm Sorry I Haven't A Clue* and *Just a Minute*, didn't feature anyone that sounded like me. I hadn't considered it before. My radio debut would have to wait.

1985 saw me continually playing the ever-expanding London cabaret circuit, and the return of The Comedy Store in new premises in Leicester Square, just along from the Odeon cinema. In April of that year I was approached by Dave Cohen to do a show in Edinburgh, with him and another male comic yet to be decided.

I knew that my previous Edinburgh experience with *Brave New Comedy* was a real one-off. A large venue, a major promoter, rave reviews and a sell-out run isn't what 99 per cent of the festival is about. I liked the idea of going back and playing a smaller room. It felt more authentic. Also I was now three years into my five-year apprenticeship and this was the time to gain as much experience as possible.

'I like the idea,' I said. 'But last year I did a show with three other men so let's change it around a bit and get a woman in. I saw an American called Kit Hollerbach the other day who is very good. She might be up for doing Edinburgh.'

I found out where she was next playing, and Dave and I went along.

Kit had a confidence and a pizzazz that many of us British acts lacked. She had sharp one-liners and a strikingly different onstage attitude that was brash yet likeable.

We met up with Kit after her show and talked over the idea. She wasn't particularly keen at first, principally because she had only been in the country for a few weeks and had never heard of the Edinburgh Fringe Festival. She might have been slightly put off by my appearance, which during the mid-eighties could easily be described as unconsciously eccentric. For a year-and-a-half I constantly wore a pair of spectacles that had the left lens missing. This made little difference to me as it was only my right eye that needed correcting. I also got into the habit of wearing black track-suit bottoms because they were comfortable and easy to slip on. The same with shoes; cheap trainers were fine by me. There was nobody in my life to tell me any different (and nor would there be at that rate). I knew that clothes were important in what they said about you, but I deliberately flouted that pearl of wisdom. Such is stubbornness. I didn't consider myself a fashion victim, fashion was a victim of me.

At the end of our meeting, Kit agreed to do the show. I came up with the title 'The Sunshine Players present *Three Weeks To Live*' and Dave did all the organising of venue, programme entry, etc.

Once we got to Edinburgh that year, we discovered that we were sharing the venue with a double act called Mullarkey and Myers who had recently formed. Neil Mullarkey, ex-Cambridge Footlights, was somebody I met on the cabaret circuit, and Mike Myers was a Canadian who was living in England for a while. Mike and Kit hit it off, and quite quickly they were talking about the lack of improvised comedy this side of the Atlantic. Jim Sweeney and

Steve Steen, amongst others, had been staging improvised shows since the mid-1970s, but there was no weekly impro night that I was aware of. Kit and Mike said that New York, Chicago, San Francisco, LA all had venues that regularly hosted impro nights, so why not London?

Mike suggested we stage a show while we were in Edinburgh, so the five of us, Mike, Kit, Neil, Dave and I put on a twenty-minute show. I remember my main contribution being sitting at the side watching Mike and Kit improvise, while thinking *'this is impossible'* to myself. *'Making it up as you go along, how can you do that?'* And yet they were. Once everybody got back to London, a meeting was held with Don Ward at The Comedy Store. Sunday evenings were free and so were we.

Don agreed to give it a try but only as the second half of the show. The first half would be a couple of stand-ups. That format lasted a few weeks. Kit started running impro classes on a Saturday morning at the Store, and I went along every week to get more practise. It was good to be improvising at the same level (i.e. beginner) as everybody else. This was in contrast to the Sunday show, which had now become 100 per cent improvisation.

Working with Mike Myers every week was a great education. I observed how he created an imaginary world around him. In one scene we were in a Yorkshire farmhouse, and within moments he had taken freshly baked bread out of an oven and placed it on a table. He commented on the view out of the window, which was all green hills. He swept the floor. He filled a kettle at the tap and lit the stoves. All of the above was carried out around me as I stood transfixed at his invention. He was so good it was rather daunting. In fact, I don't think I really improved until Mike left us and moved to America to take up a job on *Saturday Night Live*. His phenomenal success as first Wayne Campbell in *Wayne's World*, and then to top that with the *Austin Powers* movies are testament to his talent and his extraordinary capacity for hard work.

One night Mike, Neil and I were travelling back from a Comedy Store Players gig* in Highgate.

I started talking about the cartoon series *The Flintstones* and I adopted a tone of outrage as I complained that Betty Rubble, a very beautiful woman in my book, had really married beneath herself looks-wise when she hitched herself to the frankly thickset and stumpy Barney. Mike had near hysterics at this point. He was greatly tickled by the comic conceit of treating cartoon characters as if they were real people, and when I saw *Wayne's World 2* I was rather chuffed that the Betty Rubble marrying Barney controversy was in the screenplay, more or less verbatim as I had said it in the back of a car a few years before. I didn't view this as stealing material because I never talked about the Betty Rubble stuff onstage. Instead it gave me a secret thrill to have one joke in a hugely successful Hollywood comedy.

I had an idea one day, inspired by one of my favourite British War films, *Albert R.N.* Based on a true story, a bunch of British POWs built a dummy, which passed as a prisoner in a rudimentary headcount. Another prisoner hides in the shower block and then escapes later. The Germans, courtesy of our dummy Albert R.N., are fooled into believing that no one is missing by counting the heads. I took this idea to its illogical conclusion and worked it into a routine, but planned it well to keep the audience with me by not jumping too far ahead in a single bound.

---

* Our new show at the Store demanded a group name, so we became The Comedy Store Players.

I wrote the routine up and rehearsed it in my bedsit, complete with appropriate arm movements. It was about three minutes, which was a long bit for me to introduce into the act in one go.

I hoped that the storytelling part of the routine would carry me through any dead spots I might encounter. The first time I performed it, at a club in Islington, I was as nervous as a kitten attempting the trombone. I'd been playing around with the idea of manufacturing a catchphrase, so I wrote a little preamble to the beginning of the sketch.

'I'm looking for a catchphrase. I've tried several over the years. "Not another pound of apples please Margaret." That never took off, but I've decided on "In it marvellous". I'll drop it in later to see how it works. During the Second World War, I was in a German prisoner of war camp and one day I had an idea.'

No hanging about here in terms of scene setting. For me, a live stand-up gig concentrated the writing.

'So I said to the other prisoners, "Why don't we build a dummy six foot high, stick a uniform on it? One of us escapes in the middle of the night, the dummy takes their place. The next morning at roll call all the Germans count the heads, nobody's missing!" The other prisoners said, let's try it, so we did. It worked like a dream. So the escape committee said, "look this is great but can you do more than one at a time?"

'And I said "Yeah."

'So one night twenty-six prisoners escaped. I had to go down to breakfast the next morning holding a ten foot pole in each hand.'(Here I stretched my arms out to each side.)

'Thirteen prisoners on this side, thirteen prisoners on that side, trying to keep a polite conversation going.

'"So what you having for breakfast then?"

'"I thought I might have the thin gruel followed by eggs Benedict."

'I did this every day for a week. Soon I was the only prisoner left in the camp. Meanwhile the Germans were losing the war. Every available man they had was fighting at the front. There was only one guard left in the camp and I didn't know that; I didn't know that, because that one guard was putting dummies on the gate, dummies in the watch towers – all dressed in German uniforms. And then one morning I was pushing a wheelbarrow full of prisoners towards the exercise block when suddenly this German soldier came round the corner pushing a wheelbarrow full of storm troopers. The German looked at my dummies, I looked at his dummies, and then the German said in almost near perfect English ... "In it marvellous."'*

The first time I performed the routine it was nerve-racking but the audience enjoyed it. They went with it – they could see the pictures in their heads. Always the ultimate aim. Afterwards, I was naturally thrilled with how well it went. A new sizeable chunk for the act was more than welcome; it happened very rarely for me. It was an impressive new three minutes that built nicely with strong laughs throughout. So I was confident and looking forward to doing the routine again, which I would do, two nights later, on the other side of town, at the Bearcat club in Twickenham.

It's Monday night. Just forty-eight hours after my Islington triumph. I'd always enjoyed playing the Bearcat club and the gig was going well until I got to the brand new part of the act. I did the 'in it marvellous' catchphrase set-up and ... a voice from the crowd said loudly amidst the laughter, 'This is the prisoner of war bit.'

Now, this wasn't a heckle but it momentarily wrong-footed me nevertheless. I started on the prisoner of war bit. The laughs

---

* The earlier bit about trying to come up with a catchphrase was invented simply to provide me with this punchline. Before thinking of it I struggled to come up with an ending for the POW monologue. I had everything up to 'And then the German said in almost near perfect English ...' I couldn't think of anything that wasn't an anticlimax, but the invention of 'In it marvellous' worked a treat.

were coming in the same places as Islington, which proved that the previous gig had not been a one-off. I was delivering the words properly, but there was bubbling discontent inside my head.

And then I got to the bit 'Meanwhile the Germans were losing the war. Every available man was fighting at the front ...' and the same loud voice as before said, *'There's only one guard left in the camp!'* followed by a huge laugh from the same man.

Who was this man in the audience, and why is he saying the lines out loud before me?

I have the sure knowledge that he must have seen me in Islington on the one previous occasion that I had performed this material, so why has he travelled twenty-odd miles across London to deliberately ruin the act? He is sitting six rows from the front. He is wearing a striped blazer and his friend has blonde hair.

I didn't want to react to him and lose the flow of the story, and he wasn't exactly heckling me but it did put me off somewhat and I lost some funniness along the way. The gig was still OK, but its beginnings had promised better. This was tough for a young stand-up to bear. I took it to heart.

I looked straight at the guy with the loud voice sitting in the audience. Him and his friend were both laughing heartily amongst themselves, in a room that was otherwise quiet. They were odd. They were evil.

I would never forget them.

Life continued back at the bedsit. I was getting around thirty quid a gig and doing three or four gigs a week. I didn't like to do more than that, as the stress involved in going to a different room every night and endeavouring to entertain an audience who hadn't come to see you, could become debilitating. I once had thirteen consecutive gigs at different places on the circuit in the space of a fortnight. I was exhausted at the end of it. And trying to find a venue you're not familiar with, particularly in the strange unfamiliar world of north London, could easily induce plenty of anxiety. One Saturday night I played five gigs between eight p.m. and one o'clock in the morning. This one-off marathon coincided with a producer from a television talent show called *The Freddie Starr Showcase* trying to catch my live act. He turned up at The Comedy Store, where I was the first comic on. He arrived late and missed me by fifteen minutes. I had given him my itinerary for the night, so as I hadn't seen him at the Store I assumed he would be at my next gig, which was at the Oxford Arms in Camden Town. This was a lovely room that was fairly small but still comfortably sat eighty people in a convivial, lively, intelligent atmosphere. After the gig, which went well, I hoped to see the producer but he wasn't there. I had a mobile number so I found a call box and phoned him. He told me he had left The Comedy Store and was now on his way to my next gig.

'I've just finished there,' I said. 'I'm now on my way to The Finborough Arms in Earls Court.'

'I'll see you there,' he said, but he didn't. I did very well at The Finborough Arms, a lovely little room above a pub, but I had no time for a celebratory pint because I needed to get to the Jubilee Gardens on the South Bank of the Thames, where a circus tent had been erected. I followed a fantastic juggling act and died on my arse. That's slightly unfair, I got some laughs, but my lack of visual content worked against me. I came off after twenty minutes of sweat only to be met by the producer who told me that I wasn't the sort of act they were looking for (i.e. he was looking for a funny one). On the basis of what he had just seen, I totally understood. I hurried back to The Comedy Store where I went on shortly after 1 a.m. and, Sod's Law, had my best gig of the night.

Meanwhile, John also established himself on the growing cabaret circuit as one of those comedians that other comedians enjoyed watching. John had the most inspired opening to his act. At the time, he had hair reminiscent of Charles II or a judge's wig, and he would wet it then pile it all up on top of itself under a hat just before he walked on. Once centre stage, he would remove the hat and the released hair would stick up at odd angles as John moved his head from side to side to see what people were laughing at. This movement caused the hair to collapse spectacularly on one side while he continued to look seriously bemused. Halfway through his third joke the hair would again move in a strange way, provoking laughter which John again amplified by reacting with puzzlement. On a good night this hair business could last a good two or three minutes.

The new Comedy Store soon settled in and became a favourite spot for comics like us to gather due to its back bar away from the auditorium. The dressing room was essentially a short corridor, but the back bar was spacious and away from the public. In those early days there was a carefree spirit abroad. In *The Comedy Store* book by William Cook, Hattie Hayridge recalled that 'Paul Merton would go on under an assumed name (Len Badger). He'd do his act really badly, deliberately, just to get heckled off. He'd get punchlines wrong and all the comics would be killing themselves laughing, and the audience would be going "fuck off!" He'd do the heckle put downs very badly. People would tell him "You shouldn't do that. They're going to think you're really shit." He'd say "I don't care. They won't know it's me."'

It's all perfectly true, but I should emphasise that the Len Badger stuff was an unpaid ten-minute spot at the end of the evening when I dare say drink had been taken.

10

Look at the Size of that Chicken

Julian was tall, elegant, rather quiet off stage, but what really impressed me was his total commitment to his act and to the world of glamour. He had a lot in common with me in that he was a new act finding his feet in the ever increasing world of cabaret. In other ways, he was very different.

I first met Julian Clary in 1985 at a south-east London college of further education. Gigs were beginning to appear all over the place, and great inroads were made into building up a college circuit. The gig that night was typical of its era. The room had a bar at one end and at the other was a tiny makeshift stage, constructed from a dozen blue plastic beer crates with a layer of cheap green-and-brown carpet laid across the top. Attempting to balance itself on this erratic surface stood a microphone stand on a dodgy tripod that lent the whole setup an unnecessary sway. Approaching the microphone itself risked loud acoustic feedback, and the lighting consisted of a couple of weedy looking spotlights optimistically aimed towards the stage area.

Despite these dispiriting surroundings, Julian shone that night. He set the tone immediately, making his entrance to the theme from *Gone with the Wind* while walking through a swirl of cascading colours. He achieved this effect by throwing confetti into the air and pushing the play button on his portable cassette player. Although the effects were cheap, Julian's attitude towards them was anything but. Onstage, he carried himself with the air of a golden emperor or a visiting deity, generously allowing us to look at him with our eyes full of wondrous gratitude. In those days he wore a lot of stage make-up to accentuate the theatricality and otherness of his performance. He appeared under the name of 'The Joan Collins Fan Club' but he didn't work alone. Fanny the Wonder Dog was an essential part of the act. Her range of impressions, considering she was a dog, was both uncanny and unnatural. She was part whippet and part Rory Bremner. She would sit patiently on a stool while Julian draped various props and wigs on her. A string of pearls around her elegant neck immediately conjured up the Queen Mother. Eye witnesses were startled by the resemblance. Not only was Fanny spookily accurate in her people impressions, but she could also 'do' films. No one who ever saw it will ever forget how Fanny became the embodiment of *Psycho*, merely by sitting on a stool with a shower cap on her head. Having run through her repertoire, Fanny would accept a chocolate drop and retire to the dressing room.

The three of us shared a train back into town that night. I told Julian how much I admired his onstage presence, which was oblivious to the general air of seediness around him. We talked about the nature of camp and that 'rise above it all' quality that permeates through. Camp humour strikes an attitude. You hold your head high and request that the world not only accepts but adores you.

The BBC radio series *Round the Horne* first introduced me to the concept of high camp, in the shape of Julian and Sandy as played by Kenneth Williams and Hugh Paddick. The hugely inventive scripts by Marty Feldman and Barry Took bubbled with a naughty air of near-sauciness, as double entendres flew from our radios to liven up our Sunday lunchtimes. Kenneth Horne, as the avuncular anchor with a twinkle in his eye, lent authority to proceedings. His rich tones and occasional air of mild bewilderment were employed hilariously as he could scarcely believe the words he was saying. I particularly relished his reading of the line 'My name is Ebenezer Cuckpowder', his voice conveying the thought that really nobody could be expected to take such an obviously fictional name seriously, and it was beneath him to even be asked to utter the words.

Kenneth Horne's weekly encounters with Julian and Sandy were for many listeners the highlight of the show. One exchange between the three of them that has always stayed in my memory occurred in the week that our two heroes were running a ticket agency for West End shows. Their company was called Bonar Seats. 'Bonar' means good or authentic, and was part of the street language Polari common in the gay community in the 1960s. An underground language that meant nothing to the programme's mainstream audience was part and parcel of the superb entertainment they listened to every week.

'Oh hello Mr Horne, how lovely to varda your eke' was often the opening remark. Even if you didn't know this meant 'how lovely to see your face', the words sounded funny and were delivered with such brio. Kenneth Horne is enquiring about the various shows they have on offer. At one point Julian says, 'Or then of course there's your actual opera.'

'Mozart?'

'Please yourself, we only book the seats.'

This exchange, played at some speed, drew massive laughs from the then studio audience and is still very funny today. But on closer inspection as a pure joke it doesn't really stand up. What on earth does it mean? It's not a double entendre because Mozart doesn't sound like anything else. Through brilliant characterisation and diamond sharp delivery, though, we laugh. The quickness of the words deceives the ear.

Homosexuals were invisible in everyday life in the 1960s, and so the Julian and Sandy sketches had a special power to shock us in a mild and comic way. At a time when homosexuality had only recently been decriminalised, Julian and Sandy's 'Most of our time is taken up with a criminal practice' was daring and on the nose. If that's the way you like it.*

This was what I loved so much about Julian Clary's act. That defiance. That looking the world right in the eye and saying this is me and this is my stage make-up, and tickets are available at popular prices. His onstage charisma and physical beauty, allied with an often waspish cutting humour delivered with impeccable timing, made for a very exciting package.

Julian excelled at audience interaction, sometimes inflicting mental scars that might possibly last a lifetime. One night onstage at Jongleurs in Battersea, his eye was caught by a gentleman sitting at one of the front tables.

'And what's your name?' enquired Julian with a characteristic slight wiggle of his head.

'Chuck,' replied Chuck.

'Chuck!' said Julian arching an eyebrow. 'As in heave?'

The audience fell about, and three years later I was performing a gig on a barge somewhere around Holland Park when a man came up to me and asked if I knew Julian Clary. I said 'yes', and he introduced himself as Heave, and could I pass on the message that all his friends now called him that since that night at Jongleurs.

---

* In my first few months as a performer, I was thrilled to be asked by a fellow act on the bill a question I had never been asked in the civil service, 'Do you go with boys?' he enquired. 'No,' I said, 'but it's great to be in showbiz.'

I asked him if he minded and he said, no, he'd got used to it after a couple of years. The power of the person onstage can be an awesome thing.

Compèring a benefit gig at Jongleurs one night, I stood on the stage and found myself looking at an audience of Marie Antoinettes and Charlie Chaplins, intermingling with circus clowns and cowboys and French tarts and nuns. It was all rather unsettling. For whatever reason they'd either been told, or had volunteered, to come in fancy dress. An audience attired this way, I can now tell you, don't react like a normal crowd.

I was struggling with my opening ten minutes when a small incident occurred, which completely transformed the gig. As I laboured to get the audience concentrating on me rather than looking at each other's costumes, through one of the doorways at the back there suddenly emerged a six foot two chicken. To be more accurate, a man inside a big yellow feathery chicken costume, with big orange feet and a huge chicken head with functional beak, emerged through one of the doorways at the back. My next words sprung from my lips unbidden.

'Fuck me, look at the size of that chicken.'

I certainly wouldn't claim my ad-lib comment contained much wit, but it accurately summed up the general view on offer with a passionate exhortation to marvel at the same. The audience turning in their seats roared with laughter at the sight of the gigantic fowl, and my comedy muse was up and running.

'What's your name?' I asked rather unfairly, knowing that speech from beyond the beak would be difficult to hear. A friend volunteered the info that our poor sap in the chicken skin was called Barry.

'Barry,' I repeated. 'You don't look like a Barry. You look more like a fucking chicken.' Then I changed tack. 'I bet when you hired that in the shop was it the last costume available? Or was it down to the last two left? Either a giant chicken or Adolf Hitler. Frankly you would have been better off as Hitler because at least you could have passed yourself as Charlie Chaplin like this clown sitting down the front here.' I then addressed the audience generally. 'Wouldn't it be great if under the chicken head Barry had a Hitler moustache and a Nazi uniform? Hedging his bets. The old chicken Hitler combo.' All these remarks were getting big laughs, made bigger by Barry's antics as a huge chicken at the back shaking his fist/wing and looking more miserable by the moment. By the time I was finished with him he was a beaten chicken. I brought the first act on and it all went swimmingly from there.

Twenty minutes later, through the open doorway, I half glimpsed a hot sweaty man climbing out of a chicken. I turned my head. I didn't want to know what he looked like. I owed him his anonymity. But the whole incident proved to me that there is a comedy god. Just as I needed divine intervention, help arrived in the shape of a giant chicken. The universe had provided and I was truly thankful.

Audience members would often say the oddest things to the compère. Because you're on and off throughout the show you're easily identified by even the heavily pissed. One man came up to me once during the interval at Jongleurs and demanded that I start telling jokes about a certain make and colour of car.

''Ere mate,' he said. 'Do you know any jokes about red Cortinas?'

'No, I don't,' I said. 'Why?'

'You must do. The girlfriend wants a red Cortina and they're rubbish cars. So, you know, just do a couple of jokes about them.'

So I went onstage at the beginning of the second half, told the audience all of the above, much to their amusement, and then ad-libbed few lines.

'There's this red Cortina walks into a pub' etc., silly thoughts, but it had the virtue of genuine spontaneity. I thoroughly enjoyed the freedom that being a compère brings you. Doing seven to eight minutes between each act meant that I could build up trust with the crowd, and subsequently be freer in the second half. By that time, everybody knew me and the show had built up its own momentum.

My general philosophy as compère was simple: establish myself quickly at the top of the show, make sure the audience knew that I was the boss. Bring the first act on once the crowd are happy and laughing, and keep the evening ticking over from there. If one act doesn't go particularly well then the compère needs to get the audience back in a happy frame for the next performer. To set up a platform for each act was the aim. Alternatively if a performer storms the room my job was to come back on and settle the audience back down again.

I only compèred a few times at Jongleurs but I always enjoyed the experience of running the show. The only dull bit was reading out the birthdays. The management insisted that the birthdays should be read out straight with no jokes. One night, bored by doing it properly, I started making stuff up. 'It's Helen's birthday … She's a hundred and eight, let's give her the bumps. Is Dominic here? Stand up Dominic.' A drunk man stands up, succeeding at the second attempt. 'I'm here,' he bellows. 'Ah, Dominic,' I say, 'I understand you're the designated driver tonight.' The audience laugh but Dominic is too drunk to know why so he grins foolishly and gives everyone in the room a cheery wave before semi-collapsing back into his chair.

In this game, I realised, you need luck. Dedication and talent are obvious requirements but without good fortune you're whistling in the dark, which is a fine act for radio but it won't get you to the Palladium.

The night I was clowning around with the birthdays also happened to be the night a TV producer called David McMahon was in the audience. He had been commissioned by Channel 4 to make a pilot show based on the concept of comedy sketches, written by the general public and then performed by a professional cast. He needed a compère for the pilot, which he was recording at the Astoria Theatre in the Charing Cross Road. The compère wouldn't feature in the edited recording, but his job was to keep the audience happy on the night. He told me this immediately after the show at Jongleurs and asked me to give him a ring, giving me a business card. The TV show sounded like a completely terrible idea. I knew this was the opportunity I was waiting for.

I had noticed, through my intense readings of many a showbiz autobiography, that the elusive first big break can often come about by being good in an otherwise ordinary show. You stand in stark contrast to the stuff that stinks. David McMahon also told me that Seamus Cassidy, a Channel 4 commissioning editor, would be in the audience. Given that all I needed to do on the night was split my stand-up into thirty second sections while chairs were brought on to the stage to set up another sketch, a lot of cards were stacked in my favour. Particularly as those sketches were all written by non-established writers, and some were particularly weak. Whereas I, on the other hand, had strong one-liners to hit the audience with as soon as I was back on. I felt ready and confident.

On the night of the recording I got to the Astoria in a couple of hours before kick-off. I took the opportunity to walk the enormous stage, to sniff the (really big!) empty auditorium, to see where the cameras were placed.

I felt the stage beneath my feet. It was sticky with spilt beer. The Astoria was primarily a live music venue in 1987, and alcohol was randomly thrown about without much discretion. I checked my exit and entry onto the stage, the height of the microphone on its stand, and the whereabouts of my dressing room. There was an hour or so to kill and somebody suggested we find the nearest pub. So we did. The backstage facilities at the Astoria were pretty grim, and being away from the venue for a short while means you can return to it with a buzz of excitement and purpose in your stride. And so we went to the pub. On the cabaret circuit alcohol was an ever-present trap for the performer. The gigs were in rooms above pubs with bars in them and that was the accepted atmosphere. This isn't a cautionary tale. I never believed in drinking before I went on. In the histories I read drink was often the comic's curse. A stressful job where some nights are better than others in venues with plenty of booze on sale, is a recipe for falling over if you're not careful. The trap as I saw it was you drink a couple of pints before the show and if it goes well you credit some of the success to the booze. But supposing the next time you have two pints and it's not so good, do you think to yourself 'I'd be better off with three'? That night, an hour and a half before the gig kicked off, I drank two pints of clear cool water, well aware that this was a big occasion. I went out onstage that night in front of several hundred people and wowed them. And the skilled sketch performers lifted the frequently weakish material into the realms of entertainment. There was a good spirit amongst the sketch cast afterwards, but everyone was very generous in saying that I had stormed it. I bathed luxuriously in their congratulations.

And a few days later I got the phone call I was hoping for. It was David McMahon.

'Channel 4 want a series of ten programmes.'

'Ten! Blimey!'

'And they want you to host it.'

'To be on screen?'

'Yes.'

'Wow, that's good … Yes, I'll be happy to do that.'

'You were the hit of the night. Seamus Cassidy was raving about you.'

'Well you know, it was all tried and tested stuff, David.'

Recording ten shows meant using up every bit of stand-up I had but I reasoned that it was worth it. Being good on television gives you a credibility amongst people who work on television. They don't have to ask the question 'Will this person work on television?' David McMahon continued.

'Now do you have an agent?'

'Er. No.'

'There's a really tiny budget, we can only give you a couple of hundred quid a show.'

'That's fine by me,' I replied. The more business-minded of you might think I blew this conversation and negotiated terribly. But I wasn't concerned with the cash. Getting on to television with my own material was the most important achievement for me.

David McMahon continued. 'And we've got the title; we're calling it *Comedy Wavelength*.'

'What an awful title,' I thought.

'Lovely,' I said.

I put the phone down and looked around my bedsit. In April 1982 I'd given myself five years to try and improve myself, to serve an apprenticeship, and here I was in January 1987, about to star in a ten-part comedy series on Channel 4.

I'd squeaked in with just a few months to spare.

11

Let's Invade Poland

'Hello, could I speak to Jamie Rix please?'

'Who's calling please?'

'It's Paul Martin, sorry, Paul Merton. Jamie left a message saying he had something to offer us.'

'He's in a BBC radio producers meeting at the moment. Can he phone you back in half an hour?'

'Yes,' I said.

Jamie was a Radio 4 producer who John and I had approached with some sketches. I had seen him at a gig and we had got talking. Producers of sketch shows are always on the lookout for material and Jamie, who was working on a show called *In One Ear*, had liked the four sketches that John and I had submitted. It was a special thrill to hear our material broadcast on the radio for the first time, some eight years after we sent our first unsolicited script to the BBC. It was much easier to write for a show that already existed, and we attended the recordings noting which bits of our stuff worked and which didn't. I had changed my name to Paul Merton because back in the eighties it was illegal to work in television unless you were a member of the actors' trade union Equity, and they had a rule that no two members could have the same name. There was already a Paul Martin registered and, for a moment, I wondered if it was the kid I was introduced to at school, but further research revealed that he was a juggler in Leeds.

My ten-week stint on *Comedy Wavelength* demanded Equity membership, so I was suddenly faced with the prospect of changing my name. A number of questions immediately posed themselves. Should I alter my first name? I'd never been overly pleased with Paul but I had got used to it. It would be ridiculous to suddenly become Gerald or Wilbur, so changing Martin was a better option. For a couple of days I strongly favoured Paul Albert. Obviously as a tribute to my dad, but I also liked the cadence of it. The two words together did sound like they may be the name of a funny man. But I settled on Paul Merton for one overriding reason. In my early teens, I constantly practised my signature in the fervent wish that one day someone might ask for my autograph. Paul Merton as a signature looked exactly the same as Paul Martin. Morden was in the London Borough of Merton, so the name felt part of my late childhood. The decision was clear.

Jamie called back within half an hour with a very exciting proposal.

'Hello Paul,' he said. 'I'll come straight to the point. I'm moving to television to produce the next series of *Alas Smith and Jones*, and I want to commission you and John to write sketches for it.'

'Wow,' I said, 'that's exciting.'

Mel Smith and Griff Rhys Jones's sketch show was a classy affair, with the head-to-head conversations between the two stars quickly becoming a regular favourite. Some of the best sketch writers around worked on the show.

'I'll need to talk to John,' I said, 'but that does sound very interesting indeed.'

I phone John and arranged to meet in the pub that night to talk the offer through.

'On the one hand,' I said, taking a sip from a pint of Guinness, 'we didn't come into this business to become writers for other comedians. And the sketch show is a hungry beast. We don't want to be churning out our best stuff for other people. But on the other hand ...'

'We can't say no because this is a golden opportunity,' said John.

'You're right. Perhaps there's a middle course?' I said.

'Let's write a handful of sketches to see how it goes,' suggested John. 'It would be a good experience for us.' I agreed.

And so with some excitement we said 'yes' and attended the first of many script meetings. We walked into the BBC television centre with our official passes, and looked excitedly around the inner circle while still maintaining a cool professional air. Mel Smith didn't attend any of the meetings we were at, but Griff was always there, full of ideas and enthusiasm. The latter was a trait he shared with Jamie Rix, who was always encouraging about our writing.

One sketch we were particularly pleased with was a funeral scene at a graveside that combined physical humour with the solemnity of the service. Griff is the priest and Mel is the mourner who first drops his car keys accidentally into the open grave and on to the top of the coffin. He climbs into the grave to retrieve them and his foot goes through the coffin lid. He climbs out of the grave wearing the lid like a giant ski. He extracts himself from the wood and indicates that the service should continue. He sneezes and now his false teeth fall in to the open grave. He climbs back down, grabs his teeth and once again clambers out of the grave. He again indicates that the service should continue. As the priest carries on, Mel begins rolling his tongue around the false teeth in his mouth.

The priest says, 'Is there something wrong with your teeth?'

Mel says, 'No.'

The priest says, 'What's the problem then?'

And Mel says, 'These aren't my teeth.'

The two of them then look down into the grave with a look of horror on their faces. This sketch was the last one in the first programme of the series. A prestigious slot.

Nevertheless, as well as us each performing on the cabaret circuit, we had to keep reminding ourselves not to be distracted from our main goal, which was to get a radio pilot commissioned. We already knew who we wanted to produce it. We had first met David Tyler on the cabaret circuit when he was trying his luck as a stand-up comedian. When he became a Radio 4 comedy producer we gave him a call. He was enthusiastic and talked about who else we would have in the show. I mentioned Neil Mullarkey and Josie Lawrence, who like myself were members of The Comedy Store Players. Julian Clary was an obvious choice for me. He would be the high status individual in every sketch he appeared in, whether he was Robin Hood or Zorro. As Zorro we had him burst into a Mexican cantina saying he is hungry and demanding a recommendation from the menu. The answer comes back, 'The chef's special?' And Julian says, 'I know that but I want my dinner first.'

I also suggested that Tony Hawks could provide a comic song every week. David Tyler went away and attended a few meetings, and returned a couple of months later with the news that the BBC was prepared to commission a pilot. Bingo! This was fantastic news. A major step forward. Now it was up to me and John to write a good script. It had been nine years since we had written our first effort and we'd both gained a lot of experience performing in front of live audiences. We now had a surer instinct for what was funny.

I'd seen two or three pilot radio shows recorded at the Paris Theatre in Lower Regent Street, and I was struck by how nervous the writers and performers often were before the recording.

The Paris could be an intimidating place if you let it be. As you walked down the stairs to the auditorium you passed a number of black-and-white photographs on the wall of all the great comedians who had recorded there. Tony Hancock, Peter Sellers, Harry Secombe and Spike Milligan, Kenneth Williams, the cast of *Just a Minute*. I didn't want our pilot to be cowed by its surroundings so I came up with the title *The Big Fun Show*, which I felt would put us all in the right frame of mind. It was important that we all enjoyed ourselves onstage and didn't look like we were taking it too seriously. We were all well accustomed to the cabaret circuit with its sometimes volatile crowds, so playing the Paris Theatre with its polite intelligent audience and hopefully a funny script in our hand should be something to enjoy.

In March 1987, on the day of recording we got to the Paris around mid-afternoon. I was carrying a plastic carrier bag, which contained my copy of the script and a bottle of brandy. The brandy was a silly romantic gesture on my part. I wanted the bottle to be kept backstage on a table with a few glasses while we were recording the show, in tribute to the Goons who used to do exactly the same thing. Harry particularly loved his brandy and on many *Goon Show* recordings he can be heard shouting 'right round the back for the old brandy', followed by the sound of speeded up running footsteps. I assured our producer David Tyler that the brandy was not to be consumed during the show, for its presence was entirely symbolic.

The Paris was a beautiful space to perform in. I wanted a sound effects man onstage with us so the audience could see him opening doors and walking across gravel, or even firing guns if necessary. One show I'd seen recorded had hidden the sound effects person away from the audience, which seemed to me to be missing a trick. Out front onstage with us seemed to be more fun and might generate laughs. Luckily, it did. In fact, the recording that night went sensationally well. We could not have wished for better. The sketches worked beautifully, the music was wonderful and the audience enjoyed it. John and I as the presenters and actors in various sketches got our fair share of laughs, as indeed did Neil Mullarkey, Josie Lawrence, Tony Hawks and Julian.

During Tony Hawks's song, John and I stood backstage out of sight of the audience as I poured a tiny glass of brandy for each of us and we toasted each other. Sentimental, I know, but we couldn't help thinking about the church hall in Swansea. Everything worked that night. Our sound effects man told me afterwards that our show was the best pilot he had seen in a long time. Everyone had worked very well together as a team. His words sent me higher still.

Things were rolling. Before *Comedy Wavelength* started recording I got a call from a new chat show that was launching on Channel 4. I'd never heard of the host and was naturally wary of appearing in something I didn't know. I turned it down politely only the next day to receive a rather insistent phone call from the host himself who told me that he was a big fan of mine, had seen me several times at The Comedy Store and really wanted me to appear as his first ever stand-up guest. His enthusiasm won me over.

'OK,' I said, 'I'll do it.'

'Thank you.'

'Oh and I'm sorry, what was your name again?'

'Jonathan Ross.'

'I'm sorry I've never heard of you.'

'Nobody has and possibly never will again after this!'

'OK, I'll see you there!'

'It'll be great.'

And he was right, it was. Channel 4 created a real air of excitement around the show. The chat show format was given a different approach more closely based on the David Letterman model than Michael Parkinson's more journalistically based interviews. In the Letterman version the host is the biggest star on the show, whereas Michael's technique was to listen to the answers and base his questions on what had just been said.

The night I was on *The Last Resort* the other guests were Ray Davies of The Kinks and Mandy Rice-Davies of the 1963 Profumo scandal. Jonathan, as host, was successfully hiding his nerves before the beginning of the recording, but inside his guts must have been churning. At this point he'd had very little experience of appearing in front of a live audience. He'd been to The Comedy Store a few times and had once got up onstage to do five minutes and found it a terrifying experience. And now, here he was, about to host Channel 4's big new chat show called *The Last Resort*, so named because the choice of Jonathan as host was literally that.

Although he had no meaningful experience, Jonathan did have a quick wit, a bright brain and bags of confidence. He had the nerve to pull it off. As for myself, I was buzzing like an electric teapot. Before the recording I'd been asked if I could wear a dark formal suit because all the floor staff would be wearing dinner jackets, including the camera men. I cobbled something together from my less-than-extensive wardrobe.

Soon it's time. The packed studio audience are in the early twenties, and they feel they're up for something different and daring. These people are trendy. They want to be on the next big thing. They're fashion conscious. A large section probably live in north London and were amongst the first to adopt the habit of drinking Mexican beer from the bottle with a wedge of lime lodged in the bottle neck.

This absurd arrangement, which demonstrates the ridiculous posturing people get up to when trying to impress or be part of an in-crowd, at least flavoured the piss poor quality of the beer on offer. In all honesty, without the lime the drink tasted like it had been strained through a cat. I once mentioned this onstage and said it was a ludicrous practice and I couldn't see it spreading to more established flavoursome brews. Who'd ever drink a pint of Guinness with a potato in it?*

My spot went very well, I was doing strong, familiar material to me, but unfamiliar material to the audience. After the recording, Jonathan and friends invited me out for a curry in Berwick Street, and afterwards we watched the show go out in a nearby flat. I was pleased for Jonathan, he clearly had the big-match temperament and, although he had very little experience of appearing in front of an audience, he did a sterling job.

'Ladies and Gentlemen, Paul Merton.'

The audience made enthusiastic cheering noises while I stood centre stage and looked at them. After a pause I said, 'That's a big

---

* This was deemed a little too much racial stereotyping by another comic on the bill and I reluctantly agreed. For me the juxtaposition of the words potato and Guinness was unexpected but I didn't feel the joke was worth defending so I only did it the once. To a big laugh. Thinking about it now for the first time in nearly thirty years, I realise the joke would be funnier if it was, 'Who'd drink a pint of Guinness with an aubergine in it?' Aubergine is so much better. Far more unexpected and simply devoid of cliché. I'm glad I cleared that up.

cheer. Let's invade Poland.' This seemed to be my time. *Comedy Wavelength* was enjoying good ratings. And now, a new experience – I was being recognised in the street by people! Halfway through recording the TV series, the audience who had seen a couple of programmes were cheering and wildly applauding my entrance. This had never happened to me before.

Before you knew it, I was invited to do a three-minute spot on the Terry Wogan show, BBC1. A pinnacle, no doubt about it. It was live television and I was match fit and ready for it. Cock-a-hoop, I decided to have a party after the live broadcast with a few friends and a few bottles of champagne back at my flat. Irrespective of how *Wogan* went, it was worth marking my appearance on this iconic show and to also throw a flat-warming party for the lovely new place I was renting with my girlfriend Julie.

Well ... I remember several things about *Wogan* that night, the first of which is there was no Terry Wogan, he was on holiday. His replacement was Mike Smith. In addition, it was the hottest day of the year and several coaches packed full of *Wogan*'s fervent fans had all broken down on the motorway, and I was informed on my arrival in the Shepherd's Bush Theatre that they wouldn't be coming.

'Don't worry, this won't make any difference,' I was told by a member of the production team.

'But I'm doing stand-up,' I replied.

'Oh it'll be great. But there is one thing.'

'What's that?' I said.

'Please don't actually mention there's no audience to the viewers watching at home. It might spoil it for them.'

'But I think they'll realise, won't they, when my act goes over in silence.' I was starting to get worried about this now.

'No! You'll be fine!' they replied, full of verve and positivity.

I just about carried it off on the night by finding the situation amusing and doing my best to work the illusion that it was going well, or at least that I wasn't bothered by the complete lack of any laughter. It was really hard, but I think I got away with it.

I left the studio quickly afterwards to get to my champagne party in Streatham. The BBC car took me down Fulham Palace Road past the flats at Robert Owen House. I arrived back at our new flat in Ambleside Avenue, climbed up the iron stairs outside, and was greeted by six half-tipsy people who declared my *Wogan* appearance to be a triumph. They were other comedians from the circuit. Clearly they had been drinking bubbly for some time. I accepted their congratulations, though, and the proffered glass of champagne, and basked in the occasion. Some of the male guests were fascinated by a new piece of hi-fi technology that I had bought with a portion of my *Comedy Wavelength* earnings. A futuristic piece of kit called a CD player. Nick Hancock told me that I was the first person he knew to own such a machine.

The CD itself was a new object and one to marvel at as you held its silver surface full of rainbows up to the light. This was science fiction compared to previous methods of listening to music, which were suddenly archaic. LPs on black vinyl being played by needles scratching through the surface as they revolve sedately at thirty-three-and-a-third revolutions per minute were much loved. But their dominance would soon be over.

The LP with its much larger size enjoyed a higher status than the CD initially. The long player could be intimidating. But the CD was different. The small shiny disc played a crucial role in radically expanding my musical tastes.

When I started buying LPs, after I first got a job at Tooting employment office, I quickly built up quite a collection. The Beatles, The Kinks, Bob Dylan, Simon and Garfunkel, the Beach

Boys, music from my early years, which I'd missed the first time round. I could listen to these albums knowing they had been critically acclaimed bestsellers. I was pretty conservative. In terms of other musical genres, I had a few classical records featuring the obvious pieces such as Beethoven's *Fifth Symphony* and Tchaikovsky's *1812 Overture*.

The nearest I came to jazz was an album of Scott Joplin piano rags played by Joshua Rifkin. For years I wanted to like jazz, but I didn't know where to start. It sounds downright peculiar, but I couldn't give myself permission to relax and start listening to it. I remember thinking 'I wish I liked jazz'. I was full of self-doubt. I liked Louis Armstrong but I heard that his really good work had been in the 1920s, and I only knew 'Hello Dolly' and 'Mack the Knife'.

But these wonderful new CDs changed my frightened frozen attitudes and persuaded me to dive into a new world of sound; to be no longer put off by doubt and anxiety; to walk into a music store and buy a jazz CD. I'd heard of a young trumpeter called Wynton Marsalis. I bought an album called *Standard Time Vol. 2* and took it home, all excited trembling on the edge of a new adventure. I slid the CD in to the machine. I was fooling myself into thinking that I was listening to the sounds on the disc purely in terms of high fidelity. How good do the individual instruments sound? The thud of the bass drum and the sizzle of the cymbals? I fooled myself brilliantly. By taking away the worry of whether I would like it or not, the music seeped into me. Wynton and his band played a selection of standards. It was proper jazz. And I loved it. In a blinding flash of clarity I realised a fundamental truth. Once I had cast aside the elements of no confidence and 'it's not for me' syndrome I realised THERE WAS NOTHING TO WORRY ABOUT. I bought a well-respected jazz encyclopaedia and I slowly built up a library of albums. I followed connections. I read that Wynton Marsalis had played as a teenager with the Art Blakey group. Art was a drummer who had played with virtually everyone in a long creative career, so from him I could jump into enormous areas of jazz history.

Acquiring an up-to-the-minute hi-fi system attracted the attention of a local burglar, who kicked in my front door one afternoon. That was bad enough, but the handyman who came round to fix the door was certainly the most stupidly racist individual I have ever encountered. He arrived in his dark blue dungarees and carrying his metal tool box. He perused the busted lock.

'Is there where he got in?' he said.

You will appreciate the brilliant dimness of this remark when I tell you that my flat was three floors up and the only way in was via a flight of iron stairs, which are clearly visible from the street.

I said, 'Yes, this is where he got in.'

'I see,' says my handyman/repairer. 'Black was he?'

Although posed in the loose guise of a question, he was already creating a photofit picture in his own mind.

I said, 'No, he wasn't black, no.'

The handyman looks at me with a steady eye. He's clearly bothered by my bizarre assertion.

'Are you sure?' he says. 'Because some of them are quite clever you know. They don't look black, but they are' … Wow! How had this guy managed to get into such a mental state that not only did he fear all blacks, but the ones that you really had to watch out for were the ones who were white?

At the time of him saying it I remember my lips moving up and down but with no sound uttering. I was experiencing simple nervous spasm, whose original function is buried deep within our DNA dating back to caveman days. I had no idea what to say next.

But then, luckily, he gave me some breathing space by continuing his general theme of talking absolute bollocks.

'Well,' he says, 'look at them Indian restaurants.'

'What about them?' I said, knowing full well where he was about to take me on this informal tour of Bollockland. What he was about to say was the same old slanderous cliché that you heard in the early days of people beginning to become brave enough to try food outside of their own cuisine. If fish and chips is a cuisine.

'The thing with Indian restaurants is that the meat they are dishing up is dog.'

'Dog?' I said.

'Dog,' he confirmed.

It was my turn to employ the steady eye.

'Oh yes,' I said, 'that's very likely. Now imagine …' at the word imagine his jaw thrust slightly towards the direction of Tooting Common. Employing imagination was not a personal ambition of his.

I repeated my last two words after drinking in his jawline gymnastics.

'Now imagine you're the chef in an Indian restaurant and it's your job to buy meat for your business; a bit of chicken, a bit of lamb. What are you going to do? Are you going to go to your local butcher and say, I'll have some of that and some of that, or are you going to run around the streets of London late at night, trying to catch Labradors in a butterfly net?'

I was immediately pleased with 'trying to catch Labradors in a butterfly net'.

The handyman looked at me.

'You're talking bollocks mate.'

'Well at least we understand each other.'

Due to a lack of my real ability to generate fresh stand-up material at anything approaching a prolific rate, the same exchange with Monsieur Thicko quickly became part of my act.

The actual burglary attempt was fairly traumatic. I had come back from the shops with two heavy plastic shopping bags crammed badly with basic foodstuffs, and as I crossed the road to my place I happened to notice a man at the top of the stairs by the front door. I checked for traffic, crossed the road, looked back up to the top of the stairs and astonishingly the man had vanished. He hadn't had time to run down the stairs. He was inside my flat. I climbed up the stairs, pushed the front door open and glanced into the living room. Comically I saw a pair of black boots peeking out from under the red floral curtain. A comic cliché.

I remember from the back of my head a piece of wisdom relating to housebreakers. Don't stand between them and a route of escape. Which I am, with the neat twist that I'm forty-five feet up in the air. Nevertheless, it's clear what I have to do. 'I know you're there,' I shout into the room. 'I'm not going to try and stop you but you gotta go.' He dashes out of the front door with a big wooden mallet in his hand. He runs past and shouts 'I'll be back', before clattering down the iron steps and running down the road in a shifty suspicious manner.

So I sit down in a state of mild shock. Nothing has been stolen, a piece of glass in the door has been broken, the new CD player has been lifted off the shelf and onto the floor. My system is pumping adrenaline. I know I have to do some more shopping, but I don't want to leave the flat in case he comes back. Equally, I don't want to stay in the flat in case he comes back.

I sit down. I breathe. I think.

And then, summoning up all my courage, I quickly dash out and heroically purchase two packets of spaghetti and a tin of tomato soup before quickly walking back home.

A couple of days later I reported the crime to Streatham Police Station and my appearance at the front desk caused some amusement. In fact, the desk sergeant couldn't stop grinning at me. As I related my encounter with the burglar his grin grew wider, and when I got to the bit where I saw the burglar's boots sticking out from under the curtain he positively roared with laughter.

'What happened next?' he said. 'Did the curtains turn into a hot air balloon and he then soared up to a height of 15,000 feet before being rescued by a flying saucer?'

My mute astonishment at his words made him laugh even more. He then poked his head around the side of the door behind him and shouted, 'Here Tom, come and have a look at this bloke.' Tom arrived, took one look at the bloke, and burst into laughter. He pointed a finger at me. As I stood there, the only participant in this bizarrely jovial identity parade, I suddenly twigged what was going on. My monologue Policeman on Acid began with the words 'On Wednesday October the 14th last while patrolling along Streatham High Road …', which was the very road that Streatham Police station was in. The series *Comedy Wavelength* had been broadcast on Channel 4 and the monologue featured in one of the programmes, and obviously the policemen had seen it and were still amused by it. But what I didn't know was that they found it particularly funny because one of the young coppers at the station looked a bit like me, and whenever he walked into the canteen somebody would be bound to shout 'Seen any spaceships lately?'

Once they had explained the source of their merriment, we finally got round to reporting the crime and they taking me seriously. Upon leaving the police station and walking back up to Streatham High Road, I passed a building with many windows. And as I walked past, each one of the windows had a smiling uniformed policeman waving and whistling in my direction. A dozen at least. And when I waved back an almighty cheer erupted, followed by enthusiastic applause. I bowed, they cheered again. And then I turned and walked back into Streatham High Road and normality.

It was one of the very first times I had truly tasted fame. My very presence had set people laughing, admittedly under extremely specialist conditions. Looking like one of the coppers had greatly enhanced the monologue's comedic power.

A couple of days later a plain clothes policeman turned up at the front door to dust the same door for fingerprints. He told me that burglars disturbed in the act often said, 'I'll be back.'

'They say it to worry you,' he said. 'Oh, and by the way, would you be interested in doing a Christmas Party for the plain clothed division this year?'

'What?'

'Obviously we'd want you to do your tripping constable.'

'No, well I don't think so, but thanks for the offer,' I immediately imagined a room full of very drunk policemen and wondered how I might deal with a heckler who also had the power of arrest. A pissed policeman shouts 'you're rubbish' and I wittily reply 'and you've got a stupid fat head', and no sooner are the words out of my mouth then I find myself in an arm lock being pushed face first into an overnight cell with no talk of a toothbrush and facing a charge of drunk and disorderly.

'Oh well, you got to ask haven't you?'

He then quickly told me a story that he said was true and, although it sounded like a joke, it had actually happened to him. He said I could use it in my act. Although funny I never considered it at the time. Its essential vulgarity made it wrong for me. At that time I prided myself on having an act that had no swear words in it. This helped me appear distinctive amongst some of the other comedians. It also meant that radio and TV producers could book me knowing that my act was broadcastable. So I never used the true policeman's story, until now. This is how he told it to me:

'It happened many years ago when I was a young copper on the beat. It was a lovely summer's afternoon in the Kings Road, Chelsea. I was standing near a crossroads when suddenly this beautiful Bentley comes round the corner too fast, mounts the pavement and hits a Belisha beacon. Very fortunately, no pedestrians have been hit but the driver, a male, is looking a bit dazed. I approach the vehicle. Our driver is in his mid-fifties, very well to do, lovely tweed jacket, and as his window winds down I get a massive whiff of booze coming off him. He notices my uniform and tries to set his face into a completely sober relaxed expression.

'I say to him, "Excuse me sir, would you mind telling me how much alcohol you have consumed?"

'And he answers in a slightly slurred but perfect cut-glass accent, "Only two cunts pintstable."'

That spring and early summer of 1987 was a special time. The success of the radio pilot for *The Big Fun Show*, my television exposure on ten episodes of *Comedy Wavelength*, was all part of the buzz. There I was, thirty years old. Knocking 'em dead (albeit with no live audience) on national television. Sipping champagne (OK, in Streatham) – and even getting into jazz via new technology. Even by my own tough standards I was doing alright. Everything was coming my way and life was opening up in front of me.

Things were going extremely well.

12

I'm Not Walking Up Those Stairs Again

To add to all this excitement, I was in my first ever live-in relationship. Julie was Australian, and working over here as an actress and occasional stand-up comic. She was fun and bubbly with charming eccentricities that always made me laugh.

I had moved out of my bedsit in early 1987, having spent seven years living there. It was a long time, but in that period I went from being a shy unemployed dreamer to becoming a successful stand-up on the cabaret circuit, about to host a Channel 4 sketch show. Knowing that the *Comedy Wavelength* series was coming up, and that for the first time I would have the financial resources to rent somewhere a lot nicer, I had gone ahead and done just that. We had found a rather spacious one-bedroomed flat that had a magnificently large living room. It was the converted attic of a very big house on Ambleside Avenue, almost overlooking Streatham Common. Meeting Julie had been the motivation I needed to leave the small single room existence behind.

Here's an interesting thing: Cynthia Payne, the former Madam who rose to fame through her sex parties where customers paid for services using luncheon vouchers, lived in Ambleside Avenue at the same time as we did. Indeed, she was a long-term resident. I remember walking past her imposing house, with its generous bay windows and its intricate crazy-paved driveway, early one sunny morning. It was May Bank Holiday Monday. A man was kneeling, attending to the mortar between the cracks of the crazy paving, brushing away miniscule debris. 'That can't be right,' I thought, as I made my way down to the shops. There was something odd about the scene. As I returned with my morning paper it occurred to me that it was rather unusual to find a builder working on a Bank Holiday. He was still on his hands and knees when I walked past again. This time I noticed what he was using to remove small particles of dirt that perhaps only he could see. It was a toothbrush!

Boggling at the toothbrush, I was then rather amused to see Miss Cynthia Payne herself standing at the open doorway of her great house, wearing a tight-fitting, lime green, knee-length dress, what I suspected were slick black stockings rather than tights, and a highly polished pair of jet black stilettos with a four-inch heel.

'Haven't you finished that yet?' she snapped sternly.

'No madam,' said our man with the toothbrush.

When I later read her autobiography Cynthia Payne talked of her wonderfully effective system of using men who liked to be dominated to do all her housework and gardening for her. They were fastidious and in fear of not pleasing their mistress. He must have been one of them.

Julie and I made ourselves comfortable. We owned a cat and whenever we left the flat she insisted on leaving the radio on as company for the animal. I suppose that makes sense, but one day as we were going out the radio was tuned to the World Service, which was broadcasting in Arabic, when Julie quickly changed the station.

'What are you doing?' I said.

'I have to find something else,' said Julie, 'because she only understands English.'

Julie's Australian Aunt Shirley stayed with us for a while. Shirley was a lovely woman and once coined a phrase that has stayed with me ever since. She had been describing various strange happenings that had occurred in a house she was living in. There were bumps and noises in the night, and objects seemed to go missing before later re-emerging somewhere else. And her theory?

'Well, it has to be a poltergeist; it's the only logical explanation.'

That August I departed for the Edinburgh Fringe Festival to perform, for my first ever time, a one-man show. I stood by the front door and said my goodbyes to Julie and Shirley.

'Good luck,' said Julie.

'Break your leg,' said Shirley.

'Thank you, Shirley,' I said witheringly. 'The expression is "break a leg", that's the theatrical tradition! But I know what you mean.'

My Edinburgh accommodation was right at the top of a six-story flight of stone steps into a perfectly small one bedroom flat. There was no lift in the building, so going out was a major consideration because the journey back up was so hard and testing. Nevertheless, having checked out the flat, the next step was to check out the venue. It was a converted cellar of a pub with an intimate atmosphere, where fifty people could feel like a real buzzy crowd.

I'd seen a couple of gigs in there the year before and I'd fancied it.

I had twenty-four hours to go before my opening gig. I had a couple of 'welcome to Edinburgh' pints in the evening. This had the added advantage of delaying my ascent up the north face of the six floors to my bed. Eventually I faced the climb, stopping several times to catch my breath before, with aching legs, climbing into bed.

The next day, my first gig went well. I improvised a sequence about a troupe of Mexican female dancers who were playing the festival that year. Their finale was to stand onstage naked to music. I mused aloud how could they ever have a bad gig? My finale involved a 16 mm film projector showing a four-minute film on a screen behind me, while I sat on a chair in front of it. I'd shot the film from the back of a moving car passing through some streets in London to give the illusion that I, sitting on the chair, was driving. But the projector didn't work so my first night ending was a little strange and clumsy. I went back to the venue the following morning with a stage technician who quickly diagnosed a faulty fuse. I thanked him and left the venue, walking back up the stairs to street level. There I bumped into another comedian, Tim Clark.

'Hello, Paul,' Tim said. 'I'm on my way to the meadows for the football.'

'What football?' I said.

'A bunch of comics are playing football, do you fancy a game?'

I thought of the long hard gradient up the six flights of stairs.

'Yes, why not?' I said. 'I've got a couple of hours to kill.'

And so the two of us walked to the meadows, sides were chosen, and I volunteered to go in goal. Always my best position, so I was happy enough.

One of the outfield players quickly ran out of puff and asked if he could go in goal. I was OK with this and I started running around. On slightly wet grass. In unsuitable footwear. And, in a fairly unfit condition for a thirty-year-old man of my age. Mind you, I wasn't the only one. Nick Hancock, Andy Smart and a few other circuit regulars were huffing and puffing away, with the latter successfully smoking a fag while playing at centre forward. Andy is an adventurer. He is wiry, strong, intimidating on the pitch, intensely loyal off it. He has run with the bulls at Pamplona and slept on the roofs of Mexican trains. He once met Samuel Beckett in a Dublin pub, and he knows how to open a bottle of beer without using an opener. He is a toothsome troubadour with a touch of Ernest Hemingway mixed in with Tommy Trinder.

The ball came to me, I kicked it forward. I chased after it. I slipped. Badly. Both my legs went up in the air. The right one made a cracking sound as I landed in agony, my kneecap twisted around to the left side of my leg. One glance at that sent me straight into shock. Clear as day, I had broken my leg. As I lay there, Andy panted out that the hospital was just 400 yards away. One of the players rushed there and an ambulance arrived within minutes.

I was taken to the hospital where my leg was X-rayed and the break confirmed. The two male medical staff charged with creating a full-length cast for my leg seemed to think they were comedians themselves. They asked how I had broken my leg and I blinked at them uncomprehendingly as they then ridiculed both me and my condition. Their behaviour suggested this was a well-practised routine. To enliven their repetitive but very important job they took the piss out of stunned vulnerable people in shock.

I lay on the hospital trolley and soon found myself being pushed down a corridor at quite high speed. I begged them to slow down, which made them both laugh even more. I was then left alone in a room on my own for an hour, lying on this trolley.

I spoke to Julie on the phone. 'Julie, I've broken my leg.'

'Oh, what have you done that for?' she said, genuinely wanting to know.

'It seemed like a good idea and I've got a spare,' I said.

At one point a nurse did come in to ask what my religion was. Trying to be helpful I said 'Catholic'. It was decided I should spend a couple of days in hospital for observation and when I woke up the following morning I found the full round face of an Irish priest approaching mine.

'Ah, my son,' he said, 'I hear it was a game of football that has brought you so low. Did you know that his Holiness the Pope was himself a goalkeeper in his younger days?'

This was a bit much for me. I politely asked the priest to leave, while thanking him for his interest.

The corner of the ward I was in just had one other bed in it. A young man in his early twenties who had also broken his leg. He had gone to a far greater effort to achieve the same stunning effect. On his stag night, three days before the wedding, our young hero got totally pissed, climbed up a tree, fell out of it, fracturing a lower limb. He was discharged in time for the marriage ceremony. I'm sure that was the story, but the truth is I was so whacked up to the eyeballs with morphine it might all be a figment of a drugged-up imagination. Morphine is a very powerful painkiller and I was in agony without it. There was a television in our corner of the ward and, after one particularly effective measure of the wonder drug, I found myself watching an episode of *Minder*. This very popular programme starred George Cole as a rather dodgy used-car salesman, flitting around the fringes of the criminal world, and Dennis Waterman as his bodyguard/minder. While floating on a cloud of morphine with a big silly grin on my face, feeling no pain whatsoever, I managed to put myself into the drama on the television screen.

I appeared chatting next to the two lead actors who were standing at the bar of their local. I saw myself listening to their conversation.

GEORGE: So as long as reckless Ernie keeps away from the casinos for the next forty-eight hours we have got a definite result.

DENNIS: Yes, except we don't know where he is.

PAUL: Excuse me, but if you describe him to me I don't
            mind helping out.

But they both ignored me. Much to my frustration I couldn't make my fellow actors react to me. I'd been sent to Coventry before but never on ITV's premier drama series.

After three days I was released from the hospital and taken to a new flat, which was at ground level. My comedian friends Dave Cohen and Andy Smart had organised the move. My right leg was encased in plaster and I could just about hobble around on crutches. My immediate plan was to spend a few days recuperating before performing the last two weeks of the festival. This was a positive outlook on my behalf, I believed setting an achievable goal would help my recovery. So I settled into my new environment, lying on some cushions on the living room floor. I was so grateful. If you've been there, you know that there's no such thing as a spare bedroom in Edinburgh in August.

Something wasn't right. I had a pain in my right hand side. Perhaps I'd pulled a muscle in my back trying to lift myself up on my crutches. I was lying on the floor on cushions. I was surrounded by half-a-dozen performers, mostly female. They looked worried. I was sweating. I felt weird. I drifted into unconsciousness …

I came round. One of the women was talking to me and holding my hand. 'We've phoned for an ambulance but it's been delayed,' she said.

'Ambulance,' I repeated, and my eyes rolled into the back of my head and I drifted away again.

I'm woken by a knock at the door. Two ambulance men are lifting me onto a stretcher. Andy volunteers to go with me in the ambulance to the hospital.

As we travelled to the hospital I gazed up through the glass strip of window at the green beauty of passing trees. 'Trees are beautiful,' I murmured to Andy, who agreed. I then fell back into unconsciousness.

At the hospital I was put on a trolley behind a curtain. Andy sat outside waiting impatiently for some medical personnel to turn up. He was concerned about me, but he was also keen to put a bet on the four thirty race at York. After about fifteen minutes he pulled back the curtain to see how I was doing. In his own words to me later:

'You were a grey-blue colour. You looked nearly dead. I shouted for a nurse. "Nurse quickly, quickly, my friend is dying." She took one look at you and rushed off to fetch a colleague. You were pushed away at rapid speed. I thought that might be the last time I saw you. If I hadn't been so keen to get a bet on I might have sat there for another half hour. And by the look of you that would have been too late.'

I don't remember the trolley dash or anything else until I woke up in a hospital bed the following morning. I had an oxygen mask over my face and a tube going into my arm.

I'm connected to a machine that's monitoring my heartbeat and I'm thinking to myself '*What kind of broken leg is this?*' A visitor comes to see me. It's Kim Kinnie from The Comedy Store. Kim has been Don Ward's right hand man for a number of years and has been responsible for booking the acts for some time. He was a great encourager of talent, providing he liked you. Lots of comedians, myself included, benefited from his advice. For example, he was always encouraging of The Comedy Store Players.

Kim's head pokes around the corner of the door and the expression on his face confirms how ill I am. He looks aghast. He doesn't know what to expect but he fears the worst. He doesn't stay long as I'm clearly very tired, but he's relieved to be able to report back to the other concerned parties that I'm at least alive.

A little later a consultant appears beside my bed. He has the air of a man who would enjoy his job so much better if it didn't involve treating sick people. To be honest, he seems a bit angry with me.

'Well!' he says. 'I suppose you realise you nearly died last night.'

I'm hit immediately by a massive shock wave as my head falls back onto the pillow. My mind spins into a tight spiral and I can no longer hear what is being said to me.

'Do you understand what I've just said?' repeats the consultant.

'No,' I said struggling to reconnect. 'No, I don't.'

'You have just suffered a pulmonary embolism which, in simple terms that you will understand, means that after you broke your leg a blood clot formed in your body. That blood clot started travelling around your system and it had the option of three destinations. One, your heart; two, your brain; or three, your lungs. Heart and brain, instant death! But with lung you've got a chance. And that's where it ended up! Otherwise I wouldn't have been able to tell you about it.'

'I see,' I said in some disbelief.

'We've put you on warfarin to make your blood thin. It's also used as a rat poison.'

'Thank you very much,' I said. 'So am I out of danger?'

'Well you're talking, which is a good thing,' he said, before he left.

Once he'd gone, I resolved not to die. I thought about a three-part documentary series on Buster Keaton that I knew ITV would be broadcasting in a few months' time. I was determined to see it even if it meant staying alive to do it. I couldn't give up living now.

I was in that part of the hospital for a couple of days. I suppose it must have been Intensive Care. The next ward I remember vividly. It was full of very old, sick-looking men. Here was another indication of how ill I was. I was the youngest patient in there by forty years. The ward took on horrific qualities at night. One patient at the other end of the ward howled like a banshee once darkness hit. He was so loud it was difficult to sleep.

One night the toothless, bald, enfeebled old man next to me fell out of his bed and onto the hard floor. He lay there naked and disorientated. An ancient baby. I called the nurse and she helped him back into bed. He cried in confusion, and she held his hand and spoke gentle, warm, calming words to him. He cried softly as she stroked his hand, and he was soon comforted and fell back into a fitful sleep. I listened to his breathing for a long time until I eventually went the same way.

Everybody I knew was performing at the festival and once it was clear that I was going to survive I had no shortage of visitors. Comedians were very generous with their time. Mark Thomas and Kevin Day brought me books and CDs, and one night organised a curry to be delivered to my bed.

Everyone brought news from the outside world. Fresh gossip about who was doing well and who was dying on their arse; who was having several Edinburgh flings simultaneously; and which well-known promoter was pissed out of his head the other night at the Assembly Rooms bar and behaving like a completely drunken arsehole for the third year running.

PAUL MERTON · · · 167

All this delightful gossip kept my spirits up. A review appeared of my one and only performance. It was glowing. The headline was 'Go and see this man'. I imagined disgruntled audience members standing at the side of my bed, whispering to each other 'He's not very funny, is he?'

After about a week of lying there one of the doctors approached me and said, 'Ah now, you know we've been testing your blood every day.'

'Yes, it's a daily torture for me,' I replied, which it was. I've always hated the idea of needles and this was something I had to get through every morning.

'Well, according to your blood tests you've contracted hepatitis A.'

'What?' I said. 'How have I managed that?'

'Well,' he said, 'between you and me, you've probably caught it from the hospital food.'

'It's my own fault for ordering it from the menu,' I said. 'It sounded quite nice as a sandwich. So how bad is hepatitis A?'

'Not so bad as some of the others,' he said.

'That's reassuring,' I said not feeling reassured at all.

So that was the diagnosis. I had a broken leg, a pulmonary embolism and hepatitis A. Fantastic! It shows what you can achieve if you set your mind to it. Still, as bad as things were, I can tell you that this combination of fun is the perfect environment for giving up smoking. I had been on the roll ups for a few years at this point, but now I was fag free!

A couple of weeks after the festival was over my doctor decided I was well enough to travel back to London. I was to return to the capital on the night sleeper, but getting me to the railway station was to be a major achievement. Two female fans of Julian Clary who lived in Edinburgh volunteered to get me to the midnight train on time.

Helen and Louise came to the hospital around half past ten and the first shock to take on board was that, as I tried to get out of bed for the first time in over three weeks, I discovered that the muscles in my good leg, my left leg, had atrophied. My left leg couldn't take my weight and my right leg was in a full-length plaster. With the help of Julian's two friends and some nursing staff, I was placed into a wheelchair and pushed down the dimly lit corridors and out into the open night time. The air was very cold. The seasons had moved on since I'd last seen outside, over four weeks earlier.

Helen and Louise helped me out of the wheelchair and into a black taxi. They joined me in the back and the three of us endured the short ride to the station, bumping along Edinburgh's cobbled streets. I was terrified, in my frightened fragile state, to be bounced around the interior of a taxi with only two new friends for support. I shouted at the driver to slow down and he did. Life on the outside was clearly very scary. I could see the sense of avoiding the large crowds during the day and travelling back at midnight. My two helpers got me from the taxi to the train. A sleeping cabin had been booked for me. I offered my grateful thanks to my assistants, without whom I couldn't have got up from my bed, never mind get on a train. I waved them goodbye and the train pulled away.

My sleeping cabin was a tiny room. I had two crutches and a holdall bag under my charge and, with a swaying cabin and very few working muscles in my legs, I attempted to get into the short bed I saw before me. It took the best part of an hour. Firstly, standing up against the wall of the rattling carriage was asking too much of my weakened state, and I immediately made plans to sink to the floor the best way I could.

Then I reasoned quite quickly that that might be a bad idea in that it might be a tad difficult to get back up again. Bearing in mind as always that I couldn't bend my right leg because it was encased in a full-length plaster cast, any proposed movement needed careful preplanning.

No, on second thoughts, getting down to the floor is not going to work. I've got to make a quick decision because my back's against the wall and the train is speeding up. There's only one thing to do. If I can get my left buttock down onto the edge of the bed, then things are looking up. From there I can edge myself along, and then try and lift my heavy plastered leg up onto the bed. All the while jiggling along at an increasing speed.

After twenty-five arduous minutes I had achieved the objective of not only getting onto the bed, but also managing to lie down. It was only then, as I struggled to make myself remotely comfortable, did I realise I was lying down the wrong way and my feet were resting on the pillow. Easily fixed? I got myself up into a seated position and swung both legs off the bed. My heavy unbending right leg continuing to provide me with worthy opposition, I tried moving the pillow, but unbelievably it was sewn to the mattress! To stop it being stolen I suppose. I struggled back round the other way and managed with enormous effort to get my right leg off the floor and into bed. This happened around about the time we went through Newcastle.

I didn't get much sleep that night, and when Julie and my good friend Andre Vincent met me off the train at Kings Cross in the morning I must have looked pretty ropey. I could see they were both visibly shocked by my appearance. They had a wheelchair and they helped me into it.

I sat down with a huge sigh of relief, as I could truly relax for the first time in eight hours. Travelling the 300 miles back from

Edinburgh in a jolting moving train, with every weakened muscle in my body tensing with anxiety, was akin to being constantly assailed by evil gnomes wielding tiny hammers. Now being pushed slowly in a seated position towards a London taxi struck me as the lap of luxury. It took a while to get into the cab and even longer to get me up the four flights of iron fire escape that led to our flat. I was helped across the threshold and into my favourite chair.

As I sat down I immediately recalled the last time I was in that living room. Julie's Aunt Shirley had shouted out 'break your leg'.

I had corrected her, but it turned out she was right all along.

13

Woof Woof Boom

In the time I was bedridden in hospital one good bit of news came through. The BBC had commissioned a series of *The Big Fun Show* for Radio 4. In light of my recent health problems, the producer David Tyler suggested that John and I could postpone the writing of the show until I was fully recovered but, of course, I was keen to get on with it. Beyond the radio series lay the ultimate prize of a television sketch show, so I was keen not to lose momentum. Writing the radio show would fill my days.

We started the process of creating the next five shows with John coming over to my place every morning, five days a week. We gave ourselves two weeks to write every episode, although we also relied on written contributions from Neil Mullarkey and Tony Hawks as the Timid Twins. Tony also provided some beautiful songs during the series, sung brilliantly by Josie Lawrence. The format was the same as the pilot, with John and me presenting a series of sketches, finishing on a big set piece featuring Julian Clary in a high-status role ordering people about. In Julian's world everybody was a straight man existing solely to feed him a line into the next gag.

At this time our work on the *Alas Smith and Jones* series had been recognised and Geoffrey Perkins, a producer on *Spitting*

Image, had commissioned us to write sketches for the show. This was the most prestigious comedy writing credit on television. Latex puppets lampooning the rich and famous were being watched by audiences of 15 million and more every week. It quickly became apparent that my limited stamina wouldn't permit me to write our radio series and *Spitting Image* sketches at the same time. This caused a bit of a fuss, because John and I had signed contracts and Geoffrey, who had championed us with the show's chief producer, John Lloyd, was left embarrassed by our almost instant departure. We had tried attending a writers' meeting near Canary Wharf, but the meeting was on the third floor and importantly the lift was out of order. There was no way I could climb three flights of stairs. Getting in and out of the back seat of John's car with my full-length cast was exhausting enough. Reluctantly we drove back home. We tried to write a couple of sketches but I just didn't have the energy. We were probably the only two writers to ever turn down a commission for *Spitting Image*.

Also at this time, I started to make the odd appearance back on the cabaret circuit. At one gig the compère Steve Frost introduced me by listing the various medical problems I had recently encountered. I started heckling from the wings.

'And he's still alive.'

'Yes, he's still alive,' said Steve. 'Oh no, he's just died,' he said looking into the wings.

'No, it's alright, he's up again.'

By the time I came on the audience were extremely sympathetic as I staggered onstage on crutches, heading for the safety of a stool. I couldn't stand up but I was doing stand-up.

One consequence of cancelling three weeks' worth of shows at the Edinburgh festival was that I was now £3,000 in debt. Renting the flat, hiring the venue, publicity costs, all mounted up. At Kim

Kinnie's suggestion the comedians on the circuit agreed to do a benefit gig for me at The Comedy Store. It was touch and go whether I would be able to attend myself, as I was only a few weeks into my convalescence and the prospect of getting down the iron staircase outside my home, and then tackling the many steps down to The Comedy Store only to face the even more challenging journey back, was not appealing. As well as the plaster and being on crutches, I was still on warfarin to keep my blood thin and I was forbidden alcohol. But as virtually every comic on the circuit was doing five minutes and the gig was sold out very quickly, it would have been extremely bad form not to have attended!

The solidarity of my fellow comics was overwhelming that night. I was deeply touched. Most of the acts that evening did something different for their allotted five minutes. Arthur Smith sang 'Fings Aint Wot They Used To Be', and Mark Thomas and Kevin Day did each other's act. John Hegley, Ronnie Golden, Arnold Brown all proffered cracking sets, and Julie went on wearing one of my jackets to tell a few of my old one-liners.

'I went into a newsagent the other day. I said, "Have you got a copy of the *Psychic News*?" and he said, "You tell me."'

The show was recorded on audio tape and photographs of the performers were later mounted in two special albums for me. It was a wonderful night, but completely exhausting. The money raised cleared my debts and I will remain forever grateful to the performers and the audience who bought tickets on the night. It was one less thing to worry about.

We completed writing *The Big Fun Show* with the final programme written in the five days before the last recording date. This was a fast rate, but we rose to the challenge.

I was very pleased with how the recordings went and David Tyler, the producer, led an excellent team of technicians. It was a particular pleasure to record at the Paris studios. Our scripts very rarely changed from the printed page to what ended up in the show. Occasionally, a member of the cast would suggest a different line and we would certainly judge it on its merit. But we had put a great deal of work into the script and we were generally in favour of keeping what we had done. When we presented our scripts to David Tyler, it was with the understanding that we regarded this as near-finished work. We had already done a couple of drafts ourselves and were proud of our efforts. This didn't mean that tweaks and adjustments here and there could not be made, but they had to be improvements on what we already had. David always seemed to really look forward to getting the script from us, and he would read it for the first time in our presence. He was a very good audience and would laugh frequently, which would send me and John into a flurry of 'which bit was that you read?', and sometimes a quick glance of anticipation between the two of us as we looked forward to David turning the next page where we believed a great joke lay. When he laughed explosively, as he often did, a great warmth of satisfaction flowed through our veins. We worked hard and were proud of our efforts.

Having said all of that, none of the above would be worth a rat's wristwatch if the audiences on the nights hadn't enjoyed and applauded the show. David's appreciation was our first indication outside the two of us that we were coming up with the goods, despite my diminished energy. And I thoroughly enjoyed sitting onstage with a script in my hand, playing around with different characters. I had great fun in one scene with Julian Clary. I was playing a pirate and Julian was Captain Cockles. Neil played a young man who wanted to know more about his father's past. Captain Cockles filled him in. He talked of living with his father, Ted, as husband and husband on a remote south sea island.

COCKLES: We settled down in a rude hut. I spent my time thinking up innuendos while Ted went out catching crabs. Of course, children were out of the question because I don't have a womb.

PAUL: I have.

COCKLES: But you're not normal.

PAUL: At least I'm not married to a man.

NEIL: Are you telling me that my father batted for the other side?

COCKLES: Not only that, but he used to open the bowling.

PAUL: (Pause) I heard a whisper he took the stumps home as well.

On radio it's very straightforward to conjure up some atmosphere with a few well-chosen sound effects. An eighteenth-century pirate galleon is firmly fixed in the mind's eye with judicious use of a seagull's cry, a ship's bell and the sound of wind in the rigging.

One particular sound effect I was extremely pleased with took place in a late Victorian music hall. It was a speciality act that exploded poodles to music. The description sounds cruel but the sound effect didn't. Some pleasant fairground music was interrupted by the sound of a dog bark, followed rapidly by an explosion. It's a gag very much in the style of *The Goon Show* and the technical team put together a funny sequence of noises. La, La, La, La, Woof, Woof, Boom.

Radio can magic up anything, and having the script in front of you takes away a whole level of worrying about memorising the words. We entered each show with quiet confidence and the reaction was deeply gratifying.

*

To continue my convalescence at the end of the year, Julie and I planned to go to Australia where her mother still lived. Julie would travel there before me and I would arrive three days later, just before Christmas Eve.

By this point I had long left the full-length plaster behind, although the removal of that heavy object proved to be a traumatic affair. It happened at St George's, Tooting. The procedure was carried out with brutal indifference by a young man wearing a white coat and armed with a mini buzz saw. I don't know whether he was being paid by the leg, but he certainly wasn't hanging about. Without any consideration for my sensitivities, he tore into the cast with his trusty revolving blades as if he was an expert sheep shearer going for the world speed record. I cried out because I thought the buzzing blade could so easily tear into my flesh, but what my tormentor knew and I didn't was that my right leg had atrophied considerably in the weeks while I was in plaster, and there was a huge gap between me and the cast.

This horrendous experience neatly bookended the whole broken leg episode for me. The application of the plaster had also proved to be an endurance test back in Edinburgh, when it had first slapped on to the leg with some vigour. But now, that was all behind me. I still needed a stick to get about, but undoubtedly a few weeks in the Australian sun would boost my recovery.

First, though, I had to get there.

I couldn't breathe properly, my eyes and nose were running, and I was befuddled by virus and frankly didn't know where I was. This wasn't a great situation to be in on my first long-haul flight. I arrived in Athens suffering from a very heavy cold. There I was, ill again. I found a taxi driver who drove me to the hotel, where I checked in and then retired to my room for the night. Or until three thirty in the morning, when the telephone beside my bed broke my slumber with its shrill, ringing, urgent, annoying tone. It was clearly not good news but at first I wasn't sure what it was. A very annoyed foreign gentleman was shouting at me incomprehensibly, and as his rant developed the main thrust of his displeasure became apparent to me. There was a coach in the car park waiting to drive people to the airport and I should be on it. In my knocked-out cold stupor, it really did take a fair amount of shouting before my brain clunked into gear. I got dressed, I left the room, I checked out of the hotel and made my way to the car park.

And there it stood in the darkness. A brightly lit throbbing coach with rather unusual contents. There was one empty passenger seat waiting to be occupied, so I sat in it. Every other one of the fifty-nine seats was taken by a Boy Scout from Lichtenstein.

They all wore the traditional green uniform with matching shorts. 'Lichtenstein' was embroidered on the front of their shirts, and they all stared at me with mild hostility. Arriving at an airport on time must be quite important to a Lichtenstein Boy Scout.

My deep cold and the fact that I was half awake left me in no fit state to worry about reality. I sat down and let reality get on with it. The bus left for the airport, and so did everybody sitting on it. Once at the airport, we eventually climbed on to the plane for the next leg of the Australian flight – Athens to Singapore. This staggered way of getting to Sydney must have been the cheapest option other than swimming. On arriving in Singapore there was a three-hour stopover, and in that time a technical fault was found on our plane and so we were driven by another coach, myself and the Boy Scouts from Lichtenstein, to a hotel in the heart of the city. There we stayed the night.

The next morning my head had cleared to the extent that Singapore's air pollution was much more noticeable. The air smelt brown and hot. The hotel was small. This made the presence of fifty-nine Boy Scouts from Lichtenstein, in their green-shirted uniformity, even more obvious as they clogged up the breakfast queue for orange juice and flavourless croissants that tasted of soft foam. I began to resent the boys' similarity and suspected them of secretly being robots. I played a game to see if it was possible to travel up and down in the lift for more than two minutes without a Boy Scout from Lichtenstein getting in. It wasn't. Our plane was delayed for a further twenty-four hours and so by the time I arrived in Sydney, it was eight o'clock in the morning on Christmas Day. Julie was there to greet me at the airport. It was a boost to my spirits to see her and to have finally landed at my place of recuperation, even though I felt like I needed a holiday to get over the flight.

The weather was very warm, a cloudless sky, and it was going to get hotter throughout the day. My trusty walking stick had made the journey with me, which was some kind of triumph given how out of it I had been for most of the three-day journey. I was dependent on that stick, and it was never out of my sight and rarely out of my hand.

I would be staying for six weeks with Julie in a room that her mother kindly provided us with. Pauline was delightfully eccentric but always in a well-meaning kind hearted way. One example springs immediately to mind. We had our own bedroom and early one morning, around 7 a.m., the phone rang by our bedside and Julie answered it.

This is what I heard: 'Hello, what? Why are you ringing us? … Where are you anyway? … Where? Oh you're not! … Why? Oh I don't believe it … OK, alright.'

Julie puts the phone down and turns to me.

'Guess what?' she says.

'Who was that?' I say.

'That's the point,' she says. 'That was my mother!'

'Your mother! How can she be phoning us on this line? Do you have two phone lines in the house?'

'No,' said Julie. 'She's not in the house. She called from a telephone box down the road.'

'What!' I said. 'Why did she do that?'

'She didn't want to disturb us by knocking on the door.' I pondered this as I struggled to comprehend how I'd woken up in the middle of a music hall routine.

'She didn't want to disturb us?' I repeated.

'No.'

'What does she want?'

'She's made you some sausages and she wants to know if she can bring them in.'

'Ah yes, why not,' I replied, trying to remember what it used to be like living in the real world. A few minutes later I heard the front door open and close.

Then there was a knock at the bedroom door.

'Come in,' I said. The door opened and a large plate filled with a dozen beefy, meaty sausages entered the room at waist height. Behind them, carrying them delicately, was Pauline. I thanked her profusely, and ate the offered breakfast slowly over the course of the next half hour. I fell back asleep and woke up two hours later with a bellyful of sausage.

Having taken so long to get there, the first time I met Pauline was in fact Christmas Day 1987. And it was getting hotter by the minute. At my request, we were having Christmas dinner by the beach. Julie's Aunt Shirley was there and so too was a male friend of the family, Stuart. Stuart quickly established himself as a funny, kind, considerate, entertaining man. He liked to affect mock outrage – his recurring line at least once every mealtime together was, 'Call me a taxi, you've called me everything else.'

We clinked our glasses of Seaview sparkling wine, which was proving to be very drinkable, and wished each other Happy Christmas in the blistering heat. Ten minutes later, I fell asleep for eight hours. That's jet lag for you.

Mum, Dad and Angela celebrated Christmas at home, and I phoned at the appropriate time to wish them Season's Greetings. As was our way, we exchanged a few pleasantries about presents and respective weather conditions.

The Big Fun Show was being broadcast while I was away, and so David Tyler had kindly given me copies of the show on cassette. I resolved to listen at weekly intervals as close to the transmission time back home as possible.

Sydney has the most beautiful heart of any city. The harbour, the bridge, the ferries, the big, open blue skies, colourful pastel shades on shorts and skirts and tops and frocks, merging in and out of view as commuters jostle past each other to board either ferry, train or bus. Before I arrived in Sydney, Julie assured me that all Australian men could be divided into two categories. They were either sports obsessed, sexist beer drinkers with huge bellies and no interest in any conversation outside of their specialist subject of 'being a bloke'. Or they were gay.

Julie knew a lot of gay men. They were interested in culture, fashion, the performance arts. I found it highly unlikely that Aussie men could be divided into such blatantly contrasting factions, but much to my amusement it turned out to be perfectly true. I didn't meet a single man in the six weeks I was there who didn't belong to one camp or the other. Not that all gay men acted 'gay', but if you found yourselves discussing the films of Orson Welles, you could bet your bottom dollar that you were talking to a friend of

Dorothy's. Whereas your 'ocker' type, with his fiercely competitive urge to be the best in all sports, be they rugby, cricket, tennis or swimming, would become antagonistic and tiresome once he realised I was a 'Pom'.

I got talking to one bloke in a bar.

'Here's one mate,' he said. 'How do you know when a plane full of Poms has landed?'

'I don't know!' I said, even though I did.

'When you turn the engines off, you can still hear the whining.'

I looked blank at him.

'Really?' I said. 'And is that because Australian planes have a curious delayed echo effect that maintains the sound of the engines even though they've been turned off?'

'Are you being funny?' came back the hostile rejoinder.

'Clearly not,' I said, 'but I thought one of us should give it a go.'

Oh dear. That didn't go down very well. People with no sense of humour suspect that every joke they don't understand is about them, and that makes them angry. Luckily we were sitting with a group of friends and somebody laughed it off, and then successfully changed the subject.

The live comedy scene in Sydney in 1988 consisted of one permanent venue, The Comedy Store. The name had travelled around the world. Occasionally pubs with spare backrooms ran comedy nights, which soon fizzled out after a few weeks. I compèred one such night and had a great time. On a busy bill a compère doesn't have long between acts, which suited me fine on the night. I made some observations about the absurdities of some of the Australian slang then prevalent, e.g. the men who emptied the dustbins were known as garbage men officially, but 'garbos' by common consent.

To my English ears 'garbos' conjured up images of cloned Greta Garbos walking in elegant long gowns with purposeful strides, pulling great bins full of rubbish behind them. The audience loved this image. My favourite Aussie abbreviation was reducing 'berserk' to 'berko', as in 'don't go berko mate' when somebody became agitated.

Julie had to meet someone at The Comedy Store one day and I tagged along just to have a look at the place. I'm standing in the foyer of The Comedy Store, in Sydney, Australia, at half past two in the afternoon. It doesn't open until seven in the evening. A man walks in from the street to check the opening times. He sees me and stops in his tracks. His mouth falls agape and his eyes open wide.

'Paul Merton,' he says, 'here in Australia, I can't believe it.'

'It's true,' I said. 'I wouldn't lie to you.' I was a little surprised to be recognised, but Brits do travel everywhere.

'I saw you once at the Bearcat Club,' he continued. 'Me and a mate of mine were there and you did this routine about being a prisoner of war.'

'Yes,' I said with emphasis. 'You sat six rows from the front, your friend had blonde hair and you were wearing a striped blazer.'

'How can you remember that?' he said. 'It must have been three years ago!'

'I'll never forget it,' I said, fixing him with a mysterious, menacing stare. I could see he was puzzled. 'But why don't you tell me your side of the story first?' I said. Which he did.

'I saw you at a club near the Angel in Islington and I thought you were fantastic. You did this routine about being in a prisoner of war camp. So I saw you were playing another club somewhere ...'

'Twickenham,' I interrupted.

'That's right, Twickenham. I took along a friend of mine to see you a couple of days later, and again it was hilarious. Especially as we'd both taken Ecstasy. I remember telling my friend about the funny bits that were coming up.'

'Really,' I said, raising my eyebrows. 'I didn't really notice.' After listening to his story I realised I couldn't stay upset with him for long. 'I'm glad you liked it,' I said, as I grabbed him by the throat and slowly choked the life out of him. Hecklers, will they never learn?

While I was in Sydney one of the local independent cinemas showed Granada TV's documentary *14 Up*. A programme following the lives of a bunch of seven-year-old kids by revisiting them every seven years. I heavily identified with *14 Up* because I was roughly that age when I first watched it in an O level sociology lesson. The upper-class kids had their life mapped out for them to an extraordinary degree. At the age of seven they knew which university they would go to, and in some cases which careers they would pursue. The working-class children had ambitions such as 'I want to work in Woolworths'. I remembered it clearly when I watched it again. Here I was now, recuperating in Australia at the age of thirty, having nearly died on the brink of perhaps building a broadcasting career.

For a boy from my background I had done very well so far, and now the important thing was to physically recover. My confidence also needed boosting, and I took great comfort in reading and re-reading a self-help book called *The Magic of Thinking Big*. I continued to soak up the sun, the sea air, the beach and the friendship of Julie's circle of gay, cultured men. It did me the world of good.

I returned to England in the beginning of February and went straight from Heathrow to a photographic session for The Comedy Store Players. I looked stunningly well (if I say so myself) and felt it. The next thing was to get back into the swing of live performance.

The Comedy Store Players on a Sunday beckoned. There is no better show than an improvised one to sharpen up your stage skills and wits. At any point you could be playing a pirate, a vet, a Greek god or singing out loud in desperate search of a tune. In comparison, the appeal of performing stand-up had worn thin for me. I was a far from a prolific creator of stand-up material anyway, and I had used it all up all over the ten programmes of *Comedy Wavelength*.

Despite this, it was around this time that I recorded what remains in my memory as the best televised stand-up gig I ever did. Although I never actually saw the show broadcast, I can only go on how it felt on the night. It was a show called *The Happening*, made for the short-lived satellite channel BSB. The programme was normally hosted by Jools Holland, but on this occasion the American comic Will Durst was fronting. We recorded at the Astoria Theatre and if the footage turns up again after all these years I'd be interested to see how it looks. I felt I was flying on the night. Afterwards there was a new look of respect in Will Durst's eyes, as he congratulated me on a great gig.

Will was one of several American comics that came here and played the cabaret circuit with great success from the mid-1980s on. The younger British and Irish comics took time to watch their more experienced, relaxed, sharper American counterparts on the bill. Charles Fleischer, who voiced Roger Rabbit in the movie, played The Comedy Store regularly on a Saturday night for the three months, while he was over here laying down the dialogue soundtrack. The other acts admired his command of the crowd, his attack, his delivery. At the end of his half hour he always walked off to thunderous applause and cheering. You didn't want to be the next act waiting to go on. My memory tells me that Kim Kinnie made a point of putting Charles on at the end.

One night Robin Williams turned up and tore the place apart with a storming forty-five minute set. I wasn't there that night, but the comics who were still rave about it now. He did once pop down to the Store during the second half of a Comedy Store Players gig, and later came up to me and said, 'You were good.' It's a tremendous lift when somebody of Robin Williams's stature pays you a compliment, and you tend to remember it forever and then shamelessly stick it in your autobiography twenty years later. At least that's been my experience and I can't be the only one.

In contrast, I witnessed a few spectacular deaths amongst the open spots at the end of the evening. My favourite was the man who came on to the tiny stage to the tune of 'There's No Business Like Show Business' wearing a glittery waistcoat, a black bowler hat and holding a silver-topped cane. Unfortunately he followed a terrible impressionist, and the audience were in no mood for a hearty tune sung without irony. 'Get off!' they screamed almost at once from every part of the auditorium. This did not deter our plucky songster. He didn't miss out a single word of Irving Berlin's original lyrics as he danced back and forth, doffing his bowler hat and twirling his cane. But he also hit back verbally at his hecklers while maintaining his cheesy façade, which lent his act an unintended hilarity. He delivered the song in a camp angry voice:

SINGER: 'There's no business like show business. Like no
              business I know ...'
AUDIENCE: Get off!
SINGER: 'Everything about it is appealing' – you're
              vermin you lot. Absolute vermin – 'Everything
              the traffic will allow. Nowhere could you have
              that happy feeling ...'

AUDIENCE: Get off, you're rubbish!

SINGER: 'When you're stealing that extra bow' – I wouldn't piss on you lot if you were on fire – 'There's no people like show people they smile when they are low' – and sod the lot of you.

This went on for three minutes until the end of the song. I was holding on to the wall roaring and shaking with laughter. You'll never see a better version of that song.

Offers of television work kept cropping up here and there. I appeared on a show called *Scruples*, recorded in Liverpool and hosted by Simon Mayo. It went very well and as good luck would have it, one of the other guests in the show was Nicholas Parsons, who I had listened to with great enjoyment as the chairman of Radio 4's *Just a Minute* for many years. Nicholas was as charming and debonair and entertaining in real life as I always hoped he would be. After the recording, fortified by a glass of wine, I took the opportunity to complement Nicholas for *Just a Minute* and say that it was an ambition of mine to one day appear on the programme.

'Oh, you'd be very good on the show,' he immediately said, which of course placed a great big smile all over my face. '*Well maybe one day*,' I allowed myself to think.

The *Scruples* show went well too and they phoned to say they wanted me back for a second appearance. My second time wasn't so good. I got annoyed by Tony Blackburn's puns, and that made me a little more mean-spirited during the recording and I could tell from people's reactions afterwards that I hadn't been so effective. I had been over confident after my first success and this had led to complacency. An important lesson to learn.

In the spring of that year, 1988, word started going round that Dan Patterson, the producer of an improvised radio show called *Whose Line is it Anyway?*, was developing a television version for Channel 4. One night he came to see The Comedy Store Players. We knew he was in, and for those of us who wanted to impress, here was our chance. That night Josie Lawrence and I played a game called Last Line. At the beginning the audience is asked for a location and a last line of dialogue. The last line is chalked up onto a blackboard and placed in full view of the audience. The key to the game is to build up a scene between two characters, which after ten minutes or so arrives at the last line in a satisfying surprising way.

There is a danger. If the line is uttered in a predictable manner that everybody can see coming, the scene finishes on an abrupt downward note. On the other hand, if the scene is involving and the characters are strong, the Last Line game can be a fantastic crowd pleaser.

On the night, Josie and I stepped forward to ask the audience for a location and a last line of dialogue. Somebody suggested 'attic' and 'see you next year'. Josie moves to the centre of the stage and starts rocking from side to side. She's clearly in an attic. Her rocking is reminiscent of the behaviour of large animals in tight cages.

This makes my choice very clear. I'm not yet in the scene … so I'm her captor. The person who has locked her in the attic. My first entrance is therefore through a trap door in the floor. I mime coming up through the door and I'm in the situation.

The scene built over the course of fifteen minutes. Josie's character was unbalanced, while mine was controlling. I tell her she is there for her own good. She believes me. Throughout this dramatic scenario there were plenty of laughs to undercut the tension. I move centre stage and Josie opens the trap door. I realise she now

... has the upper hand. As she closes the door behind her she says, 'See you next year.' I start rocking backwards and forwards just as Josie had at the beginning of the scene. The audience exploded with delight.

We took our bows and knew we had done well. Needless to say, we got the *Whose Line* gig.

And then, hot on the heels of this, I got the call from *Just a Minute*! Kenneth Williams had sadly died in April 1988, and in the months that followed I had written to the producer, Edward Taylor, asking to be considered for the show. He spoke to Nicholas Parsons, who recommended me.

'Alright, but on your head be it,' replied Ted, which was hardly a vote of confidence.

I had some nerves but I was very familiar with the show and adopted a respectful tone while still playing the game. Something about the programme's format inspires me. Trying to speak for a minute on any given subject without hesitation, repetition or deviation is impossible, but you have a lot of fun trying.

That August I returned to the Edinburgh Fringe to prove to people that the previous year hadn't killed me. My show was on at midnight and the three weeks went by very slowly. I was on at the Assembly Rooms. A prestigious venue. Although I finished at one in the morning, the bar was still open and plenty of performers were buzzing around. I went to bed most nights just before daylight and woke up a couple of hours before it went dark.

I had full houses every night and always strove to be at my best for the people who had paid to see me. And yet. I didn't enjoy any of it. Listening to myself onstage talking for an hour was boring to me. I used to pray for somebody else to walk on. A comedy butler played by a Comedy Store Player. A bit of human interaction.

I loved the impro shows with The Comedy Store Players. In comparison, stand-up felt like I was drawing in pencil compared to the lush Technicolor pastures of group work. After all my effort, and all the dreams I'd had, the awful truth started to dawn on me – I didn't want to be a stand-up comic anymore.

It's not that I don't like stand-up. I love it, it's a true art and one I'd spent a lot time of getting good at. But when I thought back about the moments I'd enjoyed, most of them were more about camaraderie than comedy. One favourite memory from all those years of stand-up in the 1980s was of Phil Cornwell, noted impressionist best known for his wonderful work on Stella Street, and a superb David Bowie take off. He and I were booked to play Sheffield University in the summer of 1987. *Comedy Wavelength* had recently gone out and the sheer number of programmes had helped to semi-fix me in people's minds for a while.

I could detect a buzz about me. Phil was having the same tantalising experience. He had made a few TV appearances and people in the business were noticing him. And so were members of the public. He was getting used to signing autographs, and so was I. As we sat in the dressing room with a couple of hours to kill before the show, we got a little carried away with our exuberance and delight in our newly found 'fame'. We laughed and enjoyed ourselves as we splashed around the notion of celebrity. And here we were in Sheffield playing a 500-seat theatre – just the two of us. We were at the height of our mutual congratulation when the organiser of the event walked in and told us that the gig was cancelled. They hadn't sold a single ticket. Not one.

Our response clearly puzzled him. Phil and I looked at each other and burst into explosive laughter. Here we were bigging each other up about how well known we were, and even how we dealt with the difficulty of fame, and we hadn't sold a single ticket. The poor organiser had been dreading breaking the news to us and we were in hysterics. We explained our response to him and after a bit more laughing we decided to take the next train back to London. A very important lesson had been learned, but in such a delightful way. Never take yourself too seriously.

Every so often someone will say to me, 'Oh I'm working with Phil Cornwall at the moment.'

And I always say, 'Phil's great. How is he?'

And they say, 'Fine. He says "remember Sheffield?"'

And I do.

Another memorable gig featured a comic called Mark Hurst who was in those days working under the name of Mark Miwurdz. The two of us were booked to play Aberdeen University and we were travelling by train there and back. It's a long, long journey to Aberdeen, so we left Kings Cross at the unholy hour of eight o'clock in the morning. We arrived around four and found the hotel. After checking in, we went to the university to have a look at the room we were playing in.

The bad news is that we're on a stage set up in the Student Union bar, but the even worse news is that all alcoholic drinks are fifty per cent off. We meet the organiser. He says, 'Thanks for coming, lads. Just to let you know that nobody's expecting a comedy show tonight because the posters didn't arrive in time.'

'Oh,' we say. This is a major problem because a roomful of students having a drink are not an audience. They're not expecting comedy and may react badly if it's forced upon them. Or more likely, just ignore it.

'Can't we just put up a hand-written poster advertising the gig?' Mark suggested. The organiser appeared stunned by the suggestion, it clearly not having occurred to him before.

'I'll see what I can do,' he says, as if we're asking for something difficult to arrange.

'Oh, and one thing,' he says, 'there's no proper lighting onstage and the microphone is a bit dodgy.'

'That's two things,' I say. The guy shrugs his shoulders. The organisation of this gig has clearly got nothing to do with him.

We were due on at ten. Mark and I tossed a coin to determine who would go on first. I won and decided it would be me. I would have no warm-up act before me and so it was vital to get their attention straight away and laughing soon after. The second act has the advantage of seeing how the first one copes, and can adjust their performance accordingly.

Some stage lighting had been secured since we'd arrived, but it turned out to be a spotlight based at the back of the stage shining straight into the eyes of the audience. At best it would light the top of my shoulders and the back of my head. It was better than nothing so on I went.

'Good evening everyone. Welcome to tonight's comedy show. How you doing out there?' Nothing! Maybe ten people turned around to look at me, but they were the ones who happened to be sitting on the edge of the stage. I had yet to establish my presence. It's all very well having stage charisma, but if the microphone in your hand isn't working, neither are you. So nobody could hear me, a poor start. I gestured to the sound guy that my mic wasn't on. He found the right switch and suddenly I was.

'Good evening everyone! Welcome to the Comedy Show. My name's Paul Martin. I'm a topical comedian. As you can see I'm here now and you can't get much more topical than that. I told the Doodlebug joke. I got a few scattered laughs but it's quickly obvious that listening to me is not what the 400-strong crowd are here for. Time to change tack. Carefully constructed one-liners would not serve their master well tonight.

This crowd were not expecting comedy. In fact they were having a great time chatting amongst themselves, creating their own laughs. One joke in, and clearly more words aren't going to be enough to win them over. I've only got a few more seconds to make an impact before the heckling kicks in.

What to do? What to do?

'Let's have a sing-song,' I say. 'What do you fancy singing?' The drunker audience members are initially slightly bemused by this turn of events but they soon get the idea.

'How about "Star Trekkin"?' shouts out one man. This was an inspired drunken shout. 'Star Trekkin' had been a recent hit, and it had a catchy singalong chorus that you could bellow no matter how drunk you were. Even I, who took little interest in the pop charts, had heard it. So I conducted a sing-song, which consisted entirely of repeating the chorus but splitting the audience into sections.

'OK, let's hear from all the sober ones on this side of the room,' I led them through the chorus and then pointed to one bloke who was singing lustily along. 'Hang on mate, you're not sober. You can't sing.'

'I can sing,' he shouts back.

'No, you really can't sing,' I say to huge laughs. 'But never mind all that. All together now.'

The crowd sing their way through another chorus while I made strange silly dance moves in front of the spotlight. You have to adapt.

'OK,' I said. 'Now let's hear from the virgins. Alright, all the virgins only on this chorus. Off you go, "Star trekkin' across the universe."'

This brought more laughter as the drunker members of the crowd sing ever louder.

All in all I did about ten minutes, which is as much as you can squeeze out of a sing-song. Frankly it was a triumph. It was time to bring on Mark Miwurdz.

I introduced him as the only other act on at night. It was important to let the audience know this unexpected detour in their evening wouldn't be detaining them all night. On came Mark and he got a reasonable cheer, unlike the silence that had greeted me initially. This showed how much the room had changed.

The crowd were in some places resembling an audience, which always helps. Mark was a poet. 'Good evening everybody,' said Mark. 'Here is a poem.'

Enough people in the crowd liked the first poem so he performed another. As Mark ran through his material he knew he could only hold them for a while. There would come a point when they would drift away and the hubbub would grow. Mark judged it beautifully. He got through several minutes of his act before it was time to wrap things up. As the noise level in the room began to rise, Mark said into the microphone, 'Here's one you all know. "Star trekkin' across the universe."' And the crowd immediately took up the singing again. Mark didn't need to lead them. They were up and running on their own. Our work was done.

He looked over to where I was standing on the side of the stage with a broad beam on his face. He bowed to the inevitable. Mark came off to a bigger cheer than the one he walked on to, and the audience went back into being groups of people standing around in a bar. We drank a few bottles of beer, and went back to the hotel to grab some sleep before the eight-hour journey back to London.

To pass the time on the train journey back, Mark and I started testing each other's knowledge of show-business trivia. One of the early questions I can remember was Mark asking, 'What was the name of the show that Hughie Green presented featuring celebrities' favourite film clips?'

'Is this a TV show?'

'Yes.'

'Hughie Green?'

'Yes.'

'Film clips?'

'Yes.'

I was stumped. 'I have no idea, what's the answer?'

'*Moon Movies*!'

'What?'

'*Moon Movies*. Hughie Green interviewing celebrities. They pick eight films they would take with them to the moon. Like *Desert Island Discs*, only lunar.'

'I've never heard of it.'

'Oh. Perhaps it was only shown in the Yorkshire area, but it definitely existed,' said Mark.

'OK. Let's establish some ground rules,' I said. 'No regional programming.'

We argued a bit and Mark didn't want to concede his advantage, but eventually we settled on a more level playing field. I then threw in one of my favourite questions.

'What do Boris Karloff, P.G. Wodehouse, Raymond Chandler and Bob Monkhouse all have in common? Apart from appearing as guests on *Moon Movies* that is.'

Mark didn't know. It's a tough one, but they all went to the same school, Dulwich College, in south London, although obviously not at the same time. And so we swapped questions backwards and forwards. As the train sped southwards, we each dug deep into our respective comedy knowledge. Frankly, as the hours passed, we were going slightly barmy with it all. There was lots of laughing and occasional agreed breaks from the ceaseless probing of each other's earliest TV memories. Images that went out live and were never recorded on video tape were lodged carefully inside both our heads. Preserved in our comedy memory museums.

As the train pulled into Kings Cross, Mark and I realised that we couldn't stop. We were now completely and hopelessly addicted to quizzing each other.

'Shall we go for a drink?' Mark suggested.

'Absolutely,' I said.

After eight hours of early memories, *Moon Movies* and comic trivia, I was buzzing and needed to quieten down. A slow contemplative pint to restore the mental facilities back to a gentler landscape. That was the idea. The nearest pub to Kings Cross was a dingy old dive, but it didn't bother us. We each settled around our pint of Guinness, which rested on a dirty beer-stained table. Ten, fifteen seconds passed.

'OK, Mark,' I said. 'Here is my ultimate question.'

'Have you been saving it up?'

'Yes I have. If you know the answer to this question I shall get down on my hands and knees and crawl around this room barking like a dog,' I said rashly.

'Are you sure?' Mark said.

'Look, I'm not taking a risk,' I said. 'There's no way you will know the answer.'

'OK,' Mark said.

'What was the name of the double act who appeared a couple of times on *Sunday Night at the London Palladium*? They were French, they wore black tights. They had bowler hats, they did acrobatics in slow motion.' It was a killer. Impossibly obscure.

'The Two Maxwells,' Mark said, barely drawing breath.

'You *bastard*,' I said. 'How did you know that?'

'I remember them clearly,' said Mark. 'They had really mournful faces as they performed their routine.' I roared with laughter and amazement.

'Now, Mark,' I said, warily. 'You've got to let me off the crawling around the pub barking like a dog bit. This is not the sort of place to do something like that.' Looking around the deeply hard-bitten clientele, with their impressive number of facial scars and thick air of heavy menace, my dropping to all fours was likely to end in a kick in the teeth. Mark pretended to think about it and then let me off. That we both remembered the Two Maxwells from a television broadcast twenty-five years earlier was a fitting finish to over eight hours of intense mental activity.

And when I staggered out of the pub after a couple more pints to make my way homeward, I reflected that the whole point of the journey, i.e. the gig in Aberdeen, was actually the least entertaining part of it. Unless of course you like fifteen minute sing-songs. But the joy that the two of us shared, testing each other's knowledge of show business and laughing so hard, is a memory that will stay with me forever.

One other gig from the 1980s comes to mind. I had stopped performing stand-up but there was a venue just half-a-mile up the road from the tiny bedsit I used to live in, and the guy running it was keen to get me on. He kept phoning me every so often, so one day I said 'yes'. It was a fifteen-minute walk to the back room of a pub on Brixton Hill. I turned up early before the doors opened to walk the stage, check the route on to the stage, and check the sight lines. I always liked to familiarise myself with the performing space. I watched the first half from the back of the room. The two acts in the first half were well established, but both suffered because of the strange persistent heckling from two men sitting at a table in the front. 'Where do you buy your T-shirts?' was bellowed out, killing one punchline in its stride. Put downs thrown in their direction simply whistled over their heads. The two men were greatly amused by everything they said. During the interval the promoter came up to me to make sure I was alright.

'Don't worry,' I said. 'I've formulated a plan.'

'What is it?'

'It's heckle-proof. Wait and see,' I said.

So the second half kicked off and so did our two hecklers. The next act struggled, and then it was my turn. The compère introduced me and on I walked from the back of the room. I approached the microphone.

'Good evening, ladies and gentlemen.'

'Yeti Bear,' said one of the two hecklers, to their hysterical pleasure. I ignored them without missing a beat.

'I'm getting a bit long in the tooth to work under these conditions,' I said. 'Now ladies and gentlemen, pick up your drinks and follow me. Just outside is a garage door with a light above it. I shall perform my act there. Follow me everyone, grab your coats, let's go.' And within moments I was ushering the thirty or so people from their seats out into the warm April evening air. I gathered them around me in a semicircle as I stood with the garage door at my back, and the light above me illuminating a pool of ground at my feet. The act would be performed in the manner of a conspiratorial meeting. I had fresh information to impart to the troops.

'Did you know that the very first Tube station ever opened was Baker Street in 1863? What was the point of that? Where would you go? What was the rush hour like?' It went well as the audience and I stood around each other, bathed in a halogen light. We were all rid of our common enemy. The two drunken hecklers had stayed inside the pub, as I was sure that they would. I doubted they would understand what was going on until way after everybody else had left the room.

Just towards the end of my twenty minutes, the light above me suddenly went out. The audience booed and so did I. I looked around our surroundings.

We were standing outside some factory estate, with big iron gates and barbed wire on top. My first thought was that a security guard had come back from his patrol to find thirty people outside a garage door and he didn't much care for it. The light may have been turned off by a timer, but I preferred the thought of some human agency that I could directly appeal to.

'OK,' I said to the darkness. 'I'll do two more minutes and then finish.' The light came back on – to a huge roaring cheer and I finished with a flourish.

'And thank you whoever you are for providing us with light,' I said. 'You have illuminated our gathering. We salute you.' We all held our drinks up and cheered. The light went off and we returned to the back room of the pub that was now minus its two irritating hecklers. In their drunken state, once they had become aware that the show was gone they had got up and left. There was a delightful buzz in the air. The wreckers had disappeared and the audience resumed the same seats they'd been sitting in before our brief sojourn outside. Everybody was happier.

The promoter thanked me profusely. I finished my pint of Guinness, accepted my thirty quid, and made my way home. It was my last ever stand-up gig on the London cabaret circuit.

14

The King of Pinball

'Would you be interested in writing a sitcom for us?' asked Seamus Cassidy, the commissioning editor for Channel 4 comedy. I quickly looked around to make sure there was no one sitting behind me, but no, there was just the two of us in the room. I was having my very first face-to-face meeting with someone who was in a position to commission my long-cherished dream of a television sketch show. When I had first started writing with John, back in 1977, I wasn't a performer, but now I had nearly a decade of stage experience and a comic persona that you could build a series around. That was my thinking anyway. There was one certainty. I wasn't remotely interested in writing a sitcom.

'That sounds very interesting,' I said. 'Channel 4 has lots of big sitcoms; you're not short of them.'

'Yes,' said Seamus 'but we need more home-grown successes. *Desmond's* does very well but our other big hits, *Cheers*, *Roseanne*, *The Golden Girls*, are all American imports.'

'I'd love to do a sitcom,' I said, 'but this is really what I want to do.' I handed over a slim folder containing four sketches, which he quickly perused.

'Would you perhaps be interested in commissioning something like this?' I asked, knowing that we were a long way from that.

'Well, yes, perhaps,' he said. 'But first you've got to find a production company that would be interested in making it. And sketch shows are more expensive.'

'This is what I really want to do,' I said. 'I'd really like to give it a go.'

'OK,' he said. 'Well, you'll have to write up a pilot episode and then come back to me when you have a production company interested. No guarantees though.'

'No, I completely understand.'

I left the meeting happy. If Seamus had said 'no I'm not interested in sketch shows' then I would have known not to spend any more time on the idea.

I contacted David Tyler, our producer on *The Big Fun Show*, and we arranged a meeting with Hat Trick, who were then a young independent production company making programmes for Channel 4. To have Hat Trick pushing the idea increased our chances of getting commissioned. We met with Jimmy Mulville, Denise O'Donoghue and Geoffrey Perkins. I related the details of my meeting with Seamus, and it was suggested that John and I should set about writing the first show.

This was a real opportunity. We worked hard. That first script took a month of writing, five days a week, six hours a day. It's very work intensive for two people to write a sketch show. Normally such sketch shows have up to half-a-dozen writers suggesting settings and situations, but we enjoyed the challenge. Hat Trick liked the first show and asked us to write another. They liked the second one as well. Our writing timetable was disrupted when I took eight weeks out to work as a stand-up in Australia.

I'd been spotted at the Edinburgh Festival by an Australian promoter who ran Melbourne's only permanent comedy club, The Last Laugh. I was to be one of two Brits working his venue over there for eight weeks. The other was a Glaswegian comic called Craig Ferguson, who had played Australia the year before.

Our show was part of the Melbourne Comedy Festival, and in company with a few other British acts we were invited to have lunch with the first female Lord Mayor of Melbourne, Alexis Ord. I was used to Australians being direct but, even so, I was rather taken aback by my first encounter with a high-level politician. She strode over to where my fellow Brits and I were standing, and announced briskly that we should take our seats for lunch. Or, as she put it, 'Right come and sit down before I rip your bloody arms off.'

Never having heard this expression before I was unaware that it was in common usage in Australia and meant 'everyone take a seat at the table please'. That disregard for stuffy etiquette is typically Australian. One night I watched a TV interview with the then prime minister Bob Hawke. His response to persistent questions on the economy was to direct the TV journalist towards the finance minister. He said: 'Look, if you want to know about the economy, you go and ask Nobby Clark.'

Nobby Clark was the finance minister! Nobby! In Britain Nobby Clark is doing well if he's a painter and decorator. Nobody called Nobby would be allowed anywhere near high office, but in Australia he's running the economy. I imagined Nobby fielding questions about fiscal policy while also whitewashing a fence.

The Last Laugh residency lasted six weeks, with another two in Sydney. These latter gigs went well, although the venue wasn't as comfortable as The Last Laugh. I can't say that Craig Ferguson and I hit it off particularly, but I was hugely impressed by his stage presence and attack. He had that special charisma that some people naturally have. Throughout the first week of our run he kept offering me cigarettes and clearly took it as a challenge that I kept saying no. I had given up smoking after my broken leg, pulmonary embolism and hepatitis A adventure, but that didn't stop Craig holding the pack towards me every time he had one himself. After four nights and several drinks, I gave in and took one.

Being male stand-ups we naturally vied for the highest score on the dressing room pinball machine. Craig had lodged a total of 21,000. This record had stood for over two weeks and Craig declared it would never be beaten. I kept trying but I was getting nowhere near it. Then the last night of the Melbourne run. My last chance to set a higher score. While Craig was onstage I set to it. I hadn't had an interval drink, for what I was trying to do would take absolute concentration of the sober variety. I flicked the weighty silver ball into the heart of the table. I flipped the flippers to make sure all was well and they flipped beautifully. I sent the ball into the game with enough push to get around the top curve before falling into the first cluster of holes, which automatically scored you 1,000 points. The ball was pushed up and out of the hole by a metal strip and back into play, where it bounced back and forth across point scoring electric bollards. To cut a long story short, I scored 23,800. Relaxed, I sat back on the uncomfortable beer stained sofa and waited for Craig to finish his set.

He came bounding down the stairs and into the communal dressing room area. Without saying a word I indicated the pinball machine and its score. Craig went ballistic. He immediately put some money in the machine and played furiously while simultaneously swearing most fluently.

The king of pinball wanted his title back. He gave it ten minutes of his attention before finally kicking the machine and downing half a bottle of Heineken. His determination to succeed was obvious. As indeed was mine.

Craig and I could congratulate ourselves on eight weeks of excellent shows. I said goodbye to him at Heathrow and, apart from one early appearance of his on *Have I Got News for You*, I haven't met him since. He went on to have extraordinary success. Within a few weeks of our Australian run he appeared at the Montreal comedy festival Just For Laughs. The festival is a magnificent shop window for the intensely ambitious comedian. American TV executives saw his stage act and loved what they saw. He appeared for many years in *The Drew Carey Show* before eventually becoming one of America's top talk show hosts/comedians. He's starred in Hollywood feature films, even directing one himself. He was clearly a major talent when I worked with him, but he has done extraordinary well nevertheless. Even though his career had been vastly more successful than mine, I think we all know who the real winner is. *I* am the King of Pinball.

I arrived back in London and into the routine of writing the scripts for what we were now calling *Paul Merton: the Series*, which was originally thought of as a gentle parody of *Batman: the Movie*.

John and I knuckled down to writing programme three. Jimmy Mulville, Denise O'Donoghue and Geoffrey Perkins read our third script and liked it very much. They felt we now had enough to go to Seamus at Channel 4, and he liked what he read. But he wouldn't make a decision until he had seen three more scripts. At the time John and I were quite angry. We felt we had worked our socks off for no reward, but as Jimmy Mulville pointed out to us, we were still in the game. Looking back at it objectively now, I realise that it was a completely sensible decision, given that we were asking for a big budget to make the series, and John and I hadn't written much telly before.

And so it was that we sat down … to write the fourth one.

*

The second half of 1989 picked up speed as I was swept along upwards into the world of television. Not only was I writing my own surreal sketch show with hopefully a series at the end of it, but also an idea that I had developed with Julian Clary had been enthusiastically commissioned by Seamus Cassidy at Channel 4. I had the notion for *Sticky Moments* while watching Julian performing at The Comedy Store one night. His interaction with the audience was always a highlight for me. I suddenly saw the whole concept of *Sticky Moments* – a parallel universe version of *The Generation Game*, with Julian as the host whittling the contestants down to the final two. But in our version, provided there were no real prizes to win, we could make up our own questions and answers, and thus nobody felt too cheated if they were disqualified for wearing beige.

We had a True or False section.

JULIAN: True or False. Benjamin Disraeli was once a member of the Beverley Sisters.

CONTESTANT: (Laughing) False.

JULIAN: I'm afraid it's true. (More laughter) From 1968 to 1972.

In the autumn of 1989, I was working on two completely different styles of television comedy, and each one was refreshing the other. I worked five days a week with John from ten till four, and then over to Julian's flat just off Baker Street to create games and jokes for *Sticky Moments* from four thirty to eight. I poured my heart and soul into my work to such an extent that my emotions ran high. One night on television I watched a Harry Enfield parody of *The South Bank Show*'s interview with Sir Laurence Olivier. It was on Channel 4 and it was called 'Norbert Smith – a life'. To my extreme distress, part way through the film we find ourselves in a music hall watching an act that explodes dogs to music! Our sound joke from *The Big Fun Show* had been put on the screen, but not by us.

That night I phoned our producer David Tyler with tears of anger and real upset. He completely understood, but may have been taken aback by the depth of my emotions. Exploding dogs to music was such a specifically odd gag, I found it impossible to believe that it was a coincidence. I was very upset.

I had grown up on the cabaret circuit where jokes were considered valuable as individual entities. Other acts would tell me if somebody had 'stolen' my doodlebug joke, and that they had confronted the offender on the night. For a live comic, jokes are what puts food on the table. Without them, you go hungry.

Despite all this there was much to be excited about in my burgeoning television career. Soon it would be my go. *Sticky Moments* went into production and our words on paper were beautifully enhanced by superbly imaginative designs by Anne Tilby. Pink and luscious, florid and camp, the show looked like nothing else on television. A great deal of credit must be given to John Henderson, the director, for making it look so distinctive.

Julian superbly replicated the interplay he enjoyed onstage with people in the audience. Over the ten programmes he was strongly supported by Phil Herbert as loyal sidekick Hugh Jelly; Barb Jungr, Michael Parker and Russell Churney provided beautiful music for the finale song.

The show worked! It looked like a light entertainment production, but it had strange quirky moments that placed it ahead of its time. Barbara Windsor appeared with a cardboard box on her head and the contestants had to guess who she was. We put one woman into a flying harness and flew her around the studio, much to her evident delight.

The contestants were chosen from the people who were queuing up to see the show that night. Julian interviewed them quickly as a camera passed along the line. Once eight were chosen they were brought backstage where I met them and gathered basic information, such as names and occupation. By choosing our contestants on the night we avoided the professional game show type. We wanted people to be normal and not exhibitionist. If they became that through the course of the show then all well and good, but we didn't want that as a starting point. Unlike some game shows, *Sticky Moments* had a great deal of human warmth, helped enormously by the fact that nobody was competing for real prizes. I felt the winner should get something, so I suggested a bunch of flowers and a lift back home in a Rolls-Royce. This idea pleased everyone and was a good visual for each show to finish on. A beaming winner sitting in the back of a Rolls; waving amongst the flowers.

Sticky Moments was a breakthrough show in many ways. It was made in a different political climate to the one we enjoy today.

The year before, in 1988, Julian had appeared on a primetime London Weekend Television Saturday evening show called *Trick or Treat*. This enraged the more reactionary elements of the right-wing press, with one headline reading 'Get this gender-bender off our screens'. A year later and I'm at the *Sticky Moments* press launch. We have just shown the first episode to the TV critics and I'm now standing by Julian as he is circled by journalists. Julian is wearing his onstage make-up and lots of glitter. Giving the nature of his act and his personality, the first question comes as a bit of a surprise to me.

'Julian,' says the first reporter, 'are you gay?'

Julian's reply was immediate.

'Of course,' he said. 'Isn't it obvious?'

There was silence for a moment. Nobody had a follow up question because they weren't expecting the answer they got. In the past gay comedians on television kept very quiet about their sexuality, particularly those who remembered the days when male homosexuality was treated as a criminal offence. Julian saw absolutely no point in pretending to be lusting after women in his private life, although they certainly fancied him.

Finally the second question. This from the *Sun* journalist, 'Your dad's a policeman isn't he?'

'Ex-policeman. He's retired,' said Julian.

'So what does he think about you wearing make-up and the clothes you wear?' continued the man from the *Sun*.

'He's very proud of me,' said Julian. 'Both my parents are.'

This wasn't good enough for the *Sun*, who sent a reporter round to his parents' house in Swindon the following Sunday morning to ascertain exactly what Mr and Mrs Clary thought of their boy.

'We're very proud of him,' they said.

As I watched Julian bamboozle the press with his honesty, I realised I was witnessing an historic moment. The first TV comedian to say 'I'm gay and so what'. And the sky didn't fall in. The time was right for someone to break with the traditional showbiz denials, because audiences have always enjoyed great entertainers without worrying, so much, about who they get up to off stage.

We watched the first episode going out at Julian's flat. There's a special thrill to viewing a show at its time of transmission. Me, Julian, Phil Herbert and a few others shared bottles of champagne in the tiny living room, and wondered at the magic of it all. I phoned the Channel 4 duty log to complain that *Sticky Moments* was 'the most disgusting programme I have ever seen in my life'. After I had put the phone down I thought better of my actions and redialled the number to this time say 'how wonderful' the programme was. I'd suddenly felt superstitious about criticising our show, even as a joke. I didn't want to do anything that would change my luck.

Sticky Moments was working like a dream, and I had finished writing the six episodes of *Paul Merton: The Series* and Channel 4 had finally commissioned it! Hooray! We had written the series on the writing paper that my colleagues in the civil service had given me as a leaving present back in 1980. I had kept the boxes of paper unopened for nine years.

The second series of *Whose Line is it Anyway?* was in full swing and gaining momentum. The exterior filming for the sketch show would begin in January, and I reckoned a holiday in the sunshine over the Christmas period would help me to recharge my batteries for the work ahead. I talked it over with Julie and we decided to go to Kenya for ten days. It proved to be one of the worst decisions of my life.

15

Don't I Know Who I Am?

I knew something was wrong before the holiday even began. Five days before I left for Africa, I was one of six improvisers recording a special Christmas edition of *Whose Line is it Anyway?* at the Thames Television Studios at Teddington. I found the experience disturbing. I had what I suppose was a panic attack during the show, when I couldn't stay seated in my chair for the opening shot of the programme. As soon as I stood up from the chair and walked around the set I felt calmer. I knew people were looking at me. I went back to the chair and felt my heart race. I sat down but I couldn't stay there.

I had to get up and walk around. I felt OK moving, I just couldn't sit.

To get the shot they needed, the floor manager put on my jacket and sat in my seat while the camera came as close as it dared. Afterwards people were concerned, and I could offer no plausible explanation for my sudden fear of sitting. But there was a mood of celebration; it was the last gig of the year. I was ready to go on holiday and felt like I needed it.

At the airport I browsed in the bookshops, selecting my holiday titles for the next ten days of sunshine, beach and safari. A book investigating Freemasonry caught my eye. There was something in my prevailing mood that made such subject matter irresistible. We flew to Mombasa and stayed in the most beautiful hotel on the beach. It had a wonderful circular waterslide, which went round and round before dropping you at speed into a deep warm pool. I went down it several times.

The book I was reading about Freemasonry was also making my head spin. It was a very strange book. It wasn't like other books I had read. It kept changing its content from one day to the next. One morning I read that the Freemasons had their own minicab company in south-east London, but the following day I couldn't find reference to it. The words had gone. I couldn't find them anywhere.

One afternoon I went out in a small glass-bottomed boat, through which you could see many beautifully coloured fish. Blue, yellow, orange and white, and then the man sitting next to me said, 'Are you British?'

There didn't seem much point in denying it so I didn't. 'Yes,' I said.

'What do you do for a living?' he said. I've never been one for chatting to strangers in public and this one was asking rather direct questions.

'Me,' I said, attempting to hide behind dark sunglasses and my newly tanned skin. 'Oh, just bits and pieces.'

'Like what,' inquired my persistent questioner. I turned to look at him properly for the first time since our one-sided conversation had begun. He was overweight but he wasn't bothered by it. He looked like he was used to getting his own way and saw no reason why this interrogation should be any different.

In this type of situation it can be a risky strategy to pretend to be a motor mechanic or a tree surgeon, in case you are suddenly obliged to offer up expert advice. I decided to play it vague. 'Oh,

I'm in the entertainment industry but behind the scenes, not very interesting I'm afraid.'

It was a mistake to mention the entertainment industry, I should have said banking.

'Oh really,' said my portly interrogator. 'Do you know what my favourite television programme is?'

'I've no idea,' I said, desperately trying to think of an answer that might stop the increasing torrent of words.

'*Whose Line is it Anyway?*' he said.

I looked straight at him. He clearly didn't recognise me.

'Really? I don't think I've ever seen it,' I said, attempting to staunch the flow of conversation. Although my head was also buzzing with the delightful prospect of listening to this man spout off about his favourite programme, without him realising that one of its regular contributors was sitting in front of him wearing a sun hat, shades and a tropically colourful shirt.

'Do you know who my favourite is?' he said.

'I've no idea,' I said, bracing myself for a compliment.

'Josie Lawrence, she sings all those songs. She makes them all up you know.'

'Does she really?'

'And Clive Anderson, he hosts it doesn't he? He's very clever, a bright man, apparently he trained as a barrister,' carried on my rotund inquisitor.

'I didn't know that,' I said, rather unconvincingly.

'And John Sessions of course. He's very intelligent. He can do many different styles. He boggles me the stuff he comes up with. The same with Richard Vranch.'

By this time I was nodding and making small affirmative noises, while he ran through all the other people he thoroughly liked on the show.

'Mike McShane, Tony Slattery, Greg Proops, they're all fantastic,' he enthused.

By this point I had become tremendously annoyed by my fatty tormentor. I found myself in the curious position of striving to keep my identity secret at the beginning of our one-sided conversation, only to succumb to feelings of anger as he listed everybody else on the show except me. Did I smile knowingly to myself as I kept my secret intact? Did I fishcakes.

'I'm in that show,' I yelled. 'I'm in that,' mustering together as much dignity as a shouting man in a glass-bottomed boat can reasonably expect.

My chubby questioner looked at me and I saw puzzlement in his face.

'I bet you wish you were,' he said. He was convinced I wasn't in it.

A few days later I was swimming a dozen yards off the shoreline, when two young Kenyan boys approached me in the water. They looked about fifteen.

'Hello,' they said, 'where are you from?' Their smiles were friendly.

'I'm from London.'

They smiled more.

I floated on my back in the warmest sea I have ever been in. Multicoloured fish swam beneath me as I lay in the blistering sun.

One of the boys says, 'I have a strong ambition, but I fear it is beyond me.' He speaks very good English. I ask him what his ambition is.

'I want to live in Brixton,' he says.

I was taken aback. 'Brixton!' I said, looking around at the palm trees on the sandy beach, and the clear blue sky above the clear blue sea. 'Brixton is nothing like this,' I said. 'You'd be very disappointed. Why would you want to leave here?'

One boy looked at me seriously and said, 'There are no jobs here.'

Of course, I was looking through the eyes of the newly landed tourist. I'd been in the country three days and all I had seen of Kenya was the airport, the road and the hotel. I had no proper sense of the place at all.

The two boys told me they had a friend who had a cousin who lived in Brixton. And he was earning enough money to be able to send some home. 'Tell us about Brixton,' said one, and the other said, 'The Victoria line. Please tell me about the Victoria line.'

'How do you know about that?' I laughed.

'Our friend's cousin sent home a map of the underground. And we have memorised large parts of it.' The boy spoke solemnly and it was clear that they were both deeply interested in the London Underground system. Their words tumbled together as they excitedly asked another question. 'What's it like to travel underground at high speed? Is it frightening?'

'High speed,' I said. 'Well, I use the Northern line so I wouldn't know,' I laughed.

The two boys exchanged puzzled glances. Criticising this incredible transport system didn't make any sense to them. That's when I saw it through their eyes. So I quickly added, 'Ah, but the Victoria line is different. It's a magnificent creation. From early in the morning people rush to Brixton station where they are transported 200 feet below the earth's surface, on a marvellous moving staircase. You just stand there and the stairs do all the work. This time is called the rush hour because people can't wait to have the experience.'

The boys looked at me in wonderment.

'How dark is it down there?' asked one of the boys.

'That's one of the many magical aspects,' I said. 'Everything is so bright.'

I was seeing the experience of commuting through their huge sense of wonder.

'You walk off the moving steps and you move briskly in the company of many people towards the platform. You reach the platform, which is bathed in light. At either end there is a long black tunnel that curves away into the far distance. Three thick metal gleaming tracks run into darkness. You stand and wait with everyone.

'How long do you have to wait?' asked one of the boys.

'You never have to wait for more than four minutes,' I replied.

'Four minutes!' they both shook their heads.

'Yes. And if you're listening carefully you will hear the first rumblings of a distant sound. A beast moving towards you with a sparking sound of electricity coursing through the furthest rail. The sound of the rumble becomes a roar, increasing rapidly as you realise that the fearsome monster is approaching now at a terrific speed. A light appears on the wall of the tunnel. A small beam at first, but growing bigger by the moment. The whole wall is illuminated with white light as the beast thunders out of the tunnel.' I was getting carried away. 'Its startlingly silver appearance drawing gasps of admiration as the mighty creature slows down and quickly comes to rest.

'The people board and sit on very comfortable seats. And then your journey begins.'

'How fast do you travel?' said one of the boys.

'As fast as a car but you're underground.' I replied.

'And everybody's happy?' said one of the boys.

'Yes,' I said. 'Everybody's smiling and joking and chatting to their neighbour.'

'It must really be a thrill of a lifetime.'

'Absolutely,' I said. 'And after seventeen minutes you get off the train and travel back up to the surface of the earth on another moving staircase, and find yourself in Oxford Street in the very centre of London. One of the most famous streets in the world. And you've travelled there completely underground. And millions of people travel that way.'

'If I lived there,' said one of the boys, 'I would travel on the underground every day. You must be very happy to live in such a place.'

'Yes,' I said, 'I am.'

The boys moved on and waved as they swam away, burbling with excitement.

After ten days we flew back to London, arriving at Heathrow the day before New Year's Eve. Africa had been a wonderful experience and the sights had been stimulating.

The new year opened up, 1990. One successful TV series on Channel 4, *Sticky Moments*, was behind me with my own show about to go into production. All this good news and yet strange stuff kept happening that was causing me concern. I was in a heightened state of excitement, so perhaps I was more attuned to coincidences occurring around me. One night Dave Cohen visited me at the flat. I was talking rapidly and nonsensically about Freemasons when I suddenly started crying.

'Why are you crying?' asked my concerned friend.

'Because I think I'm Jesus,' I said, tears wetting my cheeks. *'What?'* I thought to myself, *'Where did that come from? Do I really think I'm Jesus?'*

The phone rang. It was sitting on the side table next to the open window. It was a friend of mine. She said, 'Have you heard the news about Brixton prison?' Brixton prison was just a mile up the road from where I lived.

'No, what?' I said.

'There's been a riot,' she said, 'and they have had to quell the prisoners with tear gas.'

'Thank you,' I said, putting the phone down and turning to Dave in the room. 'There's a simple explanation, there always is. It's tear gas, that's why I'm crying.'

The next day Dave phoned to see if I was alright. I mentioned the tear gas, the open window and the telephone call from the day before.

He says, 'None of that happened Paul. There was no phone call, there was no tear gas. But you did start crying.'

I wonder why he's lying to me.

Strangeness kept happening. When the phone rang I immediately knew who it was before I picked up the receiver. The owner of the corner shop acted in a peculiar manner every time I walked in. Whenever I caught his eye, he was looking at me strangely. What was the matter with him? I walked backwards and forwards, undecided whether to stay inside the shop or not. This made him look at me even more oddly. No, he was strange, I knew I had to get out.

I ran back down the street towards the flat I lived in. I ran down the centre of the road, imagining the curtains in the windows in the houses either side of me twitching open like a Mexican wave. I got back to the flat and I was in a right old state. Heavily sweating, I turned the radio on. Radio 2 was playing. I knew what the next record was going to be. I was certain of it, but I couldn't say what the title was until it started playing, and then I was convinced I'd known what it was all the time. Julie was very worried.

I was scaring the people around me, but not as much as other people were scaring me.

When I looked out of the window of my front room I saw men on the rooftops dressed as builders pretending to ignore me. Their pretence was very thorough. I stared boggle-eyed at the blank white wall in my living room. I felt strongly that things I couldn't see were crawling across the surface. Thin transparent worms, fifteen inches long, created intricately invisible patterns before my unseeing eyes. A minicab arrived shortly afterwards. Julie had phoned one. The minicab driver seemed highly familiar. I believed him to be a television director I knew, in disguise. I went along with his deception believing that he must have his reasons. Who am I to pry?

We drove for thirty-five minutes before stopping in a car park. I didn't want to get out, it didn't feel right to get out of the car. The driver asked me to get out and seemed nervous in asking. I wasn't looking for trouble so I stepped out of the vehicle. Julie and I walked alongside a long building and then through a door marked 'Entrance'. We walked down an empty corridor towards a pair of swing doors. We pushed through them to find ourselves in a room full of empty chairs. Row upon row of empty chairs.

I make a silly fuss over choosing one chair over another, but as I sit down I notice a huge sign on the opposite wall. In simple terms it tells me where I am in big, big letters.

'This is the Maudsley Psychiatric Hospital.'

16

Ten Days Away From It All

SATURDAY

A male nurse explained to me that I would need to return on Monday to be properly assessed. I was telling him that 'my grandfather had invented a drink called Six-up and he was so close to being a winner but he was only one number out.

'7 Up do you get it do you see. 7 Up?'

I couldn't stop talking.

I was babbling ten to the dozen.

The nurse must have given me something to calm down, perhaps a few tablets, because the next day was a bit of a blur.

SUNDAY

?

MONDAY

Monday morning, I'm ready to leave the flat. I am dressed with my hair nicely combed, looking out of my living room window across to the flat rooftops, where workmen are erecting scaffolding. I am waiting for a minicab and big fat tears are rolling down my face. It feels like somebody – who? God? – is squeezing my brain dry.

A Paul McCartney song 'My Brave Face' is playing on the radio.

'That's it,' I say to myself out loud, 'I must find my brave face. Whatever's coming, I've got to be able to deal with it.' Julie is with me and I can see she is frightened for me.

We arrive at the Maudsley Hospital in Denmark Hill.

As I get out of the car I notice that the hospital on the other side of the road is covered in scaffolding. Are these the same scaffolders I can see out of my living room window? I can see the name of the building firm. It's a company who have an office around the back of our flat. It's clear I'm in the grip of somebody. I'm being manoeuvred into place. Then it hits me.

'*It's the Freemasons,*' I suddenly realise with total clarity. I remember now the book I read on holiday. This hospital on the other side of the road was mentioned, King's College Hospital. It's a hotbed of Freemasonry. They have a hidden room with a floor covered in black-and-white tiles, it's where people are initiated into the brotherhood. I glance back over my shoulder towards this ominous building, before I stride ahead through the door marked 'Main Entrance Maudsley Hospital'.

Julie and I walk down the main corridor of the hospital. This takes a fair amount of nerve because there's a lot of very strange people walking around. They want to make eye contact with me but I won't let them – some of the passers-by are sliding along the walls or crouching by the cold drinks machine, but I'm not getting involved in their game. The machine sells 7 Up but I pretend not to notice. We find the room I've been told to sit in. I sit, waiting, preparing myself for something, but I don't know what it is. I sit upright. If I look brave, I will be brave, and now I'm saying the same thing to a doctor in his office. 'I'm very brave, doctor,' I say.

'Why do you have to be brave?' he asks me as I start crying.

'Because I don't know what's going on. Look at me, I'm crying,' I sob. 'My head is spinning the whole time. I don't know what I'm doing here or why I'm being watched. Why?'

'You need to rest,' the doctor says. 'I think you should spend a few days with us here. As an inpatient. Do you understand?'

'Yes,' I say. 'As soon as I saw the scaffolding on the other side of the road I knew I was caught up in something bigger than me. This is the place for me now.'

Julie goes home to collect some clothes for me while a male nurse asks me to empty my pockets. He asks, 'Are you on any medication?'

I say, 'Nothing apart from my anti-malarial pills.'

'Do you have them with you?' he says.

'No, but I can describe them. They're white and quite small. There's two types. A daily pill and a weekly pill. I have to take them for another five weeks.'

'Can your girlfriend bring them in?' I'm asked.

'Yes she can,' I reply. Amidst all my current troubles I'm determined not to risk contracting malaria as well. I don't think I was bitten on holiday, but why take a chance?

I am shown a bed in the corner of a male dormitory. There are seven other beds. I am given a yellow syrupy liquid in a small plastic container. I drink it all down like a good boy.

I sit on my bed for a while.

Ten minutes becomes half an hour.

I look at my watch and see that actually it has only been ten minutes. I stand up in slow motion because I can't move any faster. My head is precariously balanced on the top of my neck and body.

I shuffle towards the shared common room. I'm aware of faces looking at the new boy. A television is on in the corner of the room and all eyes flick back to that once I've been quickly assessed. I'm finding walking a struggle because my feet are sinking into the carpet. I need to sit down now. I see there's a chair behind me. I make my way down slowly. I look around at the cream-coloured walls, the different types of green armchairs, the tinfoil ashtrays, and I soak up the happy heavy atmosphere in my head. My brain has stopped speeding and for the first time in ages my mind is resting.

The windows in this room start very high up the wall. There's no easy way to throw yourself out of them. The armchairs are arranged against the four walls of the room. As well as being a common lounge/TV area, this space also serves as the location for the group therapy sessions every morning. I will see a lot of this room over the next ten days.

I slept heavily last night, my first night here. I feel generally woozy. I speak to one of the other patients.

'Where do we go for breakfast?'

He says, 'Follow me.' This man is keen to show me the way. We walk down the long corridor of our ward, with its purple carpet and various doors on the right.

Most of them lead to single room offices but the last one is intended for visitors. We leave our ward and join the general throng in the main corridor. We turn a couple of corners and walk down a flight of stairs. I am now in the hospital canteen. In the queue there's thirty-odd people ahead of me. As we shuffle forward towards the serving area, I see two rows of grey cardboard bowls. One row of bowls contain bran flakes while the other row of bowls each has a single hard-boiled egg. The hard-boiled egg has been peeled of its shell. You can't hurt anybody with a cardboard plate or a peeled egg, and that's why there are no hot drinks here either. No scalding teas or coffees to be slung into people's faces. There is orange juice in a plastic cup. The only cutlery is a grey plastic spoon and good luck trying to stab somebody with that.

Group therapy starts at nine o'clock and it's that time now. I'm sitting in one of the shabby green armchairs. There's about twenty of us. I've just been given my first yellow syrup drink of the day. I will get another one at eight this evening and it's so dreamy. I listen attentively for the next forty-five minutes with a slightly dazed look on my face. Many of the other patients speak of their problems. My position is not that serious in comparison to their stories. I've just got to wait my time. My television programme *Paul Merton: The Series* isn't due to start filming for another three weeks, I'll be better by then. After this first group therapy session I see a psychiatrist.

'How are you feeling?' he asks me.

'A lot calmer,' I say. 'The yellow syrup they give me is lovely.'

'It's called Largactil. It helps to take the edge off things.'

'It certainly does. Any chance of getting an extra glass a day?'

'No.'

'I don't mind paying for it.'

'No,' he says. 'In fact we will be looking to reduce the dosage over the next few days.'

'Oh,' I say.

'Well, you don't want to be here for long do you?'

'No I don't,' I said. 'I've got important things to do.'

'Let's see how you are for the next few days,' he says. 'A period of rest will do you good.'

So I keep myself to myself. I attend the group therapy sessions. I watch television with some of the other patients, and I get lots of rest.

A week passes without incident. The psychiatrist sees me again. 'You seem to be well rested,' he says.

'I feel it,' I say, and I mean it.

'Let's see how you are on Wednesday,' he says.

Wednesday arrives and I'm sitting in a room surrounded by eight psychiatrists.

'I feel calm,' I say, 'and ready for the work ahead of me.'

Psychiatrist no. 4 asks a question.

'No,' I say, 'I'm not anxious about making my television series. We worked very hard on the scripts and there's tons of visual stuff that I'm looking forward to filming. I can't wait.'

The eight were satisfied by my responses and I was told I could go home later that day.

Arriving back at the flat, I sat back in my favourite chair and had a nice big cup of tea. I kicked off my shoes and breathed a deep sigh of relief.

17

Home

The next morning, at the request of Hat Trick, the production company who are making our television series, I am examined by a doctor who will independently assess my fitness for the filming ahead. This is needed for insurance purposes. I've no doubt my ten-day stay in a psychiatric hospital has caused a great deal of discussion. A lot of people have been hired and studio space has been booked. If the doctor sitting in front of me gives me the OK, then it's full systems go. I've met this doctor before and I remember that he is very fond of name dropping.

'You look well,' he says to me.

'I feel well,' I say.

'I tell you who is looking well,' he says, 'Billy Connolly.'

'Is he?' I say.

'Oh yes,' he says, 'and the other day he said to me, "Doctor, I enjoy coming to your surgery",' and the doctor impersonates Billy Connolly for the next thirty seconds while I grin weakly at him. When he finishes, he tells me that I seem fine and that the consultation is over.

I take a taxi to Hat Trick's production offices where there is much to discuss, particularly casting actors for the various roles in the sketch show. A location manager has a dozen photos of locations he would like me to look at. Car parks, parade grounds, bridges, prison gates. I love looking at this stuff. It's exciting but not too exciting. It's important I keep control of myself. The trouble is there are people looking at me. I start noticing it the following day, Friday. I take a taxi from my flat to the Hat Trick offices and the interior of the cab is coloured purple. A notice inside informs me that this cab can be 'hired for special occasions'. I wonder what these 'special occasions' could be. The purple is disturbing me. I haven't thought about the Freemasons for ages but I now realise they haven't gone away. They're driving me now. The colour purple tells me that. I associate it with royalty.

'Alright,' I think to myself, 'I won't let the driver know that I know.'

He takes me into Hat Trick. Unlike yesterday, people are looking at me strangely.

'What's wrong with the people in this office?' I think to myself. 'They all have a very odd look in their eye.'

Laurie Rowley, a comedy writer who happens to be in the building, passes me a note which reads 'Everybody knows'. He will later categorically deny ever doing this. I need to get out of these offices. I leave and impulse leads me to the London Planetarium. Here I sit in the dark, observing the night sky while casually over-hearing two people behind me muttering about my appearances with The Comedy Store Players. It's hard to catch many words but they are there.

I've left the Planetarium now and I'm looking for a cash machine. I misremember my PIN number three times in a row and the machine retains my card. It's pouring with rain and I have enough cash to get me back to Hat Trick's offices, where I will be able to borrow some money for the further journey home. But I'm not going to get that far tonight. I get a cab to Hat Trick. This driver also knows all about me, but he's cleverly saying nothing.

David Tyler is there. My thoughts are running wild and I realise that all the rooms in Hat Trick are fitted with hidden recording devices. They can hear and see everything. Who do I mean by they? The Freemasons? The Establishment? I don't know anymore, I just wish to God they would leave me alone! David says we have to take a car journey together. I look out of the cab window at the grey, wet streets and lose myself in thoughts of raincoats hanging in dark brown corridors, dripping drops of London rain onto sodden carpets.

The car stops and I know exactly where I am. A wave of melancholy engulfs me. Julie is already here. Together we walk down a corridor and this time I don't have to wait long. We see a doctor and Julie suddenly becomes convinced that I'm trying to get *her* admitted. She panics and to placate her I volunteer myself back in.

'Look,' I said, 'now you're safe.'

'Do you know what you're doing?' asks the doctor.

'Yes,' I said, not knowing what I was doing.

And so I re-admitted myself into the Maudsley Hospital, confident that after a good night's sleep I would be allowed home in the morning.

The two male nurses are annoyed with me.

'Will you please empty your pockets?'

I'm annoyed as well.

'I don't have to empty my pockets, I'm only staying the one night.'

'Are you refusing?' asks one of the nurses. 'That has serious implications.'

'I don't care,' I say, not caring about serious implications. 'I'm not staying here.' One nurse moves away but quickly reappears with a form and a clipboard.

Written across the top of the form in bold lettering are the words, 'Mr Martin refuses to disclose the contents of his pockets.'

'Do you know what happens next?' says one of the nurses. 'You will be physically restrained and you will be searched whether you like it or not. To put it bluntly, you may have a knife.'

I ignore the unintended humour of his remark and simply reply, 'You have a point.'

I empty my pockets of coins, keys, etc., and once the nurses are satisfied I'm shown the same bed in the same dormitory that I had before.

The next morning Mum and Dad arrive at the hospital. They do their best not to show their concern.

'Mum, I need to go home, coming back in here was a huge mistake.'

'Paul,' Mum says, 'you have to stay here. This is the best place for you. They will look after you here.'

I scream in frustration, and to prove my sanity I want to bang my head against the wall. It's too late for that. By coming back to the hospital and readmitting myself I have changed everything. It's made clear I'm here to stay for the foreseeable future. I calm myself down when I notice a couple of the nursing staff approaching me in case I become violent.

'I'm not going to be violent,' I tell them. My head drops in despair. 'I'm here now. I can't fight this.'

My position is hopeless. I'm back in this place.

Technically I could walk out of the building, but that's likely to lead to me being sectioned under the Mental Health Act. Seeing my acceptance of the situation, Mum and Dad leave. I watch them walk away down the corridor. Mum's nursing experience for the last twenty years of her career was in psychiatric care, so she is not fazed by her surroundings. I have to accept her calm certainty that this is the best place for me now. She would have changed her mind if she had seen me five hours later.

I'm shuffling up and down the same corridor that I spoke to Mum and Dad in, but my state of mind has changed completely. I'm mixing with the other patients. Some are surprised and are disappointed for me that I'm back again. Some are suspicious and are throwing me angry glances. They are the least of my worries. My feelings that I'm being observed and held in place by some authority other than this hospital have overwhelmed me once more. I am obsessed by the public pay phone on the wall of the corridor. I believe it's bugged. Specifically to listen in on my telephone conversations. I've been thinking about nothing else for the past half hour or so, at least what passes for half an hour in this place. A stern voice within tells me not to be so silly. I approach the phone to make a call.

A female patient pokes her head around a corner and says to me, 'Don't touch that phone. It's bugged.'

She looks like my mother but she has a heavy smoker's face. Heavily lined. I move quickly away from the phone as if it's radio-active. I walk into the kitchen area for a change of scene.

This is where I can make myself a cup of tea. There's an electric cooker, no gas or matches obviously, that would be madness. I fill the electric kettle over by the sink. I'm the only person in this kitchen but when I turn around I discover that I'm not. I've been joined by a hospital cleaner. She's wearing a sky-blue light overall, and she has a grey bucket and a dirty-looking mop. She fills her bucket at another sink. She has a little traffic cone with red and white stripes running across it. She begins to mop the floor. She is plump and West Indian.

My ward is not a locked ward, unlike many of the others. The patients here are judged to be safe enough. I hold my cup of tea and think about the phone in the hall again. The cleaner moves her little traffic cone, and as she does she reveals the word

C
A
U
T
I
O
N

written in bold black letters down one side. This immediately confirms that I'm right to believe that the phone is bugged. This cleaner, who I don't know, is taking a risk in warning me. Caution! This warning tells me I have allies, although I may not recognise them at first. I have tears in my eyes as I tiptoe out of the kitchen and back into the corridor. I look back through the door.

'Thank you,' I say to the cleaner, my voice trembling with gratitude.

'You're welcome,' she says, moving the traffic cone once more, this time hiding 'CAUTION'. I give her a knowing look.

My first group therapy session back isn't like the ones I've attended before. There are a couple of new people, but I'm different too. I can feel it in my head. I have a constant feeling of high anticipation. It's going to happen soon whatever it is. But for the moment, I'm not saying a word. One of the new patients has shoulder-length hair with a centre parting and mid-length beard, so it doesn't come as a complete surprise when he announces to the group, 'Hello. I am Jesus.'

This infuriates a man sitting three green armchairs away from me. He is bald and portly.

'No, *I'm* Jesus,' he says, which takes some chutzpah given his physical appearance.

A female patient decides the matter by pointing to the first Jesus and saying, 'You are the one, I know you are the one.'

A male nurse is sitting amongst us. I sometimes find it difficult to tell the difference between the staff and the patients. They don't wear a uniform and neither do we. The nurse gently moves us away from the business of authenticating Jesuses, and for the rest of the session I concentrate on the smaller details around me. Shirt buttons, the pattern of light and shade on the extra-heavy coffee table. Shadows on walls. At the end of our forty-five minutes a female patient approaches me and looks me straight in the eye.

'Why are you trying to kill me?' she says.

I'm stunned. This place has changed radically since I was last here. Her words float me away to somewhere else. My brain is throbbing and reeling with this fresh perspective on reality. Am I trying to kill her and don't know it?

I walk up and down the corridor with my left arm folded across my chest. My behaviour concerns a member of staff who asks me to sit down for a moment.

'Do you hear voices?' he asks.

'All the time,' I say. 'I can hear yours now.'

'Do you ever hear voices when there's nobody there?' he says.

'Yes,' I say, 'all the time.'

'All the time?'

'Yes. I call it talking on the telephone.' I laugh. I'm running rings around this guy and he doesn't look very happy about it. Then I remember 'caution'.

'I'm trying to assess your mental state,' he says.

'Oh I'm perfectly fine,' I say, 'and don't let me tell you any different.' I'm not sure if this guy is a doctor, a nurse or another patient. There is no formal identification about him. A word on a piece of paper on the noticeboard behind him leaps out at me. Psychotherapist. The letters rush towards my eyes and I instantly decipher them. The hidden message in 'psychotherapist' emerges simply by splitting one word into three. Psycho the rapist. The very opposite of what they pretend to be, a 'caring' profession. I tell him I'm fine, but I'm not. I go back to walking up and down the ward corridor. I feel powerful. I feel caged. I'm prowling, my head is jutting forward. I'm going to smash something. An irresistible need for violence is overwhelming me. A male nurse is walking past me and I quickly grab him by the shoulders and scream at him, 'For God's sake, give me something to calm me down or I'm going to go fucking crazy.'

He runs off and quickly returns with two big tablets and a cup of water. I swallow the tablets and gulp the water down, some of it dribbling down my chin. The nurse says calmly, 'Now take a deep breath. And now breathe out. That's it, relaxed breathing.'

The breathing is helping and in a few minutes I'm sure the tablets will kick in, but I'm still at a high level of agitation. I stand in the corridor with the nurse observing me and other patients moving around cautiously. I'm suddenly hit by a massive revelation. A thought has just leapt into my head. I know why I'm like this.

I say to the nurse, 'It's my anti-malarial pills, you're giving me the wrong ones. For the last three days you have been giving me the weekly pill instead of the daily pill.'

'How do you know?' he said.

'I sense it. I know I'm right. Please can you check the bottles?'

He disappears and looks inside the medicine cabinet. He comes back and holds up a bottle of weekly pills.

'These are the ones we've been giving you,' he says and checks the label for himself. 'And this bottle was pushed right to the back of the cupboard,' he says, showing me the bottle of daily pills.

'For the last three days you've been giving me the weekly dosage?' I say.

'Yes,' agrees the nurse. 'It's a big mistake to make.'

'That's a relief,' I say, feeling genuinely relieved, which may also be the effect of the two white tablets creeping up on me. 'To suddenly know why I am the way I am right now, it's good to know,' I say. 'I've overdosed on the weekly pill and that's why my head has been bouncing about.'

I relax into that knowledge and smile at the nurse. I'm feeling calmness. For now the storm has moved away. Tonight I will sleep well. It's tomorrow morning that I'll be given the really bad news.

My Channel 4 television series has been postponed. I was told this news a couple of hours ago by one of the psychiatrists here. He emphasised that it had been postponed and not cancelled.

'Oh,' I said, half-expecting the news, although that didn't make it any easier to hear. I knew there wasn't much chance of filming *Paul Merton: The Series* while Paul Merton himself was unavailable.

'Perhaps you can talk about it in group therapy,' suggested the psychiatrist. 'Apparently you haven't made any contribution so far.'

'Well there's a reason for that,' I said. 'The other people in the group have genuine real-life problems brought about through poverty, stressful living conditions, drug addiction, mental illness, other factors I'm sure. My problem is that Channel 4 have postponed my television series. I've become chronically unavailable for wig fittings. That's not a world that anybody here can empathise with. It's not normal.'

'You could try,' says the psychiatrist.

'I'd feel self-conscious saying it,' I say. This proves to me that at least I haven't completely lost my sense of perspective. Sitting in the group therapy gives you plenty of perspective. Some of us have scar tissue across our wrists, while others can't tell their stories without sobbing into their hands. Everyone is going through their own pain. When someone cries the group feels sympathy towards them but none of us vocalise our concern. There's a feeling of not wanting to intrude, perhaps that's English reserve for you.

I know what I have to do now. I can just ride out the time I'm here and not cause trouble or make waves, although there is a small difficulty on the horizon. There are a number of people in psychiatric hospitals who believe that the people on television are talking to them directly through the screen, and Channel 4 start broadcasting the new series of *Whose Line is it Anyway?* this coming Friday.

My appearance in the hospital canteen for my breakfast of either hard-boiled egg or bran flakes the following Saturday morning does not go unnoticed. The young lad behind me in the queue nearly jumps out of his skin when he realises he's standing next to a semi-famous person.

He stutters a question. 'Are you Paul Merton?' he asks excitedly. He is about nineteen years old and he is shaking. I'm the wrong person to convincingly deny that I am Paul Merton so I quietly say, 'Yes I am.'

He looks around nervously. 'What are you doing here?'

I feel a sense of responsibility. I could play with this boy's head by concocting conspiracies about people from Tellyland jumping out of TVs and into real life, and by the expression on his face he wouldn't need too much convincing.

'I'm just being quiet here,' I say conspiratorially. 'Nobody knows I'm here really.'

He looks satisfied with this. I'm entrusting him with a secret. I am now more in control of myself. After the horrendous over-dosing on my weekly anti-malarial pill, my psychiatrist has stopped me taking them. I have clarity and the mania has gone, which helps me deal with the rather uncommon problem of living in a psychi-atric hospital while simultaneously appearing on a very popular television show.

I'm talking to my psychiatrist about it. He says, 'How are you fitting in with the other patients?'

'Well,' I say, 'some of them are giving me strange looks. I know it sounds paranoid but it's the truth.'

He asks, 'And why are they doing that, do you think?'

'Because I'm in television,' I answer.

He's looking at me like he doesn't believe me.

'No I am, really,' I find myself insisting, but he looks uncon-vinced. 'I know I'm not that famous and if you don't watch *Whose Line is it Anyway?* you won't know who I am, but please don't take away from me my budding TV career.' He doesn't smile.

Some of the other patients need no persuading that I'm from another world. To help pass the time, I join up to a printing course. I'm not remotely interested in printing but I'm trying to fit in and it will help to while away the time. It's either this or sitting in the communal living room watching Robert Kilroy-Silk on the televi-sion in the corner.

There's six of us in this class and one of us is a big, thickset thuggish, big-headed type with huge fists. We are not destined to be friends. We are having a tea break and are sitting around a table, each with a hot mug of liquid in front of us. Three of us are smoking cigarettes and I'm one of them. I'd smoked for a couple of weeks after coming back from Australia and then successfully stopped for seven months, but I've picked it up again in the last few days.

When I roll my own cigarettes I for a moment feel in control of the situation. The simple ritual of filling the single cigarette paper with rolling tobacco and caressing it into a tube, brings me pleasure before I even light the damned thing. The thug is also smoking. He exudes a threatening menace as he leans towards the light plastic ashtray. He passes over the ashtray with his cigarette and deliberately flicks ash into my cup. He is looking straight at me, waiting to see if I'll be mad enough to retaliate. I pick my cup up and rinse the contents down the sink. I leave the kitchen area and return to my ward just in time to catch the last five minutes of Robert Kilroy-Silk.

The patients on my ward are more used to me now, but outside of this environment I can anticipate hostility because I represent show business and being funny, and more 'What are you doing here?' questions can be expected, perhaps next time expressed with a more hostile edge.

David Tyler comes in to visit me and is rather shocked by my surroundings. I show him the bed I sleep in every night, one of eight in the male dormitory. There is water on the floor, which comes through if you run the shower next door. Consequently, I've been put off using the shower and I haven't shaved for the last few days because I find it rather demeaning to have to sign a request form for a plastic disposable razor, which I must then return immediately after shaving.

David looks around. 'This is shit isn't it?' he says.

'I tend to agree,' I say.

'Can I get you anything?' he says.

'Yes, you can,' I say. 'Can you hear the music that is playing in the communal room now?'

David listened. 'What is it?'

'It's called "Nothing Compares 2 U" and it's by Sinead O'Connor. There's a female patient who plays it every time we get back from breakfast and lunch. She recorded it off the radio and the sound always distorts if you play it back too loud. Which she does every day. So could you bring me a personal cassette player and some head phones?'

'Of course,' David says.

'Thank you,' I say. 'I can put those headphones on and listen to my *Round the Horne* tapes. A world within a world.'

It doesn't take long to start feeling institutionalised in a place like this and to lose sight of normal behaviour. My reluctance to shower and shave is interpreted by the nursing staff as an inability to look after myself. I can see it clearly in their eyes and they're wrong, but I change my behaviour anyway. I need to be a model patient and, although I'm reluctant to soak the floor in our dormitory room, it's much better that I shower every day and seek official permission to shave.

Now that I'm no longer taking the anti-malarial pills I feel I have my full wits about me, but I'm far from ready to leave.

At the suggestion of the psychiatrist I'm going out this evening. Julian Clary is going to pick me up in his Citroën. It's the first step towards leaving the hospital permanently.

It's a filthy wet stormy night. The rain hurtles horizontally across the windscreen as the foul weather bumps us around in Julian's lightweight car.

'Where shall we go?' asks Julian.

'There's a restaurant in East Dulwich that doesn't look too bad from the outside,' I say, so we head for there. Along the way we drive down tree-lined roads, branches whipping through the air. The visibility is dreadful. It's like driving through an endless carwash or a deep vertical pond. When we get to the restaurant, the only improvement I can see in the atmosphere is that at least inside it's not raining.

The Edgar Allen Poe theme of the night is maintained by the restaurant's gloomy decor and lighting. As the storm rages outside, the two of us toy with plates of indifferent spaghetti. There is one other couple in the restaurant, which is dimly lit by oil lanterns and draped in fisherman's nets. A man and a woman have recognised Julian and so are talking unnaturally loud over the admittedly noisy weather.

'I thought we'd go back to Madrid this year,' he says over the top of the wind howling at the door.

'As long as we don't have to meet any Spanish people this time darling,' she shouts back. I attempt to say something to Julian and they immediately stop talking and stare straight at us.

The meal didn't last long. We drove back through the storm, with windscreen wipers failing to cope with the elements, and as Julian drops me off outside the main entrance, I realise it's a relief to be back home.

A man has appeared in the hospital bed opposite me. He is around five foot five. He is in his early forties and is thickset with black hair. His name is Louis and he doesn't speak English. He has disturbed crazy eyes. I find it best not to meet his gaze. He has the intense air of a caged animal biding his time. Louis doesn't look like he belongs on this ward. He spends most of the day lying on his bed, staring daggers at the ceiling. He's waiting for something.

It's Thursday evening and one of the female patients is celebrating a birthday. A cake is produced with candles and we all gather in the common room singing 'Happy Birthday'. In the thirty seconds that this takes, Louis, unseen by any of us, walks down the corridor and out of the main entrance of the hospital.

He returns to where he lives, a tower block, and throws himself off the top of it. We are told of his death the following morning. The ward is in shock. Yesterday I had arranged with one of the nurses to leave the hospital this lunchtime for a couple of hours in the company of John Irwin. In the aftermath of Louis' suicide, the nurse had forgotten this.

So, without thinking much about it, I meet my friend at the front of the hospital at midday and head off for a pub lunch. We sit around for a couple of hours, playing a few frames of pool, drinking two or three pints of Guinness, and wolfing down a mediocre shepherd's pie.

I return to the hospital to find my ward locked from the inside, and I'm placed in the rather embarrassing position of knocking firmly on the door in order to be let back in.

My appearance back in the ward is met with great relief by the staff. While I was enjoying some outside time they were desperately concerned that, in imitation of Louis, I had topped myself. I had apparently disappeared without permission and they feared the worst. Psychiatric patients are easily influenced by the behaviour around them, and people were very worried about me. I apologise for being the inadvertent cause of so much concern.

A small memorial service is held for Louis in the tiny chapel of the hospital, and one of the doctors asks if I could say a few words. I'm comfortable speaking publicly so I agree. When it comes to my turn, I get to my feet and begin. 'I didn't know Louis particularly well ...'

'That's not going to bring him back,' shouts an irate woman from the front row. I look to where she is sitting and I control my instinct to come up with some withering put-down. 'Shut your mouth, there's a bus coming,' isn't really the appropriate tone for a memorial service, so I simply say, 'No it won't.' I say the words that come to me.

'In the brief time he was on our ward, he never spoke to anyone and he seemed to be in some sort of turmoil. Well he isn't now. It's been a terrible shock and perhaps it will help us to focus and remember the important things in life. Love and respect for our fellow human beings.'

Afterwards, I reflect on the very dubious honour of being heckled at a memorial service, and also my reaction to it. Have I undergone a subtle but fundamental change? I feel my desire to be the schoolboy with all the funny lines, or the person holding court at the party, or the comic competing against all the other comics to be the funniest person in the room has melted away.

I want to be a different person off stage to the one I am on.

It's been a few weeks since I stopped taking the anti-malarial pills and now my psychiatrist is happy for me to go home this weekend. I ask him if I get a special certificate to prove that I'm sane, but when he gives me a funny look I quickly add that I am only joking.

Shortly before I leave the Maudsley for the last time, one of the male nurses asks me a question as we walk from one building to another.

'Is it possible to make a joke about anything?' he wants to know.

'Yes,' I say. 'Jokes can be made about fatal illnesses, kidnapped children, whatever taboos you care to mention. If nobody finds the joke funny, it's a bad joke. A joke can be tasteless but still hilarious to some people. Humour is essential to people's lives.'

'Is it really?' he says.

I say, 'It's helping me every step of the way.'

As I leave the Maudsley, immensely grateful to all the medical staff for their professional care and expertise, sunshine hits my face. It feels like freedom. I've been here for two months and now it's time to go. It's spring.

The daffodils are out and so am I.

18

Zsa Zsa Man Dies

I was in no hurry to do anything except take it easy. My days were spent rereading Sherlock Holmes stories and pottering about.

My first gig after leaving the Maudsley was with The Comedy Store Players, in Glasgow on the Renfrew Ferry. Andy Smart, Richard Vranch, Lee Simpson and I were four of the regular players. As a group of improvisers we have always socialised well together. You become friends with the people you regularly improvise with, and the good feeling you engender onstage carries over into real life. Travelling together, particularly by train, can be great fun. Making each other laugh at 125 miles an hour is one of the perks of the job. We had a guest player with us, Caroline Quentin, who I had never met before.

The train journey from Kings Cross to Glasgow was a lovely, gentle reintroduction to The Comedy Store Players' world.

I'd brought a book with me to read on the journey, the auto-biography of Sir Alec Guinness, called *Blessings in Disguise*. As the journey progressed I tried my best with the paperback but I couldn't get engaged, and somewhere between Peterborough and Newcastle, I threw it out of the window.

I suppose this was for effect. In a single flamboyant gesture, I had hopefully painted myself as an eccentric and interesting fellow.

The gig in Glasgow went well, and I remember Caroline finding me very funny. She was a strong character and wasn't at all fazed by the fact I'd recently spent time in a psychiatric hospital. She was confident, clever and talented. I liked her.

Julie had moved out by this time, and I really couldn't blame her. So following Glasgow, I saw Caroline occasionally at Comedy Store Player gigs, and then, after the Edinburgh Festival, we started going out together. Caroline gave me stability. She was well-grounded, and had a great deal of theatrical experience and knowledge.

Also, rejoining the Sunday shows with The Comedy Store Players was greatly therapeutic. Focusing on creating comedy out of thin air with my friends in front of hugely appreciative crowds was – and still is – a weekly tonic.

Three months after I'd left the Maudsley, Jimmy Mulville at Hat Trick phoned to ask if I'd be interested in making a pilot for a television programme. My sketch series had been postponed for a year and so was still some ten months away.

'What's the show about?' I said.

'It's a quiz based on the week's news,' he said. 'We haven't got a title yet.'

'That's not for me,' I said. 'I don't do topical jokes. In fact, I know nothing about current affairs.'

'It doesn't matter,' he said. 'Just be funny. You can do that.'

I wasn't going to give him an argument so I agreed, and on a truly beautiful day, a gloriously sunny Sunday afternoon, I, and 200 other people, sat in a swelteringly hot TV studio in Wandsworth for well over an hour-and-a-half, all wishing we were somewhere else, like outside.

The programme's working title was 'John Lloyd's Newsround', principally because John Lloyd was hosting and introducing rounds about the news. There were two teams of two. I searched for laughs wherever I suspected they may be, but without much success.

On the opposing team, the youthful editor of *Private Eye*, Ian Hislop, did his best to enliven proceedings, and in the company of two other journalists, we stumbled through a morass of uneasy banter and tedious bickering over the scores. I was pleased to meet Ian, and as a loyal reader of his magazine I had noted how it had improved under his editorship over the past four years. I told him this. He mistook me for a minicab driver at first, but when we were properly introduced he seemed to be a genuine fellow.*

'*Well,*' I thought to myself at the end, '*that's the last we'll see of that idea.*'

I continued to rest and also reflect on my Maudsley experience. Hat Trick arranged for me to see a psychiatrist to try and understand why, and how, I had ended up in a psychiatric hospital. He quickly confirmed that my anti-malarial pills were to blame; the weekly ones in particular. As I thought back over my recent experiences, I realised that my mania peaked every weekend, which coincided with my weekly pill. I was first taken to the hospital on a Saturday and the second time I was readmitted it was a Friday. When I stopped taking them, I began to feel better. I'm not worried about ever finding myself back in such a place because, to my mind, it was down to a severe reaction, rather than an existing mental health problem. I don't feel ashamed or guilty. But I do

---

* To be fair, I thought Ian had shone but later they applied some powder to the top of his head and it stopped being a problem.

feel incredibly lucky that a year later, we finally made our sketch show, *Paul Merton: The Series*.

We spent ten days filming all the exterior material, and that was a total joy. There's an enormous pleasure to be had working on location with a director, cameraman and everything else that goes with it. Prop makers, set designers, wardrobe, make-up, other actors. Sitting around dressed as a British POW in a Nazi camp, awaiting the arrival of an authentic looking German army lorry to lend period atmosphere to the scene, is an experience I wish everyone could have. The thrill lies in seeing your ideas transformed into reality by experienced, clever people. And seeing those ideas work for an audience completes the thrill.

We were adventurous in our filming. We had a man with an elephant's head discussing architecture in a car park. We threw a telephone box off Hammersmith Bridge. This was part of a dream I once had. A stuntman on his way to a laundrette is assaulted in sequence by a man hitting him over the head with a bottle, a fridge dropping out of the sky, a massive grey ball and a woman pushing a pram that's on fire. We also dropped a horse on him.

The studio-based material was generally more verbal, and a lot of it revolved around me standing inside a newsagent's kiosk in a London Underground station. I could present my stand-up material without it looking like I was doing stand-up, and the kiosk setting meant that customers could interrupt me at any time.

One habit that John Irwin and I got into was to visit the studio the day before the recording, to marvel at the fantastic sets that were being constructed for our show. One favourite was the Transylvanian hostelry, circa mid-nineteenth century, full of old lanterns, wooden floors, a dozen actors dressed as peasant folk, and authentic looking bottles and tankards. A good set evokes the atmosphere of the real thing. In the sketches, I would look for opportunities to make a dramatic entrance and this set was just about my favourite. After a few moments of scene-setting dialogue, I burst through the front door in full Frankenstein's monster make-up.

'Good evening,' I say. 'Has the Wolfman been in?'

This got the huge laugh from the studio audience that we were looking for. This was our first sketch of the night, chiefly because it was a two hour make-up job. I was careful to speak to the audience from behind a curtain before we began. I wanted to greet them, but not give away the make-up's impact. It's one of my favourite sketches from the two series that we did.

The kiosk stuff always went well too. It was a fresh way to present stand-up on telly, and by placing myself in a box I was in fact creating a little theatre for myself. Surrounded by props and customers. The director for our first series was Geoff Posner, who at that time was working extensively with Victoria Wood. His involvement lent prestige to our show, and he assembled a very talented team of people around him.

Victor Lewis-Smith, then working as the *London Evening Standard* TV critic, gave the show a stunning review. '*Paul Merton: The Series* is the funniest comedy series I have seen in decades. Part Arthur Haines, part Joe Orton, and painstakingly written with John Irwin, it bristles with comic invention ... This series demonstrates that great comedy can be produced on a small budget, if the writing is good and the central performer strong. Merton is emerging as a comic genius, a one-off maverick devoid of the smug self-satisfaction that surrounds the Oxbridge coterie.'

Wow! And believe you me, if reprinting ecstatic reviews in my autobiography proves anything, it's that I am totally devoid of smug self-satisfaction.

I once spoke to an Oxbridge comedian at a TV drinks reception, and he told me that he and his working partner were writing

248 · · · ONLY WHEN I LAUGH

some great dark comedy together. 'It's like Galton and Simpson,' he said.

'Really,' I said, slightly reeling from the favourable comparison. Galton and Simpson, the writers of *Hancock's Half Hour* and *Steptoe and Son*, set standards that the majority of comedy writers can only dream of.

'Yes,' he said, without missing a beat, 'and we write separately and then bring our material together like Lennon and McCartney.' Wow, that's first-class boasting, I remember thinking – comparing yourself to the very best in two different disciplines.

When I told the story to Ian Hislop, he had the perfect punchline, 'Yes, and I write on my own, like Shakespeare.' Ian went to Oxford, which goes to show that you can trust some of them.

But there was also some brilliant stuff coming from the next wave of comedy talent. The early 1990s also saw the meteoric rise to huge acclaim of Eddie Izzard. who made the journey from street busker to a brilliantly different stand-up who bounced brains to Neptune and back, with comic rhythms, timings, and verbal glidings that slipped you into pictures of worlds, inside your head, where raised eyebrows became caterpillars doing press-ups for charity.

Vic Reeves and Bob Mortimer eschewed the cabaret circuit altogether, and by putting on their own gigs initially, quickly made the journey from cult live act to cult TV comedians. *Vic Reeves Big Night Out* brought full-blown surrealism to the screen, and heavily influenced many comedians a generation behind them. Vic, a potent cross between Bryan Ferry and Monsewer Eddie Gray, hit the ground running, and was a fresh and radically alternative voice to that of the regular stand-up.

*

One of my favourite Galton and Simpson episodes, 'The Radio Ham'.

⬆ With Ian Hislop and Angus Deayton, in an early publicity shot for *Have I Got News for You*. Our suits were tailored in Fleet Street.

The Big Reveal.

⬆ *Paul Merton: The Series*. Reworking the familiar 'elephant and tea cup' routine in 1991.

⬅ Onstage at the Palladium with some of the original Tiller Girls.

⬇ Caroline and me in Arthur Smith's *Live Bed Show*.

→ A brief parody commercial in an episode of *Jackanory*.

↓ The late, great Spike Milligan in 1999. This was to be his last major television interview.

ROOM 101

⬅ Shooting *The Suicidal Dog* with Jack Cardiff.

⬅ Sarah and me shortly before I won a BAFTA in 2003.

➡ Left to right:
(back row) Mick,
David, Paul, Ricky.
(Front row) Eddie.
My local darts team.

➡ A *Just a Minute*
photo opportunity
with Jenny Eclair,
Gyles Brandreth
and my dear friend
Nicholas Parsons.

Richard Vranch, Lee Simpson, Mike McShane, Suki Webster, and me. The Impro Chums – coming to a town near you.

Suki and me. Coincidentally this was also the day we got married.

The pilot of *Have I Got News for You* was deemed promising enough for a series to be commissioned, but John Lloyd as our chairman would not be with us. I believe he found reading the autocue rather tiresome and restricting. This brilliant producer/creator, of such iconic shows as *Not The Nine O'Clock News*, *Blackadder* and *Spitting Image*, wasn't happy casting in this role, but he would continue to thrive with the creation of *QI* and other successes.

The question was, who would Hat Trick find to replace the Oxford-educated John? Two candidates were auditioned. In the spirit of diversity, although they had both been to Oxford, they had attended different colleges. Angus Deayton got the job and immediately made it his own. He played the host partly as a newsreader, which, combined with his impeccable timing, gave the show a subversive weight. He said things no newsreader would say, which helped the comedy along. Ian, as the opposing team captain, was slightly unsure of the programme at first. He was concerned that it might threaten his natural dignity, but I told him he had nothing to worry about.

'I'm a serious journalist,' he said.

'Don't worry,' I said. 'Your secrets are safe with me.'

The chemistry between the three regulars was immediately apparent, and the show slowly built up an audience over the first two series. I found myself becoming more recognisable, and somehow this led to me meeting other recognisable people.

On a couple of occasions, in the company of Julian Clary, I was invited to Peter Cook's flat in Hampstead. It was situated in a private mews, and the inside was spacious and furnished in a contemporary but comfortable style. There was a small, attractive patio garden out the back. Peter was one of my great comic heroes when I was growing up. His wit, elegance and charm inspired me, and here I was, standing in his living room while he asked me what I would like to drink.

'We have vodka, Scotch, brandy, white or red wine.'

I struggled heavily with the surrealism of the moment. 'Er, all of it sounds fine. Er, perhaps a white wine.'

'Certainly Paul, come through to the kitchen.'

I follow him into the kitchen and there is Eric Idle standing next to the fridge! Eric Idle, ex-Monty Python, Eric Idle! Eric is immediately friendly. 'Hi Paul,' he says, 'I really enjoyed your television series.' His accent a mixture of English and Californian.

'Oh, *Have I Got News for You?* Thank you,' I reply.

'No,' he said. 'Your sketch series. The one with the newsagent's kiosk. It's great.'

And time stood still for a moment, and then whisked me back twenty years. I was fourteen years old, and someone in a dream was telling me that I will make a television programme, and that Eric Idle will enjoy it and tell me so. I thanked him and tried to make my head stop spinning for a while. But as we talked, I soon relaxed into the situation. Although there was plenty of alcohol available, I resolved to take it easy as I was keen to avoid turning into a drunken babbling fanboy, exhorting praise on the two titans of comedy.

There were seven or eight other people at the party, and one of them produced a bag of grass and suggested that anyone was free to help themselves. I said to Peter, who was sitting next to Eric on the sofa, 'If you're happy for me to sit here,' I indicated a nearby armchair, 'I'm happy to roll you joints all night.'

'What a sensible arrangement!' said Peter, with a grin. 'What I like about cannabis is it does what it says it's going to do.'

'I don't know how to stick the papers together,' I said. 'So I hope you're happy with a single Rizla joint.'

'That's how they smoke them in California,' said Peter.

'I'm happy just sitting here,' I said, 'rolling away. I'll just let you guys talk.'

And that's how it panned out. I sat back from their conversation and took in the rest of the room, while occasionally rolling a jazz cigarette and passing it around the room.

I met Peter on a few occasions, the last of them being the most memorable. He and Dudley Moore were launching a video release of their hilariously filthy double act Derek and Clive, in a former working man's club in north London. I had bought the original LPs when they were first released. Julian and I had been invited, along with a hundred other people. I saw Dudley from a distance, but I never got to speak with him. Whereas I was having a quiet drink in the corner when Peter suddenly appeared at my shoulder, a glass of white wine in his hand. 'Ah, Mr so-called Merton, if that really is your name,' he said. 'Do you know this place reminds me of my working-class roots.'

I immediately laughed. 'What working-class roots?' I said. 'Your father was a diplomat.'

It was Peter's turn to laugh. 'I do have working-class roots,' he insisted. 'I bought them at a garden centre,' he said chuckling away.

'And did you grow them in the salt of the earth?' I asked, but before he answered he was off with a wave of his arm and a big 'hello' to a group of people walking immediately towards us, two of which happened to be members of the Rolling Stones. Keith Richards and Ronnie Wood greeted Peter as an old friend, and the three of them disappeared off together, perhaps to discuss the ins and outs of the pharmaceutical industry.

The party progressed until around midnight when Peter discretely invited a few people back to his place. Unfortunately, I had an early start the next morning, so I rather professionally in my view declined, and got a cab home. It was the right thing to do, but if I'd known that this was the last time I would meet Peter, I would have gone for a couple of hours.*

Amongst his many achievements, I rank his film *Bedazzled*, which he made with Dudley Moore, as the highest. A variation on the Faust legend, Peter plays a devilishly good-looking Beelzebub, while Dudley works as a minion in a burger bar. The film has acquired sociological value since it was made, particularly with its honest portrayal of just how unhygienic burger bars looked in the 1960s.

The day after he died, I got a phone call from the *Independent* newspaper looking for a thousand word appreciation, but as luck would have it, it was the first day of rehearsals for a West End play that I was co-starring in with Caroline Quentin, and because I write by hand it would have taken me a few hours, so I sadly declined. I would have mentioned an interview that Peter had given many years before, where he talked about, and inadvertently insulted, Zsa Zsa Gabor, a Hollywood legend of limited acting ability. She made such a fuss that Peter mock-feared that when he departed, his obituary headline would read 'Zsa Zsa Man Dies'. I passed the message back that their obituary should be headed 'Zsa Zsa Man Dies', but unfortunately it went unused.

I was invited to the memorial service, which was held in a massive church in Hampstead. One row in front of me sat Chris Morris, at that time part of *The Day Today* team, while one row behind me sat Frankie Vaughan, a British pop star before the invention of rock and roll, who was best known for his theme tune 'Give me the Moonlight, Give me the Girl'. This is an indication of the range of people that Peter knew.

---

* OK, it was the wrong thing to do.

Alan Bennett made a very funny speech from the pulpit. He said that Peter had once confided in him that the one thing he really regretted in life was the occasion in which he saved David Frost from drowning.

As I sat in this huge church, I was keenly aware that I didn't really belong there. The Church of England has a whole different set of hymns to the Catholics, and so when the congregation started singing 'Jerusalem' I was fair startled. It wasn't a tune I knew, but everybody else did. They sang the words without the need of hymn sheets. It was a hymn that posed a series of rhetorical questions, the answer to each one being 'no'. 'And did those feet in ancient time?' 'No.' There was something about a green and pleasant land. Later, everybody sang 'To Be a Pilgrim'. I'm not sure why that's a laudable ambition. But if I was baffled by elements of the Mass, I was even more baffled by events afterwards.

As the hundreds of people emerged from the church and into the grey winter daylight, I looked around rather lost and wondering where I might go next. Various groups were huddled together, I knew very few people there, and I was pondering the possibility of catching a taxi home when Ian spotted me and came over.

'Hello Ian,' I said, 'I was wondering what I should do now.'

'Come with me,' he said. 'There's a few of us gathering together for a meal.'

I followed him and his wife Victoria into a restaurant in the high street. Peter, of course, was the major shareholder in *Private Eye*, so to be invited to a post-memorial lunch by the editor did not feel inappropriate. It was clear that the long table had been arranged for a set number of people, but as the room had a bar at one end of it I was very happy to perch on an adjacent stool. A man who I immediately recognised sat next to me. He was Ronnie Carroll, who had been a pop star very briefly in the early 1960s.

Neatly combed hair, a bow tie, dinner jacket with shiny thin lapels was his show-business look. He was a star before the Beatles, but not after. He recognised me and we chatted away for the best part of half an hour, each of us slowly sinking a pint.

On the official table of guests sat, amongst others, Ian and Victoria, Harry Enfield and Dudley Moore, who sat alongside Peter's widow Lin. Ronnie and I were way in the background, talking about *Bedazzled* and Pete and Dud, and when it became clear to us that the lunch was coming to an end, I said some quick goodbyes to the people I knew and made my way out of the restaurant.

I was standing on the pavement looking for a taxi in Hampstead High Street, when suddenly a very angry Lin Cook appeared at my side. I under-describe: she was spitting fury.

'What are you doing here?' she demanded, and she wasn't waiting for an answer. 'You didn't know Peter, why do you come here?'

I was deeply dumbstruck, as the widow of the man we had only just held a memorial service for screamed at me in public, 'You weren't invited.'

Before I could answer that I technically was, but not by her, an arm grabbed me and moved me towards the middle of the road. It was Ian. In one easy move he hailed a taxi, and within seconds he, Victoria and I were speeding away from the unmerry widow. Ian spoke calm words, 'Don't worry,' he said, 'it's not about you.' He explained that Lin had just just become really agitated after some unexpected news, and I was the very next person she set eyes on. Ian, hearing commotion outside the restaurant, came instantly to my rescue. He is a gentleman in every respect.

19

Tabloid Scandal

Caroline and I got married in December 1991, at the romantically named Wandsworth Town Hall, and after a brilliant big party we embarked on a six-week honeymoon, visiting Australia and Thailand, amongst other countries. It was the trip of a lifetime. We returned to our ground floor flat in Lavender Sweep in Battersea, a cosy three-roomed affair, ten minutes walk from Clapham Junction.

The play I had been rehearsing with Caroline when I heard the news of Peter's death was called *Live Bed Show*, which she had already appeared in with the play's author, Arthur Smith, at the Edinburgh Fringe. *Live Bed Show* began with me and Caroline sitting up in bed. The momentum of the evening was entirely in our hands. We had to immediately engage the audience, and once the play was up and running we made sure we kept a tight rein, as we steered it home across an hour-and-a-half. The concentration was immense. We had no interval, and it was just the two of us and the play. We played exactly a hundred performances and we kept it fresh throughout the run. Every performance sounded like we were saying the words for the very first time – in other words, spontaneously.

Caroline, with her extensive experience in live theatre, showed the way by subtly changing the intonation and thought behind her

opening speech every night. Because I was listening I responded
to her different delivery with an alteration of my own. Perhaps an
underlying sadness or a tinge of anger might colour the opening
exchanges. We kept it moving.

You owe the audience, who have paid to see you that night,
your best possible effort.

Approaching the dialogue and action with a slightly different
emphasis helps to keep the performance dynamic. And on those
nights when the audience is so transfixed and focused on every
move that a turn of the head rightly timed gets a huge laugh, there
is massive satisfaction in making it work. However, the Friday
matinee, which was at the silly time of six thirty, was to prove a
struggle throughout the three-month run. No doubt the time was
fixed to appeal to people who had just finished work, but that was
what was wrong with it.

Leaving the office and going to the theatre without changing
clothes, queuing up for a gin and tonic in a crowded bar, and then
sitting down to watch a play that the wife/girlfriend wants to see,
is not how most men ideally start their weekend. It's understood
in theatreland that heterosexual couples tend to go and see what
the woman wants to see, so it was mainly men who sat there early
Friday evening, exuding grumpiness.

On those performances, you could feel it in waves rolling towards
the stage from the auditorium. As the curtains parted at the top of
the show, you could sense a male rumble of discomfort. An uneasy
shifting in seats as it dawned on the poor buggers that the play was
beginning. No matter how much we tried, we never rarely managed
to turn those six thirty Friday audiences completely round.

Arthur Smith, our author, would pop in to see the show every
few weeks, choosing to take residence in one of the boxes stage
right. Arthur, tall, slim, craggy, with a perpetual cigarette waving

in his right hand, is a comedian enjoying some success as a play-wright. I was always alerted to his presence by a telltale cloud of tobacco smoke appearing from behind the velvet curtain at the back of the box. Arthur was quite rightly enjoying the kudos of being a successful West End playwright, but also listening out for laughs that were missed or general slackness creeping in. This can easily happen in a long run, but Caroline and I kept on top of it. The alternative of boring people rigid for ninety minutes was too awful to contemplate.

It took me three weeks to memorise the play, and after our last performance a matter of moments to forget it completely. My brain simply wiped the words away. The moment I no longer needed to remember the play it went instantly, as if my brain had decided, 'Well you won't be needing that anymore.' The only words that remained were, 'I like pubs. Big beery rooms with carpets.'

Apparently, this is a common experience amongst theatre actors, but I marvelled at it nevertheless. I was also surprised by how much mental energy is needed for a stage play, particularly one where you remain constantly in front of the audience for ninety minutes. No entrances or exits, you stay put, right there onstage. During our three-month run I had planned to write a book, but I found I needed to rest during the day to make sure my energy was right for the evening performance.

Once the run was over, the book began. Unlike this one, it was a fictional autobiography with the make believe Paul Merton, who was born in 1920, finding immediate fame as a baby performer, before embarking on a long roller coaster of a career involving Hollywood, secret tunnels and murder. The last was inspired by an argument I had with Caroline, which led to my entirely fictional Paul Merton suddenly bumping off his wife without any prior indication that murder was in his mind.

I took a delight in painting a portrait of a terrible person and calling him me. That Paul Merton was egotistical, tyrannical, without talent and ruthless in pursuit of glory. It's amazing how the imagination allows you to conjure up a character completely different from yourself. Isn't it …?

To indicate that the main character was intended to be a nasty piece of work the book was called *My Struggle*, which is the English translation of *Mein Kampf*.

In that same year, 1995, John and I wrote up an idea called *Paul Merton's Life of Comedy*, which was a framework for a clip show featuring pieces of television comedy that I specifically remembered, but hadn't seen since the original broadcasts. I looked at dozens and dozens of video tapes from the BBC's extraordinary archive, and found great treasures, whether they were black-and-white Morecambe and Wise clips unseen in thirty years, or Bob and Ray, a Canadian radio double act, performing their classic sketch the 'Slow Talkers of America' on *The Bob Monkhouse Show*. Such richness of comic material poses problems for the presenter.

Essentially, trying to be funny in competition with the best comedians you can find is guaranteed to make you look silly in a bad way. Yet there must be humour in what you do. It's a question of tone. Lightly does it. The idea developed that I would first of all present the programme in fairly straight presenter mode, wearing a nice purple jacket, before moving into a recreation of the small council flat I lived in during the first half of the 1960s. The production designer visited Robert Owen House to measure the interior. When the flat was replicated in a studio, I was amazed by how accurate some of the details were. Although there were no grotesque goblins on the wallpaper in the children's bedrooms, the kitchen cupboards were full of exactly accurate objects.

The green round metal tea caddy, and the milk jug with its thick blue and white horizontal stripes, took me back to childhood days. The pots and pans, and the knives and forks with faded yellow handles, all spoke of the past. As much as I always enjoyed walking around sets, it was odd to revisit my extreme youth. I spotted the designer and after congratulating him I asked, 'How long have you been psychic?'

'What do you mean?' he said.

'All the kitchen stuff is identical to what I grew up with.'

'Ah well,' he said. 'It's not difficult because there was so little choice in what people could buy in the 1950s that a lot of houses had this stuff.'

Other aspects of the production were not so harmonious. John and I had written up linking scenes between the clips that portrayed family life in Robert Owen House, with me playing a fictional version of my father, Tilly Vosburgh as my mother, and Timothy Bateson, a distinguished actor with a superbly rich and characterful voice, appeared as my fictional grandfather. Our family scenes were not performed in front of a live audience, that would have been disastrous. We were there to support the extracts, not compete with them. The deliberate absence of a laughter track informs the audience where we are pitching our family story in the context of the whole show.

Whenever John and I wrote together, I was in the habit of writing it all down in longhand and, because I've never yet learned to type, someone else would undertake the task of transferring my scrawl into print. I handed a member of the production team our handwritten script and was told, 'Fine, I'll get it back to you in a couple of days.'

A week before we began filming these family inserts, I received the latest version of the script, all typed up neatly. I didn't bother reading it until the next day, and when I eventually did, I had one of those jaw-dropping moments where your jaw not only drops, but it physically bounces back up off the carpet with such force it passes your face on its way upwards to the ceiling, before gravity eventually settles it back into a rough equilibrium with the rest of your head. I suspect my facial expression took on the characteristics of a heavily sedated salmon, as I leafed through the typed pages.

The opening piece to camera where, as the purple-jacketed presenter, I set up a tone and expectations for the programme ahead, had been completely rewritten. The care that John and I had taken had casually been thrown aside, and replaced with utter toss consisting of lame puns and weak non-jokes of such bad quality they immediately compromised the entire approach we were taking. To appear to be trying to be funny and failing would cast me in a terrible light, especially when we are about to see Tommy Cooper, Frankie Howerd and others excelling. Much better to keep the presentation fairly straight and have the humour in the family settings emerge through characterisation and familiarity. The programme, after all, won't be short of laughs.

But much worse was to follow. I turned the page. This time my jaw not only dropped, it flew out of the window and circled the moon. It didn't come back for several hours. Not only had the words for my speech to camera been completely changed, but also where I was delivering them from had been radically altered. Instead of standing by the kitchen door I was now, in our new script, sitting on the toilet with my trousers around my ankles. A perfect set-up for me to introduce *Dad's Army* while pretending to have a shit!

I went ballistic.

We had an emergency meeting the next morning. The member of the production team really thought they hadn't done anything wrong by totally rewriting our lines and placing me on the toilet. Their efforts were described as a 'discussion document', which prompted my furious reply, 'What the fuck's a discussion document, we're writing scripts here?'

What possessed this person to treat our work with such contempt I really don't know, but maybe they thought my introduction needed to be desperately funny and so suggested something desperate. I needed to be informative and entertaining at the top of the show, and the best way to do that is to not insult the intelligence of your audience. For a twenty-second speech, there is no need to panic. Moments like this were deeply upsetting because I cared so much about trying to get it right.

There was something about the mid-nineties and me. I appeared on the front cover of *Esquire* magazine and television executives were falling over each other offering me tantalising projects.

Have I Got News for You really hit its stride, and *Whose Line is it Anyway?* was also extremely popular, and alongside Lee Simpson and Richard Vranch, I played a two-week season at the London Palladium. The show we put on was a little rough and ready in places, in fact there's one or two moments principally involving me that make me cringe down to my boots whenever I recall them. But working at the Palladium over the course of a fortnight gave me the opportunity to use their legendary revolving stage, which I remembered fondly from all those waving performers circulating round at the end of every *Sunday Night at the London Palladium*. The Two Maxwells included.

Torvill and Dean had just triumphed at the Winter Olympics, which prompted a very happy thought in my head. If we used dry ice, I could stand still as the stage revolved unseen beneath me and look as if I was skating simply by extending one leg out in front of me.

By clouding the floor of the stage with dry ice the illusion was comical, but clearly it wasn't enough for me to simply circle round and round, we had to up the ante every time. I reappeared in front of the audience, this time reading a newspaper before disappearing through a gap in the wall, which was hiding one half of the revolving stage from the audience's view. Out of sight is where all the hard work took place. As I disappeared, half-a-dozen burly stage hands quickly placed an armchair, a side table and a working lamp on to the moving surface. Just before the above emerged into view, I jumped into the armchair and circled round while reading a book and making ice skating movements with my feet.

Again, I disappear from view, very careful not to get out of my armchair until the audience can no longer see me. I re-emerge seconds later – the lamp, armchair and side table are gone, and instead I'm playing pool on a pub-sized table, chalking up my cue and breaking into the pack.

This always got a huge laugh, but what the audience didn't see was the sheer physical effort needed to lift that table into place inside the eight seconds that they had available. This difficult operation was only possible if the revolving stage didn't exceed a certain speed.

When I looked at the sketch on television, the action seemed a little slow but it wasn't safe to go any faster. We should have speeded it up for the screen and re-arranged the music accordingly, but either way I loved doing that sketch. As the music started and I waited backstage to be revolved, I knew that for the next minute and a half I would be gently motoring through a comedy land-scape with one leg up in the air, sitting in an armchair and then playing pool.

Being flavour of the month meant that the TV offers I was getting ranged from the tempting to the downright barmy. It was the downright barmy that caught my eye.

Paul Spencer, a producer I had known from radio, had recently moved into television and he had a proposal that no sane man would touch with a bargepole.

He'd been contacted by Ray Galton and Alan Simpson, and it seemed that a friend of theirs had suggested they remake some of their old scripts, with myself playing the central role. The idea was to re-do some of the famous *Hancock's Half Hour* scripts in colour.

So I said, 'Well I'd love to meet them. I'm a long way from agreeing to something like this, but a meeting won't do any harm.' So we met up, four tall men together. I expressed my concern about the flak I would get critically for having the audacity to take on a script originally written for Tony, and they agreed there was a potential for disaster. After an amicable meeting we strolled to a nearby pub where, with Paul Spencer, we had a couple of pints.

Meeting men from the same working-class background as myself, who also knew the same parts of south London as me – Streatham, Morden, Mitcham, St Heliers Avenue – was extremely exciting. ITV were very keen to make a pilot episode, but Ray, Alan and I were more cautious. After our first meeting, they agreed to look through the old *Hancock* scripts to identify one that we might plausibly do. I wasn't yet convinced that it was a good idea, but I was open to persuasion. Ray and Alan suggested 'The Lift'.

I read the script and gave it some hard thought. On one hand, critics would have a field day attacking my attempt to 'do' Tony Hancock, who is rightly considered to be one of the greatest interpreters of comic material this country has ever seen. His performance of Ray and Alan's scripts, particularly on radio, are masterclasses in comic characterisation and timing.

There was no way I could begin to compete with what Tony had done, and so the sensible answer had to be 'No'.

And yet. On the other hand …

If I say yes to a one-off pilot, I'll have the magnificent experience of working with Ray Galton and Alan Simpson in the rehearsal room, just like Tony Hancock, Frankie Howerd, Les Dawson, Arthur Lowe and many others!

If I say no, I can spend the rest of my life telling people, 'I could have worked with Galton and Simpson, but in the end I decided not to risk it. I was worried about what people might say.'

I said yes to the pilot, although there was no way of knowing then that a major front page newspaper scandal would erupt during our week of rehearsal, stunning myself and the rest of the cast.

'The Lift' was one of the last shows Galton and Simpson had written for Tony Hancock, and would be our pilot. On the first day of rehearsal Alan said, 'This is the first time I've been in a rehearsal room in seventeen years.' Alan had interests outside show business, including being life president of the Hampton and Richmond Football Club.

The large cast gathered around a long trellis table in a not-too-draughty church hall in Kensington. Amongst them was Peter Jones, who I had met several times while recording episodes of Radio 4's *Just a Minute*. Our producer, Paul Spencer, made the introductions and we began the first read through.

The rehearsal period for 'The Lift' was the usual five days, but towards the end of the week the actors sitting around that table would be fearing the abrupt ending of my television career.

On the Thursday evening I received one of those phone calls that you remember for the rest of your life. We had finished recording *Have I Got News for You* at the London Studios and were enjoying drinks at the bar, with Ian and Angus, when a member of the production team approached me. He said, 'Your wife Caroline has just phoned and could you ring her back immediately.' Then, as now, I didn't own a mobile phone, so I borrowed somebody else's and phoned home and this is what she told me.

'Paul, I've just had a phone call from a publicity agent who says that tomorrow's *Daily Mirror* is publishing six pages about your cocaine habit.'

'What?'

'It won't be in the first editions because they want to delay their rivals getting hold of it for as long as possible,' she said.

'But I don't have a cocaine habit,' I said. It was true, I've never been a sniffer.

'That's what I told her,' Caroline said.

'So how can there be six pages on something I don't do?'

'I don't know. It must just be a rumour,' she said.

'Six pages of rumour?' I said.

'Yes, I know it does sound odd. Oh, and there's photographs as well,' she added.

'Photographs of a rumour?' I said. I was confused and slightly in a state of shock.

'OK, I'll be home soon.' I handed the mobile phone back to its owner. How could there possibly be photographs of me indulging in my non-existent habit? Is it someone who looks like me? No, that's not credible.

Faked photos perhaps? My head on someone else's body!

I'll have to hire lawyers, put out press statements, this is going to be a nightmare. How could this happen? Why is this happening?

Then I had another thought. Waterloo station! Looking at my watch, it was half past eleven. The next day's papers appeared at Waterloo station at around about midnight. The station was only ten minutes walk away, so I said my goodbyes and left. I stood around, as late night drunks and business people scuttled quickly across the forecourt towards their home bound trains. One newspaper seller, a solitary man, was opening up his bundles of newsprint, cutting open the plastic strips with practised ease and scissors. I watched him from a distance as he went about his routine. Once he was done, I wandered over casually, trying to desperately look like I wasn't splashed all over the front page of the *Daily Mirror*.

Which I wasn't. I bought a copy and there was no mention of me anywhere.

The whole business was just some stupid joke.

It was only then that I remembered Caroline's words 'it won't be in the first editions'.

I tucked the first *Daily Mirror* of the night under my arm, descended those long white steps back down to street level, and hailed a passing taxi. Once back at the house I still couldn't rest.

'It can't be part of a blackmail plot,' I reasoned, 'because I can't be blackmailed over something I haven't done.'

'You need to get some sleep,' Caroline said.

I looked in the bathroom cabinet and found a quarter of a sleeping pill. It was two o'clock in the morning and I needed to be up at eight to face whatever the day would bring. I took the quarter and fell thankfully into sleep.

*

The next morning I woke up with a start. I went straight to the bedroom window and looked out on to our quiet suburban street. There was something very noticeable about the crowd of press photographers that were gathered outside our front gate. They weren't there! Nobody. None. The whole thing had been a hoax, or just a strange rumour. I'd got worked up over nothing.

The car turned up to take me to rehearsals. On the way there I asked the driver to stop at a newsagents. As soon as I walked in and saw the front page of the *Daily Mirror* with the word 'Cocaine' emblazoned across it, my heart skipped a beat. The front page headline carried the sensational exclusive that the Arsenal foot-baller and Highbury favourite Paul MERSON had a cocaine habit, and the story was on pages 1, 2, 3, 4, 5, 6, 7 and 8.

The newsagent must have thought I was a particularly heartless individual, because I was chuckling away to myself as I bought two copies.

But nobody was laughing by the time I arrived at the rehearsal room. Some of the other actors had already arrived and were huddled together an anxious group. One of them had misheard the Radio 2 news headlines and firmly believed it was me that had been exposed. There was much relieved laughter all around when I arrived flourishing the front cover of the *Mirror*. I briefly told the cast around me the story of the previous night. The initial phone call. The visit to Waterloo station and then getting back home and being unable to sleep.

'It was then,' I said, 'that I took a sleeping pill.'

'Oh,' said Peter Jones, 'so it's started then!'

The fun bubbled along for a few minutes and then peaked when our last member of the cast arrived in a flurry. 'Oh my God I've just heard the news,' he said.

I went over to him, sniffed a couple of times and said, 'Have you got any coke?'

Playing the lead in the middle of a highly experienced cast was one hell of a big step for me. I had performed plenty of sketch comedy where I had also written the material, but this was something completely out of my range of experience. But there was a lot of goodwill in the rehearsal room and the presence of Ray and Alan every day helped to make the process a joy.

When we first sat down to read the script Ray said, 'If there's any lines you're not sure about please do say. We'd be more than happy to change them.' A generous remark, but I certainly wasn't going to start suggesting lines. I had far too much respect for the original material and after all, that's what we were doing, performing Galton and Simpson, not a script we had bashed about a bit in the rehearsal room. A couple of actors suggested changes, and Ray and Alan listened politely, and if they preferred the alteration they would agree but generally the scripts remained unaltered.

The story is very simple. A bunch of people get into a lift, which then gets stuck between floors. One of the occupants is a bit of a loud-mouthed big head, determined to keep up morale. 'We're coming out of this lift singing mate,' was one of my lines that I cherished during rehearsal. At the end we were released by firemen, and during the technical rehearsal I ad-libbed a line as we walked off, 'Right I'm ready for my counselling.'

Ray thought this was good and that I should keep it in. Regretfully on the night, I forgot. Nevertheless I was immensely relieved to have got through the show, and the audience responded warmly.

All the important people were happy. A series was commissioned – Oh blimey! After some discussion between us, we settled on the seven scripts that, along with our already completed pilot, would give us a series of eight.

Five of the shows were written for Tony Hancock. One for Bernard Cribbins, one for Stanley Baxter, and one for Jimmy Edwards. We filmed the first script 'Impasse' in a very quiet country lane nestling in the Derbyshire hills.

On that first day of location, Ray and Alan talked of their memories of filming *The Rebel* with Tony Hancock. The two of them stood on a green hillock overlooking a country lane bordered by low stone walls, although it was October they were bathed in glorious sunshine.

Alan said to Ray, 'Do you remember the day we first met George Sanders?' George Sanders, a Hollywood star from the 1940s and 50s, was playing a major role in their first film. Ray and Alan were impressionable teenagers when George was playing The Saint in a series of B movies, and couldn't believe he was appearing in a film written by them.

I completely understood their boyish enthusiasm because I shared it. I was working with Ray and Alan who wrote *Hancock's Half Hour*, a show I used to tape off the radio on a reel-to-reel tape recorder. I held the microphone up to the speaker, shushing Mum and Dad if they dared walk into the room during the thirty-minute broadcast. I bought the tape recorder from a boy at school specifically to record radio shows that, in an era before this material was commercially available, could not otherwise be heard again. Ray and Alan were prolific writers. Hundreds of scripts poured from them over the years.

On very rare occasions, they got stuck. The two shared an office and the usual practice was that Alan sat at the typewriter while they threw lines back and forth between them. Once they both agreed on a line, Alan typed it into the script. A show a week was their usual rate. They were in the middle of writing twelve different scripts for a series called *Comedy Playhouse*. Each one had a different premise and was cast accordingly. But one week nothing came.

Whole hours passed without words being spoken. The two men desperately trying to think of a situation that could be developed into half an hour. Wednesday became Thursday became Friday. Then, in the nick of time, the comedy gods said in heavenly union, 'We can't have this. We've got to help the boys out with a little divine intervention in the shape of friend and actor Graham Stark.' And so the gods intervened. Graham turned up at Ray and Alan's office late on Friday afternoon with a newspaper clipping in his hand. He said, 'I cut this out of *The Times* today. I thought it might amuse you.'

It did.

It was a report about an incident in a country lane. Two cars approaching from either end of the lane met in the middle with no room to pass on either side. One car was a simple family saloon and the other was a Rolls-Royce. Both drivers refused to back up and the situation deteriorated into threats of fisticuffs.

Bingo! Ray and Alan immediately knew they had their premise. They started work fresh the next morning and wrote the entire script in less than three hours!

And here I was, thirty-five years later, standing in beautiful autumnal sunshine filming it.

The weather held for the rest of the filming days and the finished show turned out well. 'Impasse' didn't create any major problems for me. The script hadn't been written for Tony Hancock, and I was reasonable casting for the part I was playing.

The first script we recorded in the studio was another matter. This was a Hancock script. In 'Twelve Angry Men' I was all at sea at times. My main problem being the hugely iconic speech that Tony, as the foreman, delivers to the rest of the jury.

'Does Magna Carta mean nothing to you? Did she die in vain? A brave Hungarian peasant girl who forced King John to sign the pledge at Runnymede and close the boozers at half past ten.'

All I could hear when I read the words was Tony's voice and his delivery. I made sure that I was steering clear of any kind of impersonation, but I think this inhibited me. There was a natural rhythm to the lines that I was deliberately avoiding in case I fell into a poor copy.

I'm not quite sure what I did with the speech, but I'm sure it wasn't particularly effective.

From this challenging moment in our first studio recording of the series I started to improve. It was a severe learning curve, but I learnt to relax with the lines and by the time I recorded the final show in the series 'The Bedsitter', I was on top of what I was doing. This last script featured a cast of one. Me.

It was a funny moment that first morning, when I walked into the rehearsal room as the sole member of the cast. It was obvious that the sooner I learnt the script, the better. Unlike the other seven shows, I had no actors around to give me cue lines. At my suggestion, on the night of the recording we placed a homburg hat and a coat with an astrakhan collar on a coatrack by the door. These items were part of Tony's costume in the 1950s. The night of the recording went like a dream, I never once forgot a line and I found a freedom walking around the set on my own. I was tremendously relieved afterwards, and Alan paid me the ultimate compliment by saying, 'You didn't miss a laugh.'

We finished the series on a real high. Although the critics didn't like it, at least the audience stayed with it. Someone recently pointed out to me that Wikipedia says the programmes were 'very badly received by critics and public'. On the contrary, our viewing figures for the first series averaged seven million viewers per show, with the pilot, 'The Lift', which went out halfway through the run, getting more than ten million. We were the highest-rated ITV sitcom of the year. And that's why a second series was commissioned. In the cut-throat world of commercial television, that only happens if you're a hit with the viewers.

In the midst of the two series, Caroline and I separated and were divorced a couple of years later. When we first met, I needed support and encouragement. When I grew back into confidence, maybe that changed the dynamic of our relationship. We just grew apart over the course of half-a-dozen years. Two famous people married to each other is absolute catnip to the tabloid press, and once the news broke that we were separating we had a photographer and a journalist from the *Daily Mirror* standing outside our front gate waiting for us to emerge.

Every so often the journalist would ring our door bell and speak to us via the intercom. At one point, he and the photographer made a big show of leaving in their car. The way they slammed the car doors and drove off at high speed down our quiet suburban road was too obvious a ploy to fall for. Still, we needed to leave the house and so, fully expecting a photographer to leap out at us, we did. He was hiding exactly where I thought he would be, so when he leapt out at me I didn't react or lash out in anger, which would have made for a much better photograph. This is a standard move designed to provoke a reaction.

On separation, Caroline stayed in the house and I found a hidden-away flat in Fulham. Somewhere the press couldn't find me. Piers Morgan, then editor of the *Daily Mirror*, was desperate. He phoned a producer on *Have I Got News for You*.

'Hi, its Piers Morgan here, we're looking for Paul, have you got an address for him?'

The producer told the truth. 'If he's not at his home address, I don't know where he is.'

'I know you're lying,' said Piers.

Of course, the press knew that I would have to go to the London Studios on the Southbank the following Thursday to record *Have I Got News for You*. On Thursday morning, several photographers took up their position opposite the studios. I phoned one of the producers and told him I would be arriving about four. 'There's a load of photographers outside the building,' he said.

'Don't worry,' I said. 'I've got a plan.'

And it worked to perfection. At four o'clock I walked through the revolving door of the London Studios into the foyer, where I met a totally startled PR woman who said, 'How did you get in here?' And then she looked over to the photographers on the other side of the road who were chatting amongst themselves, totally oblivious to my arrival. 'How did you get in here,' she repeated before adding, 'without them seeing you?'

I said, 'Let's get into the lift and out of sight, and I'll tell you all about it.'

'It was simple human psychology,' I told her, taking on a Colombo-like air. 'I reckoned that the photographers would be expecting me to arrive by chauffeur-driven car or taxi. That's how famous people arrive at television studios. And there is an underground car park, which you can drive directly into. Every time a car pulled up, no doubt the flashers picked up their cameras before disappointedly lowering them when it became obvious the passenger wasn't me. My plan to slip past them unnoticed was simple.

'I took a taxi to Waterloo Bridge and then walked alongside the Thames towards my destination, before cutting back up the side of the London Studios building, and walking fifty yards before entering through the revolving door of the main entrance. The photographers weren't looking at pedestrians and so missed me completely.'

I must say it was a rather joyous moment. If it wasn't for the fact that my marriage had fallen apart.

After recording that night's episode, I took a taxi to The Comedy Store and noticed a moped rider was following our vehicle. I knew that at least one tabloid newspaper was keen to establish my domestic whereabouts, and so I was not surprised to spot company. I had phoned The Comedy Store in advance and they knew what to do once I'd arrived. I entered through the main entrance, noticing the moped rider parking up on the other side of the road. This wasn't paranoia, this was the real thing. Noting the moped driver's position, I quickly walked down the stairs, through the club, and out through a service door further down the street and behind my pursuer. Proper cat-and-mouse stuff. I walked quickly away and caught a taxi back to the basic flat I was renting in Fulham High Street.

As my marriage to Caroline collapsed, I began a relationship with Sarah Parkinson. Sarah had been Caroline's understudy during *Live Bed Show*, but throughout the three-month run there was only one occasion when the two of us had had a conversation. Caroline was always eager to get a taxi back home as soon as the show was over, and so that was our custom.

Divorces are never pleasant, and the best of times with Caroline were life-enhancing and joyous. She really helped me to regain my confidence once I'd left the Maudsley, for which I am eternally grateful.

20

On the Cliff

Within a year, Sarah and I moved in together. I had bought a house in the New Kings Road, which was a ten-minute stroll to where I was born in Parsons Green, close enough to Chelsea's ground at Stamford Bridge to hear the crowd roar every time the home team scored. It felt marvellous to be back in an area I was so familiar with. We were within fifteen minutes walk of the beautiful Bishops Park, with its breathtaking river views and magnificent Putney Bridge, and that bend in the river around to the left that promises deeper countryside beyond.

Living so close to all this was ideal motivation to get myself fit and lose some weight. I had put a lot on during a tour in 1998. Being driven around in the back of a van, eating late-night burgers in hotel rooms, soon fattens you up if you're not exercising, and I wasn't. It was a lonely way to tour. Being onstage was the best bit, although I would have welcomed another performer on at *any* point – particularly in King's Lynn. My one-man show at the Corn Exchange started in the most bizarre fashion.

As usual, I stood in the wings as the house music faded and the auditorium lights darkened. My tour manager made the announcement on the off-stage microphone, 'Ladies and Gentlemen, will you please welcome Paul Merton,' I then usually walked onstage to enthusiastic applause but, in King's Lynn, I walked on to absolute silence. Nothing! I stood in the middle of the stage and looked at 600 very quiet people. Not one of them clapped or cheered or made any noise at all. It completely threw me.

'Why did nobody clap when I first walked on?' I thought to myself. *'They can't be surprised to see me, my name is on the title, "Paul Merton – And this is me". It must be my appearance that has surprised them into silence. I'm six foot two and often people say "Oh you're taller than I thought you would be" so maybe that's it.'* As I'm telling my opening jokes, I imagine a review of this gig appearing in a local paper under the headline 'Man stuns crowd with height'. The audience kept up the silence throughout the first half. After the interval there were some laughs, but then there's always people keen to spoil it for the rest of us.

The one-man show weighed more like two by the end of the tour, so I endeavoured to get the weight off walking alongside the river Thames in Bishops Park every morning. It hasn't escaped me that I seem to come back to Bishops Park time and time again. Perhaps it's the view of the river that draws me. The view of Putney Bridge was the first beautiful scene I ever set my eyes on. Or perhaps it is the river itself. Forever grey, lapping against the matching grey steps that appear and vanish according to the height of the tide. Steps that lie behind a locked gate comprised of iron railings. All this is unchanged since my earliest childhood memory. The river will always lap up these steps and there will forever be something white and plastic floating in the water.

I read in the *Daily Mirror* that 'Paul Merton owns a house in the country'. I reflected on the good news for a moment before I remembered that it wasn't true. I thought about it some more. Perhaps a weekend cottage, somewhere quiet, away from the constant traffic noise of the New Kings Road, might be a good idea. We found a lovely place. It was a small house perched on the top of a cliff, with view of the sea and the surrounding rolling countryside. I put an offer in and it was accepted. The sale went through and I couldn't believe I owned such a property. Eighteen years of my childhood, and ten of my early years of adulthood, were spent living in tight confined spaces with no garden, and so this now seemed beyond whatever I thought would ever be possible. To walk across a springy green lawn in your bare feet, to hear owls hooting in nearby trees, to glimpse a badger in a car light. All these delights of the countryside were new experiences for me.

That summer, quite a bit of which we spent in the welcome, healthy peace of the new house, I was approached by a neighbour to officially open the new village hall. Now, if you know me, you'll be a bit surprised by this. It's not my thing. In fact I've always vowed never to get involved in opening things … I'm not one for making public appearances in the context of being a famous person to be gawped at.

I can remember going to a garden fete around the age of ten, which was being opened by a rotund television comic of the day. A small but hostile element in the crowd had turned up to jeer at the man off the telly. As soon as he was the introduced as 'the man who needs no introduction' somebody shouted out, 'Wotcha fatty.'

That memory alone was enough to put me off the whole idea! Especially as I still wasn't the thinnest specimen. I politely declined the offer to officially open the new village hall. And yet the neighbour kept asking. I don't know how it happened, but at one point

I said 'maybe', just to try and finish that particular conversation – and that was enough to make it all official and everyone was thrilled. Apart from me. In fact, I'd felt so pushed into it that I had mischief on my mind.

The village put up a load of posters advertising the event. 'Come and see Paul Merton in person officially open the new village hall' they proclaimed. When we got to the venue thirty minutes before the opening ceremony, there were already hundreds of people gathered around on a lovely summer's day, determined to find out what a twit looked like. I would not disappoint.

Sarah and I drove to the village hall and I made my presence known to the organisers, who were frankly rather daunted by the size of the crowd that had turned up. They were nervous. I casually asked if they had a public address system, and I was shown a little plastic microphone and a tiny loudspeaker that looked like they belonged to some young child's toy disco. Clearly inadequate, I rejected this artificial aid to volume and elected to project my voice instead.

The manner of the Posh Bossy Man who was running the show was brusque and discourteous. 'You are ten minutes late,' he said. 'You were expected forty minutes before the ceremony.' I thought this rather rich considering I hadn't actually ever properly agreed to open their village hall in the first place, but I let it go.

They had a box for me to stand on so at least my head would be well above the crowd. I sat in the village hall for a while, thinking about what I might say. Without any preamble I was taken by the arm by Posh Bossy Man, who steered me towards a line of little women who were all dressed up to the nines. In high heels and colourful floral print dresses. He indicated them to me.

'These are the dignitaries,' he said.

'Dignitaries,' I said, rather startled by the very notion of such a creature attending the opening of a village hall, 'and how do you become a dignitary?' I said, 'Do you wake up one morning to find that you have become dignified overnight?' Quite rightly, they just looked at me with puzzlement. As I climbed on to the box, fully expecting a beery voice from the crowd to shout out 'Wotcha fatty', the devil got into me. I started off non-controversially.

'Good afternoon, Ladies and Gentlemen, it's a beautiful sunny day, which reminds me of my favourite joke.'

My favourite joke at the time had nothing to do with beautiful sunny days, but I told it anyway.

'A man goes into a restaurant and he orders a bowl of soup. The waiter comes over with the soup, but he's got his thumb stuck in it. The customer says, "What are you doing?"

'And the waiter says, "I do that to keep my thumb warm."

'"Keeping your thumb warm? Why don't you shove it up your arse?" says the customer.

'And the waiter said … "I do when I'm in the kitchen."'

I got a huge laugh from the main body of the crowd, many of whom were men with pints of beer in their hands and stomachs. Simultaneously to my left, three dignitaries audibly gasped in astonishment, and one of them reeled alarmingly as if caught in a sudden stiff wind.

'However, that aside, I'm very pleased to be able to announce that this magnificently newly built spacious facility is now officially open.' I hit the last nine words with a flourish of the right arm towards the structure behind me, which got me the round of applause I needed to finish on. I gave them a wave, and stepped off the box and straight into a now very angry Posh Bossy Man. He pointed at four women of a certain age, who were all standing in line wearing the most extraordinary hats and beneath them totally stunned expressions.

Closer analysis revealed these hats to be homemade Easter bonnets. One had yellow baby chicks, made of felt, placed on twigs, emanating from a nest nestling within a straw boater. Another conjured up meadow flowers and ivy, trailing across the top of a beret. 'Which one's best?' barked the PBM.

'What?' I said, boggling at the sight in front of me.

'You have to pick the winner – which is the best hat?' I pointed to the woman who looked most scared of me and said, 'Her.' A photographer who had been snapping away during my speech quickly lined me up alongside the winner for another photo, but Posh Bossy Man was having none of it. 'No pictures, no pictures,' he said to the photographer, who had been sent by the local paper to record the event for posterity. As we left I heard PBM demand the film from the photographer's camera. The overwhelmingly positive result of the whole adventure was, as planned, that I was never asked to 'open' anything in that area again.

Much to my delight, there was no photograph in the local paper the following week, so it's almost like it never happened.

I'm sure some people present on the day wished it hadn't.

A few days later I had a meeting with Jimmy Mulville at Hat Trick productions, who asked me if I was interested in taking over the hosting of *Room 101*, a programme that Nick Hancock had brought from radio and had made three series of for BBC2, but who was now keen to do something else. I immediately said 'yes' and offered up a couple of ideas that I thought would improve the presentation. Firstly, in Nick's version the objects were consigned to Room 101 via a slow moving conveyor belt, which dropped them off the edge. I suggested a trap door with a lever on the front pulled by me, which gave us the power of instantly banishing people and things into Room 101.

I also pitched Jimmy a short film that John Irwin and I had sketched out. I'd had the title, 'The Suicidal Dog', for ages and it was an unusual movie in that at no point does the dog do anything cute. Quite the opposite. He sets out to kill his owner. I was keen to direct. I had several moments that I had storyboarded and thought it would work well, but the overall story was missing a key ingredient. Why did the dog want to kill his owner? Then it struck me. Castration. What more motivation would a killer need than to have his testicles removed without prior consultation? Jimmy liked it, and asked if I knew any DOPs (directors of photography) and I said, 'Well, I've recently been reading the autobiography of Jack Cardiff who was this country's first Technicolor cameraman and he's still going strong.'

'How old is he?' asked Jimmy.

'Mid-eighties I think. He's worked with everybody. Orson Welles, Alfred Hitchcock, Marilyn Monroe, Laurence Olivier, Humphrey Bogart, he's photographed them all.'

'Well, we should meet him,' said Jimmy.

Jack was visiting London a couple of weeks later, and so I met up with him in the foyer of a small hotel in Bloomsbury. He was in fine shape. He was slim, well turned out, extremely alert, with a finely developed sense of humour. I liked him immediately. I liked him even more when he said he would do my film about a dog who'd had its balls cut off. My eyes sparkled with delight. And I certainly felt extremely light headed once I was back out on the pavement outside the hotel.

The first few minutes of the film were to be in black and white, and Jack suggested I should look at the various kinds of black-and-white film stock available. He shot a couple of camera tests for me to look at and I made my choice. We had a five-day shooting schedule. The film was very low budget and partly set in a fairground. The fairground attractions were particularly underwhelming, but I was enjoying the experience.

And so was Jack. It had been a while since he'd worked on location with a film crew, and here he was totally in his element, surrounded by colleagues, as bright as a button and bursting with energy. In the shot where our male lead, Steve Steen, approaches a tatty looking carousel with wonderment in his eyes, I wanted the effect of different coloured lights reflected in his face, and Jack was the first to grab a silver reflector and start bouncing light in Steve's direction.

Later in the afternoon, I needed an extreme wide shot of the brow of a hill, above which first appears a bunch of helium filled balloons and then Steve, running towards the camera. I described the shot to Jack and he looked at me, then up to the vast cloud filled sky and said, 'Only God can light this scene.'

Jack produced a piece of blue smoked glass from his pocket and looked up to the sky. 'Judging by the speed of those clouds,' he said, 'and looking at the gaps coming towards us I would say you will have twenty-five minutes of sunshine in fifteen minutes from now.'

I asked my first assistant to start his stopwatch as we prepared for the shot. I looked to the sky, and as the sun peeked out from behind the clouds, I asked him to give me the time that had elapsed since Jack's prediction.

'Fourteen minutes and forty-three seconds,' said the first assistant. We all laughed and clapped. I shook Jack's hand. 'Now that's what I call expertise,' I said.

Jack said, 'I could have been more accurate but I didn't want to show off.'

The Suicidal Dog, a very short film at twelve minutes long, premiered at the Raindance Film Festival in London in 2000, and went on general release to cinemas in Leeds, Cardiff and Bristol, where it supported *Billy Elliot* on the big screen.

Sarah and I hosted a wrap party at our New Kings Road house, and Jack – who regaled us with anecdotes all night – was immediately struck by an object I had hanging on my living-room wall. He was intrigued and fascinated by, what seemed to him and our other guests, something straight out of a science fiction movie. It was a large flat-screen television. Now a common vision, but back in 2000 it was one of the first in the country.

Jack was completely mesmerised by it. To demonstrate the picture quality, I played him the first few minutes of a film that he himself had photographed, *A Matter of Life and Death* starring David Niven, and written and directed by Michael Powell and Emeric Pressburger.

When our hero jumps out of his stricken plane and into clouds, there is a dissolve through to a top shot of the sea lapping against the shore. Jack asked me to pause the DVD at that point.

'There,' he said, 'that's where I breathed on the camera lens. That misted up the image, and when it cleared we were looking at the sea.'

Jack had a favourite story that revealed the ruthlessness that surrounds the picture business. Back in the 1950s, he got involved with a film project that hoped to replicate the success of Errol Flynn as Robin Hood by employing the same actor to play William Tell. The only trouble is, it is twenty years further down the line and Errol isn't as fit as he used to be. In fact, a few days into filming, Mr Flynn collapses and is taken to hospital. An extremely worried producer speaks to the doctor with Jack standing by.

'Doctor,' he says, 'when will Mr Flynn be fit to resume filming? Each day lost costs me a fortune.'

The doctor looks at the producer and says, 'My patient is very, very ill, I don't know how much longer he has got left. He'll certainly never be able to work again.'

'No doctor, you don't understand,' replied the producer. 'We're making a movie. Death is not an option.'

The film never got made.

Life was good.

We celebrated New Year's arrival at our country house. We walked in the fields and looked back up the hill to where our house was. On the way back home, walking up a country road, we saw a dog trotting towards us. We turned up our driveway and to our amusement the dog followed us. We opened up the house and the dog followed us into the kitchen. The three of us then ambled into the conservatory. She seemed to be a friendly sort, although a little low on energy. It was a cold night and we didn't know how far she had walked, but she seemed content to stay with us.

I have no idea what sort of dog she was, but she was fit, with a short grey coat, and stood at medium height for a dog. She didn't want any food or water but just seemed to want to be with us. To share our company. Or perhaps she was trying to wish us a Happy New Year, we said whimsically to each other. Although we were giving the dog shelter, it felt like she was actually looking after us.

The next morning, it was clear she was ready to leave. She was sitting patiently by the front door. I opened it for her, and off she trotted down the red brick steps and down the driveway. I felt an unbearable sadness watching her go.

21

Defying the Clouds

In early January, Sarah told me she had found a couple of lumps in her breast. On our return to London we saw our GP, who referred us to the Charing Cross Hospital on the Fulham Palace Road. The specialist ran some tests and the news was as bad as it could be. Sarah had cancer. Sarah underwent a procedure to determine how far it had advanced. While her condition was investigated, I wandered around aimlessly.

I walked to St Augustine's Church, which was only a few minutes away. It was the church in Fulham that I used to be taken to as a child. The church was empty inside. I sat down three rows from the back. I relaxed my shoulders, and let out a deep breath. A moment of quiet solitude. Within moments, the mood was broken by a bustling woman rattling keys. 'The church is closed, there's nothing for you here, the church is closed.' She was right about that, so I left without a murmur.

Once Sarah had recovered sufficiently from the anaesthetic, I took her home, and two days later we were in the specialist's office once again. He had the test results. His face told us the story. The cancer was fast growing. It had got past the lymphatic glands. The words swirled round my head, as the blood flushed from my face. He talked about the treatment, and recommended both radiotherapy and chemotherapy. I formed a sentence. 'And will these treatments cure Sarah?'

The doctor replied, 'Well, that's very much what they're designed to do.' The subtlety of language didn't escape me. His answer didn't sound like a yes to me.

We looked at each other, struggling to take it all in. It was a quarter to five in the afternoon. Three hours later, I was in a television studio asking Ricky Gervais what he would like to put into *Room 101*.

Sarah undertook to beat her illness with the thoroughness with which she tackled any task. The first thing she did was ask for a second opinion, and that was a dispiriting experience I can tell you. We went to a hospital in the Brompton Road in the middle of a thunderstorm. The doctor quickly confirmed the diagnosis with the complaining remark, 'I'm seeing more than my fair share of young women with cancer.' He, without feeling or tact, confirmed that radiotherapy and chemotherapy were appropriate. His attitude certainly helped to make up Sarah's mind.

As we stood on the steps of the hospital looking down on to the rain-sodden street, Sarah announced with some determination, 'I'm not going to have chemo or radio, I'm not going to be poisoned or burnt.'

'But if you don't,' I said my voice erupting with passion, 'you will die.'

'I'm not going to end up bald in a bed,' she said, with determination.

'Then I will support you,' I replied.

We resolved to look into things and get as much information as possible before making any decisions.

Life became full of uncertainties, and not just in terms of Sarah's health. Without warning, another part of my world suddenly turned upside down too. We were in Cornwall. I'd recorded a couple of episodes of *Just a Minute* in the Fowey Festival, and we had decided to take advantage of the warm weather and have a little three-day break. On the Sunday night we were staying in a small hotel. I turned on the television to check the latest news on teletext. I read the main headline three times to make sure I wasn't hallucinating. I said to Sarah, 'You'll never forget where you were when you first heard this news.' She looked up at me. 'I've just read on teletext that Angus Deayton has been caught with a prostitute doing cocaine.'

'What?' said Sarah. 'It can't be.'

'It says it on the front page of the *News of the World*.'

'Oh no, how terrible,' she said.

'I'm stunned,' I said. We went downstairs. There was a copy of the *News of the World* at reception, and I picked it up casually as if I might have a vague interest in scanning the headlines. There was the story in all of its luridness. We sat and ate quietly. The next day we moved to another hotel, in Tintagel, memorably sited on high cliffs, above a sea which raged and foamed against jagged rocks. A low mist hung above the grey swirling ocean. I was looking at this view from our bedroom window as I spoke on the phone to one of the many producers associated with *Have I Got News for You*.

'Hello,' I said, 'I expect things are very lively back at HQ.'

'Yes they are,' said the producer, 'and we were wondering whether you were going to mention the Angus thing on the programme.'

'Of course I'm going to mention it!' I said. 'We have to. Not only am I going to mention it, I'm thinking of having the front page made up as a T-shirt.'

The producer laughed nervously as I explained my reasons.

'Firstly, we have to mention it because we're a show based on the week's news and the story is all over the tabloids. If we don't, Angus will get attacked, quite rightly, along the lines of he can dish it out but he can't take it. Then he's fundamentally weakened and the story becomes about the future of the programme, and does the BBC condone this sort of behaviour, and it drags on, and becomes messier by the hour, until a resignation or sacking becomes inevitable. Or …' I said, '… and this is a big Or. I can rip the piss out of him and we'll all have a few big laughs at his expense. And it might be uncomfortable in places, but it will help him enormously in the long run if he's seen to suffer. It's not a case of laughing it off, but if he has a bit of a hard time on screen then it's done with. We've got two more shows after this next one, so the aim has to be to get him and us through to the end of the series, where we will find much calmer waters. And by the time the autumn series arrives it will be old news.'

'You've really thought about this,' said the producer on the other end of the line.

'I'm on holiday,' I said, 'I've had plenty of time to think.'

On the night of the next recording, the atmosphere in the studio was intense. Three hundred people in the audience sat with bated breath. Some of them journalists, discretely making notes. The theme music played and the lights came up. Everybody was on the edge of their seat wondering if the unspeakable will be spoken, and when?

This was another question the producer had put to me on the phone. 'When's a good time to mention it?' he asked. My answer was, 'We've got to do it straight away, before somebody in the audience shouts out or a guest panellist mentions it. It has to be us. We have to take the bull by the horns. Whatever the first question is, give it to Ian and then I'll interrupt with "Never mind all that" and then we're up and running.'

'Is that a bit soon in the programme?' asked another one of the team, displaying customary caution.

'No,' I replied, 'it has to be done immediately and I'll do it.' Which is what happened on the night. There were many big laughs at Angus's expense, with the biggest one coming when I unzipped my fleece jacket down the middle to reveal the front page of the *News of the World* printed on a big white T-shirt. It was a quick reveal deliberately at the end of the programme, so the image was a fleeting one and of course the audience went mad for it.

It wasn't a very comfortable experience for Angus, but afterwards in hospitality he understood that making it funny for the audience was by far the best way of dealing with the whole desperate situation.

'Thank you for making it funny,' he said. I didn't think we'd had any other choice. Hopefully, now we'd done it for one show, we wouldn't have to make any references to it all in the next one.

And this is what we did. The studio audience expected more Angus stuff from Ian and myself, but there wasn't any. We could hardly be accused of going easy on him when you considered his treatment the previous week.

The last programme of the series went well and now I thought the storm could pass. That was my wish. A large part of *Have I Got*

News for You's success was down to the three regular people and the interaction between them. I always tried to turn Angus into my straight man, a role he didn't always enjoy inhabiting, but he was a model of consistency who directly presented the show to the public in a very engaging and beautifully timed manner. We had reached the end of the series and there would now be a four-month gap before we returned. We all looked forward to returning with Angus as our host. Ian was of like mind, and believed that hopefully the worst was behind us.

The new series of *Have I Got News for You* started in the autumn of 2002, and to coincide with this one of the tabloids printed new accusations about Angus's private Life. We had survived the first revelations but, with a second story, this time there was no escape. We couldn't repeat what we'd done before and, even though I was happy to downplay the references, the guests thought it was very amusing to mention them. But you could tell from the audience response that we had gone past the point where they would laugh uproariously at Angus's predicament.

The first time around, it was hilarious because he was the authority figure caught with his trousers down, but you can't sustain that approach indefinitely. It stops being funny. The guests had no such concerns, and when Christine Hamilton challenged him on his repeated use of the word 'disgraced' to describe her disgraced husband, ex-Tory MP Neil Hamilton, the game was up.

'If he's disgraced, what are you?' she said. Angus looked into the lens of the camera and said, 'Disgraced, I suppose.'

He had become the wrong person to deliver a weekly script criticising people's actions and foibles. The recording the following week was Angus's last, a sad, low-key affair. An era was over. Angus had been an excellent host for twelve years, and had played a huge part in the programme's massive success, but the immediate problem was how were we going to get through the rest of the series without a regular chairman.

There was one obvious choice as a one-off replacement and I said 'yes' immediately. I had no worries about presenting the show. It was a well-oiled machine, and I had watched it being produced from the sidelines for a long time. In some respects, my job would be easier – with a team of five writers putting together the autocue script, for once I wouldn't be attempting to conjure up comedy out of thin air.

The day before the recording, as was the custom, the host met up with the producers to work on the presenter's script, which the writers were working on in another room. I love working in a team of people, so after looking through the material, I said, 'A lot of this is very good.'

'Yes it is,' said one of the producers, as a piece of paper was handed to him by a member of the production. 'Ah,' he said, 'here are some more options for the opening gag.'

'What a magical process,' I said. 'So where are the writers, are they faxing this stuff in?'

'No,' said the producer, 'they're in the writers room.'

'Where's that?' I asked.

'It's the room two doors down on the left,' he said, looking at me slightly oddly.

'Well I had better say hello, hadn't I? Seeing as they're doing all the hard work,' I said.

He looked at me again. 'Well, it's never happened before,' he said, but I thought he was joking. I trotted down the corridor and popped my head around the door of the writers room, and said to a startled looking bunch of scruffs, 'I need five jokes about a

Volkswagen, a Scotsman and a chicken up a tree in fifteen minutes.'
Before they could answer, the door was closed and I was gone.

Fifteen minutes later I was back. 'OK,' I said, 'the Volkswagen
is now a Bentley, the Scotsman is still a Scotsman, but the chicken
up the tree is now a horse in a synagogue.'

This got the laugh I was looking for, so this time I properly said
'hello and good morning' and that 'there were a lot of good gags
in the script'. One of the writers said, slightly mystified, 'This has
never happened before!'

'What, face-to-face communication with the person you're
writing for?' thinking he was joking.

'Yes,' he said.

I've since learnt that this is standard practice. Television hosts
rarely mingle with the writers.

On the day of the recording, Lorraine Heggessey, the controller
of BBC1, popped in to see how things were going, and she was
pleased to see how relaxed I was. Relaxed, but also ready for the
challenge ahead. Fifteen minutes before the recording started, I was
having my final checks in the make-up room when one producer
arrived to give me the opposite of a pep talk. He was well meaning,
but his nervous panic about whether I would remember to read
certain questions from the cards in my hand or others from the
autocue was infectious.

As he jabbered away, I realised I had to break the mood of
nervousness that I felt myself being sucked into.

'Listen. Leave. Go. It's going to be alright. But I need to get
off to a good start. So is it OK if I spend ten minutes quietly, not
talking and preparing?'

'Of course. I'll go,' he said.

'Will that be soon?' I said.

The producer who meant well took his leave and his nerves with him.

I focused on what I needed to do. Already some critics of the programme were predicting its end now that Angus had gone, but I knew that didn't need to be the case. I had to be comfortable, confident 'in the middle', thereby demonstrating that the show could easily survive a change of presenter.

Well, the night went very well and the people backstage afterwards were ecstatic. I suspect that some members of the production staff feared the worst, but my efforts as host alongside those of the panellists completely eliminated any thoughts of imminent demise.

I enjoyed my one time in the middle. It was great to feel more involved in the show. My usual routine is to arrive around two hours before the recording, have a cup of tea, something to eat, and then into the studio and in front of the live audience. Sometimes you feel isolated from the production staff because you don't know who they are or what they do, but then they probably think the same thing about me.

Although the producers were first of all looking for a permanent host, it soon became clear that a different person every week brought a fresh energy to the show. Soon we had a squad of hosts all capable of delivering the goods. Jo Brand, Kirsty Young, Alexander Armstrong were all highly skilled and could pull it off. Having said that, it was the crazier one-offs that I particularly cherished. Bruce Forsyth, Brian Blessed and William Shatner all spring to mind. The latter's assertion that Ilfracombe 'is laced with prostitution' still makes me chuckle whenever I think about it.

I had recently grown a beard to look less like myself while traveling back and forth to London by train. Providing I didn't talk too much, I wasn't recognised and so didn't get into conversations about 'who's going to be the new replacement host?'

One April evening, while heading back to London, Sarah commented that my beard had become a bit wild and unruly and needed trimming. We were heading back because I had a Michael Parkinson interview and a BAFTA awards ceremony to attend. All of which sounds crazy, of course, in light of Sarah's illness, but it was incredibly important to both of us that we tried to make life keep going as normal. If any of these things can be called normal.

'No,' I said, 'my beard's alright. It brings out my Irish roots and makes me look interesting.'

She wasn't buying this. 'You can't go on television looking like that.'

But I still wasn't convinced. Then the train stopped at London Bridge, and a homeless man got on and sat next to me. He was pissed and drinking from a can of special brew. He took a long deep glug from the can of beer and then looked at me and my beard.

He offered me the can.

I blinked back at him, incredulous. He had taken me for a fellow traveller along life's hard road.

The next morning my beard was neatly trimmed and my hair was similarly cut.

I always looked forward to being interviewed by Michael Parkinson.

He never failed to ask interesting questions and, more importantly, listen to the answers. Inevitably the subject of Angus came up. 'Did you stab Angus in the back?' he asked.

'No,' I said, 'I stabbed him in the front.'

This was a quick funny answer, but it wasn't true. I didn't have the power to sack Angus, but I couldn't disagree with the decision once it was made. I'd done what I could to help us ride out the storm the first time round, but events overtook us.

Sunday night was BAFTA night. I'd been nominated eleven times previously for *Have I Got News for You*, and having lost out on each occasion I was rather hoping it might be twelfth time lucky.

Bruce Forsyth announced the winner of the category I was in and, thankfully, it was me. I kissed Sarah, and bounced on to the stage and danced a quick jig with Bruce. I remembered being six years old, watching him on the same stage, the London Palladium, on our black-and-white telly in Fulham, and now I'm here with him and he's handing me a BAFTA. I never realistically thought I would win such a prestigious award. After being nominated so many times, I had sort of given up on it. I take the BAFTA from Bruce and it's reassuringly heavy. I feel its worth in my hands. Sarah beams back at me from the audience.

A few days after the glittering London Palladium night, Sarah and I found ourselves sitting in a rather gloomy waiting room in St George's Hospital in Tooting.

It's raining heavily and the waiting room is packed with wet patients, all waiting to see one of the three cancer specialists working that morning. There were about thirty of us. I read some funny story from a newspaper to Sarah, which made us both laugh. Somebody recognised my voice. An elderly man sitting a few seats away looked at me and chuckled. I said, 'It's either raining outside or they're emptying the bed pans out of the top floor window.'

Several other patients started laughing. The mood of the room lightened a little. Smiles appeared on faces as more people recognised me and seemed to feel permission to laugh. Excitement spread amongst us. Another man said, 'It really is pissing down,' which got a huge response, and then one of the women joined in. Now there were waves of laughter, much to one nurse's astonishment, who walked into the waiting room to find a happy group of people on the verge of a sing-song.

The morning was so grim, what with the miserable weather on top of people's serious health concerns, that a little laughter, once initiated, grew quickly amongst the group. There was no stopping it. I sparked it off but the group made it happen. We all embraced it. Laughing about the weather – defying the clouds.

Laughing in the face of something none of us could change.

On 21 June 2003 Sarah and I got married. Sarah left the church grounds riding a white horse at walking pace. As we stopped for photographs one of our guests overheard a journalist on his mobile dictating some words back to his office. 'Hang on,' he said, 'I'll just stay on the line in case she falls of the horse.' Sarah didn't fall off and everybody had a wonderful day.

The last six weeks of her life saw Sarah increasingly deteriorate. Her mother and father were staying with us, and the three of us cared for her with so much love and attention. Then she got worse. We called in a doctor, who arranged for a room in a local hospice. Sarah was just strong enough to walk down the red brick steps from our front door to the waiting car. The sun caught her blonde hair as she carefully negotiated each step down. She was very ill.

She was at the hospice for a week before she died.

My Irish family arrived, Mum and Dad and the cousins, and we all gathered at the cottage along with Sarah's family before making our way up the hill to the church. After a few words were spoken we escorted the coffin to the final place. We passed a wooden bench, which overlooked the cemetery. A few months earlier Sarah had sat on that same bench and said, 'I'd like to be buried in a place like this.' I looked at that bench and thought of those words as we committed her to the ground. Sarah had been dealt terrible cards, but she had played her hand beautifully.

A couple of days after she died, I saw Sarah's young three-year-old niece attempting the same red brick steps down from our front door to the driveway that Sarah had negotiated ten days before. Rosy had inherited her aunt's fair hair, and her tentative steps exactly mirrored Sarah's.

22

A Little Help From My Friends

If you've been unlucky enough to experience the sort of trauma and complications that the loss of a loved one can bring, then you have my sympathy. For me, the overriding feeling of loneliness and the emptiness of our two houses was brutal. I counted myself lucky that I had some very good friends, and plenty of work in a world that I loved. This is what ultimately saved me at this point.

I went to The Comedy Store the following Sunday. Not to be in the show, but just to be around it. I hid in the background in the shadows, observing people laughing, soaking up the positive atmosphere, talking to my friends The Comedy Store Players, in the dressing room, in the interval. I wanted to be onstage but I felt a certain decorum had to be maintained. A stage appearance so soon after Sarah's death would be likely to be misinterpreted. Standing onstage improvising comedy scenes with my friends would have been a great escape for me. Entertainment can work both ways, both as a viewer and as a participant. I left it a couple of weeks before I returned. That first night back, as I improvised, comic thoughts washed through my head and I swam with the currents that whisked me along as everything else for a while disappeared from view.

Have I Got News for You started a week later and again I was ready for it. Amidst my grief it would have been very difficult to sit at home and watch somebody replace me.

And so I played on through it all, feeling the misery of the encroaching winter and seeing my friends in The Comedy Store Players whenever I could. Every Sunday of course I was performing with them, but there were other times as well. The times I was on the phone in a bad place, or needed someone to visit me straight away. And they did. I owe them a great deal.

Room 101 was a wonderful show to do at this time. We had some fantastic guests and it also gave me the opportunity to exercise my interviewing skills honed over three years in the civil service. I saw Michael Parkinson as a good role model. He was an interviewer who listened. I wanted the guest on *Room 101* to be the focus of the show. We gave them a platform, and supported them with well-chosen illustrative clips and funny props.

Back in 1998 Jimmy said, 'Who would be your very first choice to have on the programme?' 'Spike Milligan,' I had replied, quick as a flash.

Interviewing Spike was one of the most improbable things that happened in my professional career. The man who wrote the Goons and many books, one of which I had won as an eight-year-old, was now sitting in front of me telling the world why he wanted to banish Portsmouth into Room 101. He'd had a terrible time onstage there back in the 1950s, but I tickled him greatly by showing him Portsmouth's slogan to attract tourists, which was 'Portsmouth offers thousands of French restaurants and they're all only a few hours sailing away.' It's brilliant, 'Come to Portsmouth, you can get to France from here.'

Spike was sharp on the night. His appearance marked his last major television interview and I'm so proud I was part of it.

Of the sixty-four programmes we made, spread over eight series, there was only one which led to the director general of the BBC being interviewed by the police. My usual practice with the guests on *Room 101* was to take them to lunch to discuss their choices; to make sure they had strong enough reasons to justify their selection. If they could be encouraged to nominate something quirky, so much the better. Julian Clary came up with the left side of his face, while Sheila Hancock was happy to nominate herself. Spike Milligan chose his own house, Stephen Fry picked Room 101, while Ian Hislop selected me.

Once I'd lunched our guest, I reported back to the producers with a healthy selection of choices, which we then figured out how to illustrate with props and clips. There was one guest however who was unavailable for lunch, and would only give one of our researchers five minutes on the phone. This was Anne Robinson.

She listed her six selections, but would give no indication of why she had chosen them. One of her choices was the Welsh. If I'd had lunch with her I would have strongly suggested she drop this one, but that didn't happen. I met her for a couple of minutes before the recording, and then we were up and running.

The audiences on the night never knew who was going to be walking through the doors and onto our walkway. Anne Robinson was a very good booking for the show, and she got a huge response when she walked on. She's strongly opinionated and doesn't give a toss what people think of her. We got to 'The Welsh' and she said, 'What are they for?' Some audience members laughed while others audibly gasped. There was no way I was putting the Welsh into Room 101, or genocide as it's called. I know it's pretending, but still. Her comments caused uproar and rightly so, although it was a bit much that Greg Dyke, the then director general of the BBC, was interviewed by a couple of policemen over the matter.

I was surprised by how much people wanted their nominations to go into Room 101. I found as the programme progressed that people would be miffed if I didn't put their choices in, so I tended to be generous, with some guests getting all six through. If I could surprise my guest early on then I would. Bill Bailey chose the difficulty in removing bras, and I made that the first item because I was wearing a very heavily padded bra under my jacket and shirt and I didn't want him or the audience to spot it. I revealed it to much laughter and invited Bill to take it off me.

Kirsty Young's first choice was men in cowboy boots. As she began I crossed one leg over the other, revealing that I was wearing long brown leather cowboy boots.

The day the props came in was always an exciting one. Bobby Warrens, legendary props master of the BBC, would bring in the most exquisitely made items. My favourite one throughout the eight series was inspired by Linda Smith's choice of 'Adults who read Harry Potter books'. The prop was thought up by my old friend John Irwin, who was now writing on the show. Essentially, it was a device that allowed adults to read the Harry Potter books on public transport without anybody twigging it. You sit a replica of a small child on your lap. This replica holds the book open while you look through a hole in the back of its head through to the book. It was a hilarious object that combined visual humour, immense practicality and a certain creepiness.

Working on *Room 101* was all-absorbing, and I'm proud of my involvement with it. Each show set out to reflect the personality of the person I was interviewing. We mainly succeeded.

*

Without even knowing it, all of a sudden I seemed to have clocked up thirteen series of *Have I Got News for You*. And almost a decade-and-a-half of *Just a Minute*. Both shows have been brilliant for me. The first producer of *Have I Got News for You* was Harry Thompson, who came up with the rounds we still play today. It was he who thought of the idea of replacing Roy Hattersley with a tub of lard when the former cancelled on us for the third successive time. Harry went on to write an acclaimed biography of Peter Cook, and brilliant treatise on the Man in the Iron Mask. He was a stubborn man who had brilliant ideas, but his stubbornness sometimes blinded him to other people's good suggestions. At the beginning of the second series, I had an idea that I felt was a guaranteed big laugh. I explained my idea to Harry, he didn't like it. I mentioned it again a few weeks later but he hadn't changed his mind. I tried the other producer, Colin Swash, and he didn't like it either. Series three came along and I tried pitching my idea again.

Colin said, 'It will confuse the viewer.'

And I said, 'No, it won't, it'll be perfectly alright. Why don't we just try it? If it doesn't work you can edit it out.'

'No,' said Colin, and Harry agreed with him.

Undeterred, I brought up the notion every couple of years, but they stonewalled me every time. In 1996, two new producers took over, Richard Wilson and Giles Pilbrow. On the evening of the first recording the three of us chatted in my dressing room. I broached the subject wearily, 'Now gentleman, I know you're not going to be interested in this idea but I feel honour bound to at least mention it to you.' I outlined my idea and they both immediately agreed that we should try it.

'Well, if that's your attitude, I beg your pardon,' I said.

'If it doesn't work we can edit it out,' said Richard.

The following Wednesday, Ian, our director Paul Wheeler and I convened on Clapham Common. We were there for twenty minutes. The following night's studio recording ran as usual up to the point of the odd one out round. The four photographs were shown as usual, and then the camera cut to me. I looked up towards my left in a dreamy fashion, as the picture mixed through to Ian and me running across Clapham Common in slow motion. We cut back to me continuing to look dreamy, until I snap out of it and say, 'I'm sorry, I was miles away.' The studio audience's roaring laughter confirmed what I'd always known. It was funny and it wouldn't confuse people.

The programme continued to gain momentum. It became a prestigious show to appear on. Salman Rushdie appeared, much to the audience's astonishment.* When he was announced many people laughed, assuming it was a gag. Mr Rushdie, who was then still in hiding, was greeted with extraordinary applause. The producers told me that when he had first been invited he'd sadly refused because our record night, Thursday, coincided with his two bodyguards' night off. Once the two protecting policemen from Scotland Yard learnt of the situation, one of them said, 'We like that programme, we'll come and look after you on our day off.'

When the Conservative MP Teddy Taylor appeared on the show, he believed that the best way to put across his political message was to keep talking continuously until everyone else was bored rigid. He kept going despite the fact I was sitting beside him miming hanging myself with my own tie.

Glenda Jackson, the Labour MP for Hampstead, told me the following week when she was on the show, that all the politicians on her side of the house now mimed hanging themselves with ties

---

* The author was living under heavy security at the time and was hardly ever seen, having had death threats made against him.

whenever Teddy Taylor got to his feet. At one point, in the same show, Glenda was asked what her school motto was. She wasn't sure if the question was being addressed to her, so she said, 'Are you looking at me?'

To which I replied, 'That must have been a tough school.'

It took a moment to register but then it was big laughs all round. My proudest moment associated with *Have I Got News for You*, however, didn't happen on camera but on my way back to my dressing room at the end of a recording. Spike Milligan had been on the show and I was still pinching myself that it had actually happened. But the best was yet to come. As I walked along the corridor, I saw Spike approaching from the other direction. As he shuffled towards me, I thought of everything his humour had meant to me, from my very first exposure to *The Goons*, through to his poetry books for children and his later *Q* series. I thought of him playing the traffic warden in my favourite film *The Magic Christian*. I thought of the fun and camaraderie between him, Peter Sellers and Harry Secombe during those *Goon Show* recordings. Listening to the off-mike giggles on my headphones in my teenage years was sometimes the only company I had.

Spike was now a few feet away from me, shuffling nearer. I paused in my stride, but Spike showed no sign of stopping.

'Paul,' he said. 'You are a very funny man.'

I stood flabbergasted, as I watched his back disappear down the corridor. I regained my composure to call after him, 'And Spike ... you're a wonderful man.'

He waved his right arm without looking back. 'And with that compliment ringing in my ears,' he said, 'I shall fade into the night,' and he disappeared around a corner.

The single most astonishing moment in my professional career.

Appearing on the programme can open certain doors. A few years ago, I was invited by a journalist to attend Prime Minister's Question Time. I sat in the press gallery, eagerly anticipating the tussle between David Cameron and Gordon Brown, the then prime minister, when I noticed a journalist eagerly whisper into another journalist's ear. The whisper quickly passed along the line. I looked down the chamber to see MPs on both sides quickly strike up conversations with each other. The excitement was tangible. What had happened? A sudden attack on Gibraltar by Spain? The Argentines claiming back the Falklands? No, the news was far more surprising than that. The *Daily Mirror* journalist approached me excitedly. 'Guess what?' he said. 'John Sergeant has quit *Strictly Come Dancing*.'

And so the mighty wheels of government trundled on.

One of the benefits of having guest hosts is that every so often an inspired piece of casting can lead to priceless television gold. The first time Bruce Forsyth hosted, I remember him being nervous in the wings before the recording began.

I was standing next to him.

'How are you doing Bruce?' I said.

'A bit nervous,' he said. 'They're not my usual audience out there. I wonder what they will be like.'

'I think they'll like you,' I said.

I had no doubt about that, but the response Bruce received from the studio audience when he emerged from behind a glittery curtain was overwhelming. The place erupted with huge cheers from every corner of the crowd as Bruce settled into the central chair.

He was superb on the night, brilliantly dealing with Ian's total bemusement as *Have I Got News for You* morphed into Brucie's 'Play Your Iraqi Cards Right'. Bruce had photographs of various wanted men with a price on their head, and asked Ian if the next card would feature a higher or lower amount.

An obviously embarrassed team captain replied, 'I don't think this programme can sink much lower.'

To which Brucie replied, 'Oh, you haven't seen our finish.'

As Ian's discomfort continued it became apparent that he had never heard of the original programme, Brucie's *Play Your Cards Right*, so really was at a loss as to what was going on.

'Ian had the ITV button on his television removed by Harrods,' I said, a line I repeated several years later when Bruce made a triumphant second appearance on the show. His first had landed him the role of presenting *Strictly Come Dancing* – a prime example of how one successful appearance on the programme can rejuvenate a career. Boris Johnson's political trajectory after a few entertaining appearances took him all the way to high office.

This clever, intensely ambitious man at times enjoys pretending to be an idiot. He likes being underrated and dismissed as a fool who is not to be taken seriously. Shortly after it was decided that Boris would run as the Tory candidate for the mayoralty of London, I bumped into him at Lord's Cricket Ground. I was there as a guest of Channel 5 who had a private box, which Boris wandered in to some minutes after I had arrived. My presence visibly startled him, and his right hand instinctively ruffled the front of his neatly combed hair into an untidy sticking up mess. I had seen this transformation once before on one of his appearances on *Have I Got News for You*. He left the make-up room with his hair nicely combed by a make-up artist, who takes professional pride in her work. He disappeared around the back of the set waiting to be introduced, and when I saw him again twenty-odd seconds later he looked like he had spent the previous forty-eight hours in a wind tunnel. So to see how quickly the transformation into eccentric Boris could be achieved was a rare treat.

'Ah, oh, ah, Paul, ah, how are you?' Boris burbled in that familiar manner, which heavily suggests that P.G. Wodehouse drew from life.

'I'm very well,' I replied, 'and congratulations on becoming the Tory candidate in the forthcoming mayoral election.'

'Ah yes, yes, yes,' he said. He paused for a moment. 'What policies do you think I should have?'

Naturally, I was amazed by this. Here was a man running for mayor who, by his own admission, had no idea what he wanted to do if he got elected.

'You must have some idea,' I said.

'No,' he said. 'I just thought I would make it up as I went along.'

This last remark was a misstep on Boris's part, as he succumbed to the temptation to over-egg the pudding. I smiled inwardly at his rather clumsy attempt to convince me that he was the rarest of all political animals – the politician who cared nothing about politics. Boris's subsequent political career shows a very skilful operator indeed, and had I believed his performance that day at Lord's, there would have at least been one genuine fool taking part in our brief conversation.

Many have succeeded in hosting the show, but what about the failures, the ones that completely misfired? I am often asked who is the worst host we have ever had. It was undoubtedly Neil Kinnock. His first insurmountable problem was his inability to read the words displayed on the autocue in front of him at anything like a normal speed for talking. He was extraordinarily slow, and approached every word with extreme suspicion, as if it was capable of suddenly surprising him with a hitherto unsuspected meaning. So right from the top of the show, the energy in the middle was all wrong.

'Hello,' – pause – 'and welcome' – pause – 'to Have I' – pause
– 'Got' – pause – 'News For You.'

His delivery really was that tortuous and took the recording
well past the two hour mark. The longest we have ever had. Afterwards, he told me that he could never deliver a speech unless he
had written it himself. His experience wasn't improved by Will Self
and Linda Smith, the other panellists, having a go at him for losing
the 1992 general election.

Charles Kennedy didn't fare much better in the middle. Again,
the autocue script proved to be his nemesis. The autocue is operated
manually with a nearby human operative who follows the speed
of the host's delivery. Inexperienced autocue readers often fail to
grasp that if they slow down, then inevitably so will the autocue.
The night Charles Kennedy hosted, it came to a complete stop on
more than one occasion.

Generally, Tory MPs have proved better at hosting duties,
perhaps because they feel more comfortable at being in charge.
Although I must make an exception for Ann Widdecombe, whose
second appearance as the host rivalled Neil Kinnock's for sheer
awfulness, but for entirely different reasons.

Ann's first appearance had been OK. She muddled through with
some help from the onscreen panellists, and supportive editing in
post-production made her look a little better than she had actually
been on the night. So, having seen her edited performance and
received many congratulations from her political supporters, she
undertook her second performance with a completely different
mindset to her first. The second time around she knew much better
than the producers what was a funny line and what wasn't, and her
refusal to read out perfectly good jokes or, worse, try to rewrite
them, proved immensely frustrating to the production team.

During the recording, as she blundered her way around the script like some kind of comedic King Herod strangling new jokes at birth, she suddenly snapped at me, 'Come on, be funny, that's what you're being paid for.'

To have Ann Widdecombe tell me about my professional duties when her own efforts were so appallingly awful, was one of the rare low points in what has so far proved to be a twenty-five-year run.

Another lowlight was the night that Jimmy Savile appeared on the show. This was some ten years before he died, and at the time nobody on the panel or in the studio audience thought he was anything more than an eccentric DJ and charity fundraiser with a weird way about him.

His appearance on *Have I Got News for You* inspired an internet hoax, which even these days still swims into the public consciousness. The false document purports to be a transcript of an argument between myself and Savile, in which I berate him in the worst possible terms. Accusing him in some instances of crimes that we now know he was actually guilty of. This didn't happen in reality. Although I agree with some of the sentiments expressed, the language is completely out of character for me. As an example, I wouldn't wish cancer on anybody, no matter how vile they were.

When Savile was exposed we tackled the subject on *Have I Got News for You* as a serious story, which could not be ignored. There were no laughs in it and nobody tried to make jokes, until Graham Linehan volunteered the thought that all the *Jim'll Fix It* badges should be collected together and melted down into a big stake, which should then be hammered deep into Savile's heart, ensuring that he was dead for ever. This got a big laugh, which greatly reduced the tension.

Over the years, we have acquired a busload of guests who have become experts at playing the game. Ross Noble always brings something special to the programme, usually a bit of cake. On one occasion, when he was on my team, he suggested that we should endeavour to score no points at all throughout the entire programme. This wasn't easy as a couple of questions were rather simple, but we managed to display total ignorance and were rewarded with nothing. I offer this anecdote up whenever I am accused of being desperate to win *Have I Got News for You*. My ambition on each recording it to get as many big laughs as I can, not to acquire meaningless points that have no value. Ian, on the other hand, is desperate to win and it's a shame he doesn't have the experience more often.

The show that gives me most professional pleasure is *Just a Minute*. I began listening to the programme when I was ten years old, and like a lot of its younger fans, I was attracted by its combination of simplicity and difficulty.

Nicholas Parsons' fluid chairmanship of *Just a Minute* is one of the key ingredients behind its success. He will allow surreal flights of fancy because they are entertaining, even though strictly speaking they are also deviations from reality. He judges fairly, but also he will bear in mind that a particular contestant may not have spoken for a while and he will award them the subject in order to hear from them. I used to be far more competitive in the programme than I am these days. I would challenge on every repetition and try to justify dubious claims for hesitation. This attitude was partly inspired by sitting next to Sir Clement Freud for twenty years, who was a very keen competitor. His eagerness to win rubbed off on me, and for so many years I was very quick on the buzzer. These days I tend to acquire bonus points through entertaining challenges as much as playing the game.

Just a Minute is at its best when you have four strong, experienced players of the game. Everyone understands the etiquette of the show. There are no silly challenges over small words, like 'he' or 'she', and if someone is on a roll with a subject, unless they seriously slip up, we let them go unchallenged.

A player new to the game can be brought into this environment and treated generously by the other three and allowed to find their feet. When you have two new players amongst the four, they often start challenging each other over tiny things because neither wants to be last.

Three new players of the game and anarchy abounds, as people argue over the chairman's rulings or misunderstand the nature of the show in general. The point of being on *Just a Minute* is to be entertaining. Like all successful long-running shows *Just a Minute* might give the impression that it makes itself, but its inner workings are as intricate as any Swiss watch.

One very memorable episode wasn't recorded at the Radio Theatre in London, but instead at the City Varieties Music Hall in Leeds. One of the panellists pulled out late in the day, but luckily the producer, Chris Neil, recalled that Charles Collingwood, a regular in *The Archers*, was recording an episode in Birmingham. Charles has appeared on the show several times and always gives good value. As soon as his *Archers* shift was over, he hopped in to a car and sped towards Leeds. It became clear that he would miss the first twenty minutes of the first recording unless we delayed procedures. I suggested, 'Let's start on time and pretend Charles is here. So Nicholas says, "Charles your subject is beekeeping and your time starts now." Charles doesn't say anything so he's buzzed for hesitation.'

Both Nicholas and Chris thought it was a good idea, and better than keeping the audience waiting indefinitely. So that's what we did and Nicholas played the gag splendidly. When Charles did arrive it was to a mighty cheer, as he ran down the aisle and took his seat. It was a classic recording that demonstrates that, after forty-five years, *Just a Minute* is still capable of endless variation. One joke that Nicholas often reminds me about is the occasion I started jotting down some thoughts on a piece of paper in front of me.

'What's that you're writing?' he said.

I replied, 'It's a suicide note. Now all you've got to do is sign it at the bottom.'

It's a wicked joke but Nicholas laughed as much as anyone. It's a measure of just how generous a performer Nicholas is. He remains a marvel and his continued chairmanship of *Just a Minute* for the past five decades is one of the great achievements in British broadcasting.

In the spring of 2004 a job offer came through that I would have been idiotic to turn down. I said 'no'. Six gigs in India! Performing improvised comedy to local audiences in Mumbai, Delhi and Kolkata! I said 'no' because I had become terrified of flying due to hitting clear air turbulence some years back, which had resulted in the aeroplane plummeting and one passenger breaking his arm. I had decided I need never go on a plane again. I was happy in that knowledge.

The Comedy Store Players had been approached by an Indian promoter, and amongst the regulars four people were up for the trip. Lee Simpson, Richard Vranch, Jim Sweeney and Suki Webster. Jim is one of the pioneers of impro in Britain, and his facility for creating extraordinary material out of thin air has long been admired by his fellow performers and audiences alike. Suki I didn't know very well, although I knew she had worked extensively with

Eddie Izzard's impro group, including a six-week West End run. The five of us happened to be on at the Store one night and the conversation quickly turned to India. 'We need five people,' said Richard, 'and nobody else is available or wants to go.'

'It's ten days,' said Jim. 'The gigs are in five star hotels. It could be fun.'

'Yes, but I can't fly,' I said, suddenly sounding like Orville.

'A friend of mine went on a "cure your fear of flying" course,' said Suki. 'I could find out the details. I think it was only a couple of hours.'

I thought about it for a moment. The promoter was insisting on five people, so it was up to me to somehow get myself on the plane.

'OK, I'll do it,' I said, 'I'll go to India but I'll also do this course.'

I booked myself on to the two-hour course, which completely cured my fear. Keith, an ex-pilot with a keen sense of humour, was my guide. First he asked me about the incident.

'You say the plane plummeted,' he said. 'How far do you think that it dropped?'

'I don't know, somebody said we dropped a thousand feet. I know that passengers who weren't wearing seat belts were injured and there was a feeling of panic alright,' I replied.

'Well,' Keith said, 'first of all, clear air turbulence is very rare, and secondly the most that aircraft that you were flying on would have dropped is six feet.'

'Six feet!'

'Yes. Dangerous of course, if you haven't got your seatbelt on. The trouble with clear air turbulence is that you don't know it's there until you hit it,' Keith said. 'Where were you flying to?'

'The Maldives,' I replied. 'But because of the onboard injuries we had to divert to Sri Lanka.'

'What did you imagine the mood to be like up in the cockpit, once the plane hit turbulence?' Keith asked.

I said, 'Part of me was thinking that the pilots were saying to each other, "Oh God what are we going to do, we're going to crash." But then I thought that actually they might be very calm and saying to one another, "Are you going to Dolly's party on Saturday?"'

Keith laughed and reiterated the fact that large jet planes don't crash through turbulence. It was time to sit inside the cockpit simulator. Keith and I crowded into what was a surprisingly tight area. Projectors mounted above us shone images of clouds on screens around us. The view from up there was sensationally beautiful. Keith pressed a button, which simulated mild turbulence. Although the plane shook slightly, it felt very secure and looking out of the window straight ahead was reassuring.

When he racked the turbulence up to extreme, which shook us around a bit, Keith pointed to the controls and gauges so I could see for myself how little the plane was losing height. Having pushed the big turbulence button Keith turned to me and said, 'Are you going to Dolly's party on Saturday?' I laughed uproariously. Keith then made his point.

'The next time you hit turbulence, just remember that the pilots up front will be completely relaxed and unworried. Take your mind to here. The degree of turbulence that you encountered is very rare. It's unlikely you will hit anything like that again. Look at the view and happy flying.'

It worked a treat. I boarded the plane at Heathrow, bound for Mumbai with Jim, Suki, Richard and Lee. Like excited children, on day one we ventured out and took a motorised rickshaw ride and explored the local market. On day two I woke up with a stomach bug, which laid me low for a few hours. Luckily it was a day off, but the others suggested a trip into the nearest town for an evening meal. I cried off, reasoning that I would be happier staying nearer to my hotel room. Suki had some similar kind of bug to me and wasn't feeling great either. She, too, didn't want to leave the hotel. I'd noticed that an outdoor cabaret was advertised for that evening in the hotel grounds, so I suggested to Suki that we make an arrangement to meet in the hotel bar later. She agreed.

I spent the afternoon drinking water and resting in my room. I met Suki in the bar at eight. 'How are you feeling?' I said.

'A bit better,' she said. 'And you?'

'Yes, I'm not ready to eat anything yet but I am feeling better,' I said.

'Good,' she said. 'I hear brandy is good for an unsettled stomach.'

'Is it?' I said. 'It doesn't sound right to me. Let's get a couple.'

So we took our brandies out to the hotel gardens.

It was a beautiful warm evening and the grounds were extensive. A few round tables were scattered strategically on a beautifully manicured lawn. We sat at the front, placing our drinks on to the white pressed tablecloth.

An announcement was made over discreetly hidden loud speakers, 'Ladies and gentlemen, may the cabaret begin. We present Marvo, a local magician.'

We clapped and looked around for Marvo but couldn't spot him anywhere. Well, he'd certainly succeeded in creating an immediate air of mystery. Then I heard a voice somewhere in the distant darkness.

Although it was barely audible, I thought I could discern the occasional phrase. 'Bafflement will be yours.' 'Magic will transfix you.' As Suki and I looked hard we could see that, yes, there was somebody in the semi-darkness who was standing next to a table that had some objects on it. With great delight we realised this was our magician.

The occasional scraping of metal against metal led me to believe that he may have been linking, or perhaps unlinking, giant rings. On one occasion, he threw his arms wide and said, 'Behold the magic of the Orient,' but all we could see was Marvo throwing his arms wide.

Magicians try to figure out ways to distinguish themselves from their colleagues. Some specialise in close-up magic while others work with tigers. Marvo's speciality was far away magic. In the dark. He did twenty-five minutes and was hugely entertaining. Suki and I laughed and clapped enthusiastically. We retired to the hotel bar after the gig was over, both feeling better than we had all day. We started making up publicity quotes for Marvo. 'Your eyes won't believe what they can't see,' suggested Suki, much to my amusement.

Over the coming days Suki and I fell in love. It was a wonderfully giddy time, and India is an intoxicating country. The bright colours and aroma of the spices amongst the bustling crowds, added to the heady atmosphere. And our impro shows in Mumbai, Kolkata and Delhi could not have gone better.

We played three gigs to the local Indian middle classes in function rooms in luxury hotels. I have never experienced an audience reaction like it. They had seen the American version of *Whose Line is it Anyway?*, which gives you some of the flavour, but what they particularly enjoyed were our well-meaning attempts to replicate a Bollywood dance routine.

The television in our room showed lots of Bollywood films. We copied the moves and they roared. Seeing your culture being translated back through the eyes of another culture can be hilarious if the performers are sincerely doing it to the best of their ability.

At the end of the first show the audience gave us a standing ovation. All 400 of them stood up and cheered. The same thing happened the following night. This prompted me to ask the local promoter whether this was a custom or excessive good manners, and he said, 'No, this is as rare as it would be in England.'

The rest of the Indian shows went equally well, and we five agreed to do the Edinburgh Fringe Festival as a group calling ourselves 'Paul Merton's Impro Chums'. And once we got back to London, Suki and I started a relationship.

The regular gigs at The Comedy Store on Wednesdays and Sundays carried on as normal. The Comedy Store Players have odd little rituals, which they observe from time to time. Sometimes, if a player leaves the dressing room momentarily, upon their return they will find the rest of the team standing with their trousers around their ankles.

When Suki and I went to see Neil Mullarky's one man show at the Store, we saw an opportunity to maintain this tradition. But we didn't know he had a special guest in. We were in the dressing room after the show congratulating Neil, when he suddenly made his excuses and said he would be back in a minute. Suki and I exchanged glances. No words were necessary between us. Undoing our belts and dropping our trousers was the work of a moment. Our timing couldn't have been better. No sooner had our jeans hit the floor than in through the dressing room door walked Mo Mowlam, former secretary of state for Northern Ireland. The three of us looked at each other rather awkwardly for a moment, before Suki broke the silence by saying, 'I'm awfully sorry, we were expecting Ian Paisley.'

In 2005, Channel 5 suggested I should go to China for two months, and now I had given myself permission to fly again I was able to say yes. My executive producer warned that it would be fairly gruelling at times, but I welcomed the opportunity to make a different kind of television programme. To break away from the television studio into the big wide world of China was a challenge to be embraced.

It's important to establish an easy rapport with the crew early on. The cameraman, the assistant cameraman, the sound guy, will soon work out whether the presenter is easy-going or stand-offish. The director also is important in creating the right mood. We were to be away together for a long time, and we were the only British people we were going to see for the majority of it.

On the first night of filming I was plied with beers as I sat in a popular riverside restaurant in Beijing, consuming various forms of animal penis. Donkey, ram, snake. I ate them all. By the time we had finished filming that night the crew could be certain of two things. I was a good sport – and I was drunk.

Filming in China was far from free and easy. We had a government minder with us everywhere we went. Trying to grapple with a different mindset was interesting. One of our crew was vegetarian and she explained this to the waiter in the reasonably decent restaurant we were having lunch in. She spoke fluent Mandarin and the waiter nodded his understanding. When she cut into her crispy batter dumpling she was horrified to find slices of pork. She complained to the waiter who said, 'But it's inside.' He couldn't understand that she didn't eat meat, but merely thought she didn't want to see it.

One reoccurring problem was that people were understandably very nervous about saying anything that could be misconstrued as an attack on the government. Although they thought this, they wouldn't admit it, and off camera they would confirm that they were happy to talk about pre-agreed topics. I wasn't trying to trap anybody, that would be grossly irresponsible, but sometimes fruitless efforts to get people chatting became intensely irritating. One such interview coincided with a bout of me feeling desperately unwell on a hot, uncomfortable day. I like going abroad but my stomach doesn't. We were on a farm and one farmworker had a story we were keen to get on camera.

It seemed simple enough. Our friend had at one time worked in a government shoe factory, but he had returned to working on the farm for less money because he enjoyed the camaraderie and being in the open air.

Our translator tells me that he is very happy to talk about this.

I am sitting around with a group of farmworkers and once the camera starts rolling I turn to my interviewee and say, via the translator, 'Have you always worked here on the farm?'

My friend says, 'No.'

'Where else have you worked?' I ask.

'Nowhere,' he says.

'Nowhere,' I repeat. He nods his head. The cameraman stops rolling and puts his very heavy camera down. The translator quickly talks to the man and then reports back.

'He says he's sorry. He forgot about the shoe factory,' she says. I try not to look disbelieving as we go again.

'Have you always worked on the farm?' I ask again.

'Yes,' came back the reply. I sigh, the cameraman puts down his camera, and the translator has another chat with our forgetful chum. This time she says he'll get it right.

We go again. He nods even before I ask the question.

'Do you enjoy working on the farm?' I say. He nods.

'Have you ever worked anywhere else?' I ask.

He nods. He's agreeing with me, but he's not saying anything.

I address the group of farmworkers in front of me with a strange leading question. 'Has anyone here ever worked in a shoe factory?' They all look blank. We stop filming, the cameraman puts his camera down. The man I've been trying to interview tells the translator, 'I've worked in a shoe factory.'

Frustrating and absurd as it was, our friend was trying to reconcile two incompatible thoughts. He wanted to help us, but he also didn't want to give any impression that working in the government-run shoe factory was anything other than the thrill of a lifetime. To even say he left the factory might be construed as criticism of the government.

At another location, a major industrial city in the middle of China, I was interviewing a very bright young woman who spoke excellent English. I asked her about the terrible smog in the city and she didn't know what I was talking about.

'It's very bad here, isn't it?' I said.

She shook her head. 'No, I haven't noticed,' she said.

This puzzled me. 'But the sky is orange,' I said, 'and you can look directly at the sun.'

'No, no, I haven't seen this,' she maintained.

It was only after the interview that I realised that I missed the point. To criticise air pollution was to criticise the government.

I don't normally bother with personal communication on the internet, but it was great to be able to exchange emails with Suki while I was in China. It was a line back home. The televisions in the hotel rooms sometimes offered only one channel. One particularly miserable example showed an irate man in military uniform shouting continuously at a bunch of cowering minions. The minions were dressed in overalls and work clothes, while the military man had a chestful of medals and a big hat. No matter what time you turned on the television, he was shouting at them.

Although made in sometimes difficult circumstances, the China programmes were considered so successful that Channel 5 suggested I go to India. Having filmed in China I assumed India would be easier, but I was very wrong. Firstly, on the positive side, we had the same excellent technical crew that we'd had in China. Our cameraman Will, assistant cameraman Woody, and Steve on sound, were all top notch guys to work with. Our director in China, Barbie, who had done an excellent job was not with us this time round. The new director and the producer were two people I had never worked with before. They had curious ideas about comedy, which they didn't share with me. There were problems right from the beginning of filming.

These two guys thought it would be hilarious to spring surprises on me. I took some elocution lessons from a woman who filled my mouth with glass marbles as I pronounced various vowel sounds. I turned round to face the camera behind me at one point to see the director holding up a card with 'Shout at him' written in big letters. I asked the director what he was doing, but he didn't really answer me.

A few days later I was driven to a state of exhausted tears as they dedicated three hours to me trying to sing a pop song called 'What's Up'. The idea was that I should perform with a local band in a local club. The vocal range, which would test many a professional singer, skips an octave or two, and of course was completely beyond me. The director and the producer thought this would be funny. Watching somebody fail miserably at a task they are woefully unsuited to, is in the end dispiriting. I should have maybe put my foot down about the choice of song, but in the early days of an eight-week shoot I didn't want to rock the boat. My stomach was feeling the stress of it, so I was eating very simple food. Bowls of plain white rice with plain vegetables were my main sustenance. The deadly duo thought this would be a hilarious piece to camera. One of them said, 'We can film it in a restaurant nearby. We've got half an hour from six thirty to seven.'

'What is it that you're thinking of here?' I said.

'Oh, just a funny bit about you only eating plain white rice. You can riff on that.'

'Well, let's see what I can do,' I said not feeling particularly inspired by the subject matter. Also, I didn't want to come across as crassly turning my nose up at the national cuisine.

We get to the restaurant and a bowl of plain white rice is on a table waiting for me. I sit down. Will sets up his camera and Steve wires me for sound.

'OK, off you go,' says the director, having given me no indication as to exactly what is funny about me eating plain boiled rice. Anyway, off we go and I look into the lens.

'Since I've been here in India I'm afraid I've had some stomach trouble so I'm just keeping it plain and simple by eating nothing but white rice. I'm even more cautious than that, I brought a suitcase full of white rice with me from England, rice I cooked at home.'

'Stop,' shouts the director.

'What's the problem?' I say.

'Can you not say the bit about bringing rice from England?' he replies.

'Oh, why not?' I ask.

'It will confuse people,' he says.

I struggled with this for a moment. 'You mean you think people will really believe that I brought a suitcase full of rice with me?' I ask.

'Yes. And you didn't.'

'That's right, I didn't,' I say, my spirits sinking fast.

I did a re-take that didn't reference suitcases or illegally imported foodstuffs, or indeed anything remotely amusing. The director and the producer looked at one another, nodded and declared themselves happy. Battling these people helped the rest of us to bond. The contributors I interviewed and the stories we featured had all been excellently chosen, and with Will and Woody shooting exceptional material we were able to make a decent series.

Suki came on the India trip, and although she wasn't officially part of the production, her presence was crucial. Her ease with people helped to calm troubled waters. She was effectively a go-between for myself and our director and producer, at a point when I was no longer talking to them. That was the last two days of an exhausting shoot, and I'd had enough. Suki persuaded them to let me rest.

On Christmas Eve 2008, at nine o'clock in the morning, I held Suki's hand as we both stood by our beautifully decorated Christmas tree in the living room and I asked her to marry me.

'Yes,' she said immediately.

Mum and Dad, who were visiting from Ireland, emerged from our spare room looking for breakfast. We immediately broke the excellent news of our engagement. They were both very pleased.

'I'm glad you said yes Suki,' I remarked, 'otherwise it would have ruined Christmas.' The four of us had a good laugh.

23

Bishops Park

'Bishops Park has Fulham Palace adjacent to it,' I said to Suki, 'and I think it's licensed for weddings.'

We had settled on the idea of a summer wedding and had looked at several possible venues, including the actors' church in Covent Garden, when I suddenly hit upon this particularly happy notion.

We had a look and it was ideal. A beautiful Tudor courtyard, and the room itself that we would be married in was dated circa 1495. More importantly, of course, it was where I had grown up, stayed close to all my life, and would always feel part of me.

On the wedding day itself, Suki walked down the aisle and was accompanied by her father, Bob Webster, who had shown tremendous courage and resilience in recovering from a very serious illness. She arrived next to where I was standing with my best man, my cousin Peter, and I audibly gasped when I saw her. Recovering some poise I quickly said, 'Excuse me Miss, but we are waiting for somebody else.' The registrar waited for the laughter to subside and then began the ceremony.

Lee Simpson, at my behest, read a few words that I had composed for the occasion: 'Ladies and Gentlemen, due to the austerity measures this wedding speech has been sponsored by

Mario's Pasta Emporium, 114 Fulham High Street. Today is special and today's special is cannelloni.'

At Suki's suggestion, after the ceremony the two of us climbed on to one of the many bicycle rickshaws waiting in the courtyard, and instructed our young driver to take us around Bishops Park.

'This is a moment for the two of us to be together away from everyone else,' she said as our cyclist set off.

He cycled towards Putney Bridge as people exercising small dogs cheered the two of us with our 'Just Married' signs, bridal gown and three-piece wedding suit. They cheered not because they recognised me, but because it was romantic, fun and carefree. We circled the park of my childhood before returning to our guests for food, drink and speeches.

In my speech I planned to praise my father for instilling in me a strong competitive streak by always beating me at table tennis, but as soon as I broached the subject I could see a vivid flash of anger in his eyes so I quickly moved on. Perhaps he thought I was going to embarrass him or poke fun. I wanted to praise him, but I couldn't see the way to do it.

Later, I took my bride into my arms for the traditional first dance of the evening, a waltz that we had spent some time rehearsing. I moved my feet cautiously to the rhythm of the music, but soon settled as we glided around the floor to the tune of 'Moon River'. Our dreamlike state was abruptly cut short by Bruce Forsyth tapping me on the shoulder and replacing me in Suki's arms with himself. And in the hands of a professional dancer, she excelled as the two of them waltzed expertly around the room much to everyone's great hilarity.

Towards the end of the evening we and our guests made our way over Putney Bridge to the other side of the river. There, we boarded our chartered boat that would take us back into London, past Chelsea, past Battersea Power Station and into the pier at Westminster. All our friends were there, Julian Clary, Don Ward the owner of The Comedy Store, The Comedy Store Players – Josie, Richard, Lee, Neil and Andy – John Irwin, Ray Galton and Alan Simpson, various *Have I Got News for You* producers, Eddie Izzard, Nicholas Parsons, and the prize-winning novelist Victoria Hislop who was there with her husband Ian. As we travelled up the Thames to London we raised the day's last glass of champagne to our union. The perfect end to our perfect day.

My life with Suki has made me happier than I have ever been. We have a creative partnership not only on stage with the Impro Chums, but also in other areas. In the same year we got married, I directed a documentary for the BBC titled *Paul Merton Looks at Alfred Hitchcock*. Suki not only co-wrote the script with me, but also played the small but essential role of a cigar-smoking nun.

The film was well received and led to the BBC commissioning four more on the history of early cinema. The first was about the invention and development of film in Europe prior to the outbreak of the First World War. Then came an even more exciting challenge: a three-part series entitled *Paul Merton's Birth of Hollywood*. As well as co-writer, Suki became my assistant director and proved invaluable in the making of these films.

The fourteen-year-old version of me that sat alone in his bedroom watching silent films projected onto the wall would have been utterly astonished to see himself forty years later, directing a series of documentaries in New York, San Francisco and Hollywood. Undoubtedly, the one moment that he never would have believed, no matter how much you told him, took place in LA behind a row of English-style cottages that sit incongruously on the corner of

La Brea Avenue and Sunset Boulevard. Out of keeping with much of the low-rise modern architecture surrounding them, the cottages evoke the atmosphere of a Kentish village. Which couldn't be more misleading, because behind them actually lies a film studio with an impressive history.

I stood outside the main gates with Suki, Mike Fox our cameraman, and Bill Rudolf our sound guy. I spoke to the guard on reception via the intercom and the gates opened up for us. I held Suki's hand as we walked in to Charlie Chaplin's old studio. It was built in 1918 and a fair amount of it remains unchanged. Much to our excitement, we were shown the original screening room, which is still regularly used by the current owners, The Henson Company, the people behind The Muppets.

That was a thrill but, even more exciting than the screening room, was the huge building looming in front of us. We approached a rather heavy-looking, intimidating door and pulled it open. The two of us walked into the middle of the biggest sound stage we had ever seen. A massive room. Here Chaplin made some of cinema's most enduring films. *The Gold Rush, City Lights, Modern Times* ... And here I was being given the chance to direct myself on camera in the same space inside those four walls. Suki and I looked at each other, laughed and hugged. I couldn't believe I was standing where I was, so what chance the fourteen-year-old me had of believing this story, I really don't know.

My dad never felt comfortable offering me praise, so he never did. He decided that it was his role to make sure I never got too big-headed, and to that end he would often repeat the story about the time in the early 1950s when he saw Kirk Douglas strutting around the perimeter of a London hotel swimming pool. He was a film star in his prime, and was wearing a brief pair of swimming trunks. My dad, who was carrying out some maintenance work in the hotel, watched with distaste as Mr Douglas made a big show of introducing himself to each and every occupant of the pool, and to those sitting in the surrounding deck chairs. So, to stop me being like Kirk Douglas in the 1950s, my dad never praised me. Equally, I never felt I could praise him. He really didn't want to hear it.

In 1968, when I was twelve years old, I recorded my high-pitched voice in a small recording booth at a funfair. After three minutes of speaking into a microphone, a black plastic seven-inch single record was produced. After I'd had a go, Dad said he fancied a try and he disappeared into the recording booth. I watched him from outside through the glass. I couldn't hear him but he was obviously talking excitedly. The disc popped out of the machine and we took it home. I was keen to hear Dad's record and rather wary of hearing mine. On the other hand, Dad was reluctant to play his. I insisted on playing it on the radiogram and I was astonished by what I heard. Dad, in the guise of a football commentator, ad-libbed three minutes of live commentary that was lively, entertaining and funny. His delivery of the line 'the manager has run on to the pitch and he's got a bowler hat' was so beautifully timed in its expression of exuberance and surprise that Mum, Angela and I fell about in genuine laughter. Dad really surprised me with that record, but he quickly brushed away our compliments. There was no way we were going to turn him into Kirk Douglas. I kept that record proudly for many years, until one day I found it in dozens of pieces. I'd always meant to get it transferred onto a more stable medium. I kept the pieces for a while but they were beyond repair. Dad successfully improvised for three minutes on his own. It's a feat that I would be happy to achieve at any time and he pulled it off at his first attempt.

The last time I saw Dad he was lying in a hospital bed in the Cork University Hospital. All his life he had played it cool with me. I suppose it was an attitude he might have picked up from his own father, Albert Senior. Talking about your emotions was not part of our language. As I walked into the room that Dad was in, he changed the habit of a lifetime and threw up his arms in greeting as he said, 'Paul, it's great to see you.' This was a surprise.

'Dad, it's great to see you too,' I said with tears welling up in my eyes.

'I'm looking forward to your show tonight,' he said. This was *Have I Got News for You*, but Dad was confused. We hadn't started recording the new series yet.

'Yes, it will be on soon,' I said as I held and squeezed his hand.

'I'm so pleased to see you,' he said. 'I'm so proud of you Paul.'

'Oh, Dad,' I wanted to say, 'talk about leaving it late,' but instead I talked about seeing him drive a District line train across a bridge and how that made me, as a son, feel proud of him. His pride in me flooded all around the two of us. At an early age he encouraged me to like Charlie Chaplin, and he showed me the fun in having a sense of humour. I reminded him about his days as an amateur footballer player for Owen Villa. His team were runners-up in the second division of the West Fulham Football League in 1952–3. As I asked him questions about his footballing days, he nodded off into a fitful sleep. His legs started moving under the blankets. 'That's my Dad,' I thought. 'Going for goal.' It was the last time I saw him.

Mum died in the same hospital just a few weeks after Dad, in November 2013. They were a devoted couple.

After Mum's funeral we went back to the house where Angela had unearthed a scrapbook hidden inside my parents' wardrobe.

My dad, unbeknownst to me, had cut out every newspaper article, magazine interview and review, covering my entire career. In a cupboard above the television set, Dad had carefully recorded all my television appearances. *Paul Merton: The Series*, *Room 101*, *Whose Line is it Anyway?*, all my travel and cinema documentaries, and of course there was *Have I Got News for You*. I stood with Suki looking at the extensive archive, and simply shook my head in amazement.

Epilogue

Four years ago we filmed a documentary in the Cotswolds and featured Giffords Circus, whose principal clown is Tweedy. Before our interview, I told him the about how I'd been disappointed as a kid when I hadn't put my hand up quickly enough as volunteer at Bertram Mills Circus. I told him partly to reassure him that I was a huge fan of clowns and clowning, but I had always rued my hesitancy and remembered quite clearly what it was like to desperately want to be in the ring looking out at the thousands of people laughing and clapping. He smiled sweetly. The interview went well and Tweedy introduced me to his pet iron, Keith. This was an iron that he pulled along on a lead, and his name was Keith.

Once the interview was over, I found my front row seat in the big top and awaited that afternoon's performance. The show – an ambitious interpretation of *War and Peace* – was ingeniously staged and incorporated many traditional circus acts. Tumblers, knife throwers, riding around on horses, all featured, but as always my heart lay with the clowns. Tweedy was magnificent. His sense of balance while perched on the top of a ladder drew applause and laughs in equal measure. His physical comedy was excellent. At the end of the show Tweedy invited all the children to come and join him in the ring.

'Lucky children,' I thought, and then Tweedy appeared in front of me.

'Come on Paul,' he said.

But I shook my head. I was worried I might look out of place. He grabbed my hand and with the words, 'Come on Paul, don't be shy,' he pulled me up off my seat. I had big tears in my eyes, but I didn't let them show. I let him lead me into the centre of the ring where I jumped up and down, waved my hands and felt utterly, utterly joyful. Just like all the other kids.

Acknowledgements

It's sometimes easy to believe that any success I have achieved is largely due to the fact that I'm an autodidact. Mind you, I do close the curtains. But, upon serious reflection, I find there is a list of people who must be thanked for their essential contributions to my story.

I thank John Irwin for friendship, fun and helping me enormously in the early days. I thank Don Ward for opening The Comedy Store and Seamus Cassidy for commissioning *Paul Merton: The Series*. Jimmy Mulville, for casting me as a team captain on *Have I Got News for You*, deserves my deep thanks, as do The Comedy Store Players for making every Sunday completely different. I thank Edward Taylor, the first producer to book me on *Just a Minute*, despite serious misgivings, and also Ray Galton and Alan Simpson for continuing to be the most delightful people to have a gentle pissed-up lunch with.

My thanks to all the current contributors and producers of *Have I Got News for You* for helping Ian and myself to look so good.

Many thanks to all the excellent technical crews that I have worked with over the years, and to all the commissioning editors that made it possible.

Jake Lingwood, my editor, deserves a medal for deciphering, reshaping and ultimately encouraging me to produce this book over the course of a couple of years.

I also thank Mandy Ward, my agent, for representing me so astutely for the past twenty-five years.

And of course my darling wife Suki for her continued love and support in everything I do.

And thank you Mum and Dad.

Index

PM indicates Paul Merton

This book is due for return on or before the last date shown below